Boots Poffenberger:
Hurler, Hero, Hell-Raiser

About the Author

Austin Gisriel has been hooked on baseball since watching Brooks Robinson flash some leather and drive in the winning run at Memorial Stadium one long ago summer day. Austin is a writer who applies his talents quite often to the Grand Old Game.

Gisriel is the author of three other baseball books, has been published in *Virginia Living*, *Baseball Digest*, and *The Sunpapers* (Balt.) He is also a frequent contributor to Seamheads.com, one of the country's leading baseball blogs. Austin serves as the baseball analyst on Gordy's Sports Connection, a sports-talk show on WCBG 1380 AM in Greencastle, PA.

During the summer months, Gisriel may be heard on-line providing the play-by-play for the New Market Rebels webcasts. He handles public relations for the Rebels and also serves on the team's Board of Directors.

A high school English teacher for 19 years, Gisriel holds a bachelor's degree in psychology and a master's degree in theological studies.

Gisriel is married to the former Martha Pratt. They have two daughters, Rebecca and Sarah, either one of whom would have been named *Brooks* had she been a boy.

Boots Poffenberger:
Hurler, Hero, and Hell-Raiser

by
Austin Gisriel

SUMMER
GAME
BOOKS

To the people of Williamsport, Maryland, especially Boots' friends and family who sent him off to the big leagues, welcomed him home again, and cherish his memory to this day.

Acknowledgements

Thank you to Jeremy Knode who called and wanted to know if I was interested in looking over some scrapbooks of his grandfather. I had no idea what that day in January would lead to, but here it is!

Thanks to Jerry and Joan Knode for graciously giving me so much of their time. Jerry, the main caretaker of the Williamsport Town Museum, let me in to the museum when it was closed, allowed me to borrow the complete set of *The Dug Out*, and even helped me search out a reference or two.

Thank you to Laco Anderson, Connie Cole, Jack Rupp, and John McNamara for also sharing their time and memories. All of you knew Boots; your memories and feelings for the man aided greatly in bringing him to life.

Thanks to Buddy and Bill Britner for sharing their memories of Boots.

Thanks to John Frye the curator of the Washington County Room at the Washington County Free Library and Lynn Bowman of the Buford (GA) Historical Society for their research assistance and in John's case, providing yet another Boots Poffenberger story.

Thanks to Belinda Vinson of the Mack Truck plant in Hagerstown and Don Shoemaker of the Mack Truck Museum in Allentown, PA.

Thanks to Major League Baseball Historian John Thorn, as well as Lyle Spatz and Joe Wancho, both with the Society for American Baseball Research for helping me track down details on the relationship between major and minor league teams during the 1930s.

Thanks to my wife, Martha, and to all my friends for listening to me expound on the exploits of Boots Poffenberger.

I am confident that in the future there will be more people to thank, because I am sure that there are fans, friends, and former teammates who have more stories to tell about Boots even if they are telling them from the Great Beyond through letters or other scrapbooks or passages in other narratives that are yet to be discovered. I know that folks will offer alternate versions of some of the stories, because I have already read or heard several alternate versions of Boots' more famous exploits. Perhaps baseball researchers in Charleston, Beaumont, Detroit, Brooklyn, Toledo, Nashville, San Diego, Hagerstown or some little burg or borough through which Boots passed, will unearth the exact notations for material cited herein for which there is incomplete information or no information at all. I want to insure that Boots' legacy is complete, and so would appreciate any such information being forwarded to me. I will post any updates on my blog, which is where you can find out how to contact me at **www.austingisriel.com**

Contents

Introduction

I first met Cletus Elwood "Boots" Poffenberger posthumously, through a dining room table full of scrapbooks and manila envelopes stuffed with clippings, programs, schedules, and similar souvenirs from his 13 year career in professional baseball. His grandson, Jeremy Knode, telephoned out of the blue in January of 2011 and said that he had seen that I was writing about the Hagerstown Suns of the Class A South Atlantic League for a local magazine and that he had just come into possession of Boots' scrapbooks that had been kept by his first wife, Jo. Jeremy and I had coached soccer in the same league here in Williamsport, Maryland, Boots' hometown, and he invited me to take a look at the material.

I knew of Boots Poffenberger because any baseball fan from the Williamsport area has heard of one at least one of the town's four most famous sons. The other three were also big league pitchers: Dave Cole, who pitched for the Braves, Cubs, and Phillies in the 1950s; Nick Adenhart, an up and comer with the Angels who died in an automobile accident in April of 2009; and Mike Draper, who pitched for the 1993 Mets. Boots returned to his home after his career was over and lived the rest of his life, another 50 years, hunting in the Western Maryland hills, fishing in the Potomac River, and enjoying life as a pretty big fish in a pretty small pond.

I had also heard of Boots, however, because despite playing only parts of three seasons in the majors, totaling 267.1 innings, he was one of baseball's all-time characters. He once told Tiger management that the reason he couldn't lose any weight during spring training was that they were making him rise at 8:00 which meant that he needed breakfast and lunch, whereas, if they would just let him sleep until 1:00 as he wanted to, he would only need dinner. Boots is baseball's lifetime leader in funny stories per innings pitched.

Due to the passing of his contemporaries and even of the then young fans who saw him pitch, and perhaps because no film footage of him exists, Boots has been largely forgotten. He did not make the 2009 Major League Baseball Production *Prime 9: Top 9 Characters of the Game*, for example[1]—but in his day he was probably *the* character in all of baseball, and his day included such notable eccentrics as Van Lingle Mungo and Dizzy Dean. In fact, baseball was full of characters in the 1930s and despite his short career, Boots was named to sportswriters' lists of the game's greatest oddballs for 30 years after he retired from professional baseball in 1949. Indeed, fifty years after his major league debut, he was featured in the third volume of *Baseball's Hall of Shame*, a series profiling the game's greatest flakes and oddballs.

I spent an afternoon just skimming those scrapbooks, but even that cursory look told me that Boots was more than simply one of baseball's most eccentric players, although there was plenty of evidence of that. His career reflects baseball in all its facets before, during, and after World War II. Boots went from the Texas League to the Detroit Tigers in 1937, was sent out to the Toledo Mud Hens in 1938, sold to the Brooklyn Dodgers in 1939, and sold again to Nashville of the Southern Association where he led all of organized baseball in 1940 with 29 wins. In 1941, through an interesting set of circumstances, Boots found himself playing for the Bona Allen Shoemakers of Buford, Georgia. One of the top semi-professional teams in the nation, they entered the *Denver Post* Tournament for semi-pro teams and faced the Ethiopian Clowns a Negro League team based in Miami for the championship. Boots dueled Roosevelt Davis in one of the greatest games ever played in tournament history. In 1942, Boots played for San Diego in the Pacific Coast League. Drafted into the military in 1943, he played for three different Marine teams and when he came home on leave, he pitched for the local Williamsport town team. Boots returned to San Diego in 1946, but by 1947 he was on his way down and out at the age of 32. That year Boots played only 10 miles from his home in Williamsport, pitching for the Hagerstown Owls of the Class B Interstate League before being suspended for jumping the team. He closed out the year pitching for an amateur Amvets team in Cumberland, Maryland.

Boots returned to the Owls in 1948 for the last month of the season, and for the first two months of 1949, his last in professional baseball. Major league, minor league, semi-pro, military, and amateur, Boots played at every level there was during the era.

Those clippings also readily illustrated how different professional baseball is now from what it was like then. One newspaper photo spread showed Boots bowling and playing billiards as his way of "keeping in shape" over the winter. When he played in Nashville, he was part of a seven man pitching staff on a seventeen man roster. There were no trainers and no coaches, just the manager and the traveling secretary. For appearing in a Wheaties ad, he received $150.00 (which was $50.00 more than Bob Feller received.)

Sports reporting was certainly different then, too. Reporters of the time emptied buckets full of adjectives and flowery phrases into their prose. Vivid word pictures were the only means by which most fans could "see" their favorite players, and the afternoon papers served as the *Sports Center* of the day.

I came home after skimming those scrapbooks, and wrote a 600 word blog entry about the amazing career of Boots Poffenberger, but I kept thinking about all that material and what a good story it must contain—and how long it would take to dig it out. By January of 2012, I could resist no longer and I called Jeremy. He was thrilled to have me start excavating. By the end of May, I had finally dug to the bottom of the big blue tub in which Jeremy had loaded all those scrapbooks and envelopes. And having looked at every page, it was truly amazing what they contained. In one book was Boots' Marine Corps dog tags, simply taped to the yellowing paper. In another was a letter from an anonymous fan chastising Boots for acting like a clown during batting practice. Yet a third contained a photo of Boots and his first wife Josephine looking at the very scrapbook at which I was looking. There was his 1940 contract with Nashville, a series of letters with Bill Lane, owner of the San Diego Padres, discussing his 1946 contract, his draft notice; I even found his social security card in one envelope.

In fact, Boots' first wife, Jo, who had originally assembled the scrapbooks, saved every clipping no matter how small. If the name *Boots Poffenberger* appeared in print, it was pasted or taped into a scrapbook.

Nor did it matter whether the clipping or sportswriter's column or personal letter was positive or negative. It went in a book. That told me something about the man that I was getting to know. He loved attention, but was not an attention seeker; the scrapbooks were not about that. Whether he had done something right, wrong, good, bad, heroic, or stupid, it went in a book. I got the distinct impression that Boots, or Jo and Boots together, had tried to assemble an accurate record of who Cletus Elwood Poffenberger was.

To his managers and coaches, and the sportswriters who covered him, he was the proverbial pitcher with the million dollar arm and 10 cent head or more accurately, the man's arm with the boy's brain. The former got him to the Detroit Tigers in 1937 at the age of 21 and the latter kept him in trouble for the rest of his career. After that successful rookie season during which he enjoyed the nightlife and went 10-5 besting both Lefty Grove and Bob Feller along the way, he reported late to spring training in 1938. Boots not only marched to the beat of a different drummer, he frequently heard an entirely different band and indeed, allegedly missed a game because he had been out late in a Chicago night club, having appointed himself conductor of the house orchestra. Exasperated with such behavior, the Tigers sold him to the Dodgers who, exasperated in turn when he jumped the team in Cincinnati, tried to send him down to their farm club in Montreal. Boots refused to report and was banned from baseball. Reinstated, the Dodgers sold him to Nashville where in 1941 he threw a baseball at an umpire in a fit of hung-over anger and was suspended again. A feud with manager Pepper Martin in 1946 led him to jump the Padres.

As exasperated as his managers and coaches may have been, no one ever seemed to actually get mad at Boots. He was honest and never made excuses for himself. He was an innocent. If that boyish brain got him in trouble, it also attracted a genuine affection from almost all who knew him. Boots was not just a boy, he was *the* boy. Boots fits perfectly Ralph Waldo Emerson's ideal of the self-reliant individual whose practical form is the "independent, irresponsible" boy. The boy, writes Emerson "cumbers himself never about consequences, about interests; he gives an independent, genuine verdict." More than one sportswriter compared Boots to another well-known American boy, Huckleberry Finn.

It wasn't enough for me to know Boots simply through these scrapbooks and old editions of *The Sporting News,* however, and so I interviewed among others, Boots' step-son Jerry Knode and his wife Joan; Connie Cole, the wife of Dave Cole; second cousin, hunting buddy, and Mack Truck co-worker Jack Rupp; and long-time friend Donald "Laco" (pronounced *Lack-o*) Anderson. All spoke of Boots' charm and charisma.

"He was just a guy that if you couldn't like him, you couldn't like anybody," said Anderson a Williamsport native who was a close friend of Poffenberger's for over 50 years. "There's people, I mean I know oodles of 'em that worshipped the ground he walked on."

Anderson first met Boots in 1943 when the former was 12 and the later would come home on liberty from Parris Island, where he was pitching for the United States Marine Corps service team.

> *Everybody knew when Boots was coming home from Parris Island. In my mind right now, I can see him, 'cause he lived down on Vermont Street; him and his wife Josephine, they lived downstairs and his mother lived upstairs. Again, everybody in Williamsport knew when he was going to be home on certain weekends, so it was a matter of how quick it was gonna get daylight on Saturdays that you could expect him to be comin' up that street, carrying his spikes. He always had white socks on, no shoes—no shoes on!—he would walk from Ver-mont Street . . . so you're talking about one block down, one, two, three blocks up, stop at Marsh Miller's Barbershop where he'd grab a couple of bats and a handful of balls. There's where we would spend our day, up there at the ball diamond. There would be at least 10 of us and him. And that would be 'til dark on Saturdays.*

As for not wearing shoes, "It was just one of those things! They were just the whitest [socks]—but you knew damn well they were black on the bottom, but that never bothered him."

According to Anderson, these Saturday workouts at home were a chance for Boots to continually practice his livelihood.

> *He would hit, hit, hit, hit, but he also would let everyone of us hit. Around noontime or 1:00 . . . a fellow by the name of*

Gruber had a store down on the corner of Salisbury and Artizan Street. Boots would get out around the pitcher's mound and this is where he really helped us. He would hit pop ups—not just little pop ups!—and if you caught it, you got a bottle of pop. Boots would tell us as the ball goes up, don't turn around the ring—you'll lose it. He would teach us that when the ball goes up just turn once and back up, but don't ever turn around the ring. But everybody that was there . . . he always made sure . . . because pop then was only a nickel and down to Gruber's we'd go and he bought everybody [pop] and we used to get the big ole Barq's Root Beer 'cause that was the biggest bottle that they had.

He used to have pepper games that would teach you how to get in front [of a ball] and stay in front. He was a good instructor. I can't recall him ever, ever getting' mad or sayin' it's over—we're done for the day. He never quit until it was time to go to Murray's Tavern in the evening.

Perhaps, growing up without a father in his own home or perhaps never growing up at all filled Poffenberger with the desire to spend his Saturdays while on leave from the Marines playing baseball with boys.

In any case, the image of the shoeless Poffenberger, ambling up the street to the barber shop where the town's baseball equipment was stashed, is a dramatic contrast to modern ballplayers, who because of the money invested in them and paid to them have become corporations unto themselves. The way Boots lived his life and the era in which he lived it are more than a contrast—they are an antidote—to the 21st century version of major league baseball.

I'm sure that if asked, "Who is Cletus Elwood Poffenberger?" he would have answered, "I'm Boots" and politely refrained from asking *you* why you were asking such a dumb question. He was just *Boots* to his wife, his teammates, his fellow Marines, his grandson. That makes perfect sense once you get to know him: Boots is just Boots, the common man about whom nothing is common.

A Note About Those Scrapbooks

The vast majority of information cited in this work was found in the scrapbooks which contain such a wide variety of material that a researcher would not even know to look for some of it now. Jo Poffenberger was not particular about noting the dates of some of the articles, nor in some cases did she bother to note even the author or the newspaper from which they came. In those cases, I have simply stated in the text or in the endnotes or both that the source is undated or unattributed or both. For such entries, I have noted in which scrapbook the article appears. Some endnotes contain my best estimate as to the article's publication. Some clippings contain no date, but it is clear from the article itself what day it was published and I have noted that fact. I have designated the scrapbooks and folders as follows:

SB 37-40 for the 1937-1940 seasons, the clippings from which appear in one, large scrapbook.

SB 41 for the 1941 season which includes time with both Nashville and Bona Allen.

SB 42 for the 1942 season in San Diego.

SB USMC which covers the years 1943 through Boots' discharge in March of 1946.

SB 46 for the 1946 season with the Padres.

CA En 47 refers to the manila envelope containing clippings on Boots' time with the Hagerstown Owls and the Cumberland Amvets.

Owls En refers to the manila envelope containing clippings from Boots' three weeks with the 1948 Hagerstown Owls.

SD En refers to the manila envelope containing random clippings from Boots' stints in San Diego.

Boots Poffenberger:
Hurler, Hero, Hell-Raiser

"Boots" Poffenberger
Charleston, W. Va.

CHAPTER 1

Boots' Beginnings

Williamsport, Maryland lies just a few miles south of Hagerstown along the Potomac River. Supposedly, George Washington considered the town as a potential site for the nation's capital, but this may well have been a mere courtesy to his friend Otho Holland Williams, a brigadier in the Continental Army, who founded the town in 1787, the year the Constitution was adopted. The site that Washington ultimately chose is some 70 miles downstream.

Regardless, the locals never felt slighted by the first President, as Williamsport is situated in Washington County, the first county named after George Washington. In 1915, the year Cletus Elwood Poffenberger was born, on July 1st to be exact, the town of approximately 1,600 residents was thriving with a brickyard, a tannery, and the commerce associated with the Chesapeake and Ohio Canal along which Williamsport was an important point. There were plenty of taverns in town in which farmers, factory workers, and boatmen could quench their thirst.

Williamsport's most prominent physical feature was and still is Doubleday Hill. Named after Abner Doubleday who occupied the site in 1861 shortly after the commencement of the War Between the States, it overlooks a ford that might allow an invading Confederate army to cross the Potomac. It was indeed this very ford that General Robert E. Lee used to enter Maryland on his way to Gettysburg in 1863 and then to make good his escape back to what was then Virginia after his defeat. Riverview Cemetery is located across the top of the hill and it contains General Williams' remains, as well as Boots'. U. S. Route 11, the old Wagon Road that carried settlers from Pennsylvania down through the Shenandoah Valley, was the main thoroughfare then; today, Interstate 81 runs along the east edge of town.

Steeped in history and surrounded even today by woods and fields, it was an ideal place for boyhood adventures. Boots' upbringing seems to have been less than ideal, however. According to a July 16, 1937 article in the *Detroit Free Press*, his father Charles and mother Sophia divorced when he was four years old.[1] In the interview, Charles stated that Boots was named after his grandparents on his mother's side, which was true. The article also noted that "pictures of the boy from infancy to manhood" decorated Charles' living room. Jerry Knode, Boots' step-son stated, however, that Boots never talked about Charles and indeed, Jerry stated that he didn't know about him. Neither Jerry nor his wife Joan had ever heard Sophia speak of what would have been her first husband. They always knew her as Sophia Connelly (spelled with only one *l* in the census records), the surname of her second husband, Herbert. Boots' Marine Corps records list his father's birthplace as "unk"—unknown.

Sophia was 19 when she had Boots, then had his sister Maxine one year later. Still listed as "married" on the 1920 census, Sophia Poffenberger lived with her parents, Cletus F. and Mary J. Zimmerman, her three brothers, two children, and a 17 year-old boarder. Sophia's father, for whom Boots was named, owned and operated a canal boat.

"I knew Boots' mother of course," said Jerry. "She was something like Boots. Boots got most of his stuff from her. She was dancin' and jitterbuggin' up at the Redman Club until she died." Sophia, as would Boots, lived for the moment. The family ties were not strong—Jerry did not know if Boots' sister Maxine was older or younger for example, and Boots was left to basically raise himself.

Marine Corps records tell us that Boots made it to the 7th or 8th grade depending on which form in the records one reads.

Laco Anderson provided astute insight regarding Boots' upbringing and what effect it may have had on him.

> *He really didn't have a mother and a father as he grew up. His mother raised him, how long I don't know that, but I know that he did not have the relationship of a father. How much did he miss? I don't know. And I really don't know when he got*

started and how he got started as a youngster. His reaction to people might be [a result of] something that he didn't have. His enjoyment being around people in some of the pictures that you see in those scrapbooks might be something that just popped up on him that he never had any inkling of when he was a youngster.

Interestingly, no note or any other memento from either parent appears in any of the scrapbooks other than that July 16, 1937 article from the *Detroit Free Press* about Charles, and a news photo which ran three days later of four year old Cletus and his father, who according to the caption was living in Cleveland and working as an installation man for Ohio Bell. The photo accompanied a story about Boots' 8-4 victory over Washington.[2]

An interesting cultural feature of Williamsport is that at least through the 1940s every male in town had placed upon him a nickname of some sort. Cletus Elwood was "Boots" because Charles had been "Little Boots" and his father had been "Boots" before him. Jerry Knode never heard this story, however, stating that Boots somehow got his nickname as a child while waiting tables in the tavern where his mother worked. In any case Williamsport nicknames are more than mere childhood fancies. Laco Anderson tells the story of signing the loan papers for his house with his real name of "Donald." The gentleman who ran the bank in Williamsport didn't know who "Donald" Anderson was.

According to Boots' cousin, Jack Rupp, it was Boots' Uncle Russ who taught him how to pitch, while Jack's Uncle Billy was his catcher. "One day they was goin' down to Conomac Park to play this good team from Martinsburg and Uncle Russ said, 'I think I'm gonna pitch Bootsie today. And he did, and Boots beat 'em! From then on he was a pitcher."

The brown-eyed, brown-haired Boots was a stocky right-handed hitter and thrower. Listed at 5'10" and 178 pounds at the time he debuted for Detroit in 1937, his Marine Corps service record variously lists his height as 5'7" or 5'8". It has long been a common practice in baseball for scouts to report that the players they sign are bigger than they actually are. Bigger is perceived to be better. Shortly after his big league debut, Boots began to gain weight much to the Tigers' chagrin. Perhaps, the weight gain was fueled by major league meal money. And major league beer consumption. In any case, by the end of the 1937 season, Boots had gained 20 pounds and by 1943, it was noted in the press that Boots bore a striking resemblance to comedian Lou Costello. Even now the Williamsporters who remember Boots are shocked to learn that he was as short as he was for they all remember him as a big man. His broad shoulders and barrel chest certainly must have helped create this image, along with his larger-than-life personality.

It is not until 1934 that Boots' life emerges from the unrecorded shadows to the spotlight of the sports pages. He played for the Williamsport Wildcats, the local town team and in those days it seems, every town in America had a baseball team. The games in Williamsport and surrounding towns were well attended. Crowds of 1,000 were not unusual on the weekends and according to a 1986 retrospective in Hagerstown's *Herald-Mail*, 5,000 people witnessed the three game series between Williamsport and Hancock for the 1934 Washington County championship.[3] Washington County in fact, had two adult leagues, the Washington County League for town teams and the Industrial League for area industries.

John Steadman, a long-time Baltimore sports writer reported in 1967 that Boots worked for the Civilian Conservation Corps on Maryland's Eastern Shore near Pocomoke City, making $30.00 a month, $25.00 of which he sent back to Sophia.[4] Whether he was signed there or back in Williamsport is not certain, but most sources credit Detroit Tiger scout Billy Doyle for discovering Boots and sending him to the Charleroi Tigers of the Penn State Association, a Class D league and the lowest rung of the minors, in August of 1934. According to a June 5, 1937 article in Hagerstown's *Morning Herald*, local baseball man Paul Nagy may have also helped scout and sign Boots.[5] Poffenberger had both pitched and played outfield for Williamsport and Boots was actually signed to be an outfielder. Five years earlier, Doyle had signed Hank Greenberg for the Tigers.

According to a 1941 article written by Dick Hudson, the sports editor of the *Charleston Daily Mail*, Boots played the final month of the season under the name of Zimmerman.[6] Baseball-Reference.com shows that a "Poffenberger" pitched one game for the Charleroi Tigers in 1934. It also lists a "C. Zimmerman" who pitched in four games and garnered 23 at-bats. Jerry has heard that indeed, Boots played under that name and of course, his mother's maiden name was "Zimmerman." Given the evidence, including the fact that "Zimmerman" and our "Poffenberger" share the same first initial, it is likely that the two players were one and the same. Why Boots would have played under his mother's family name is unknown as there was little concern about one's amateur versus professional status in those days. Players drifted back and forth from local teams to semi-pro teams to professional teams continuously.

At the same time that Doyle signed Boots, he also signed the Wildcats second baseman, Jack Krebs. Steadman wrote that when Krebs was released after one week, Boots figured he didn't have the talent to make it either and so he went back to Williamsport, too.[7] Krebs' daughter, Connie Cole, confirms this story. (Connie married her childhood sweetheart Dave Cole who would himself pitch for six seasons in the major leagues.)

Long after his playing career was over, Boots identified without hesitation Jack Krebs as the best baseball player to ever come from Washington County. "I figured if they didn't want to keep my pal, then they didn't need me. I came on back to Williamsport, but the Tigers came here and got me," Boots told Steadman.[8] This would hardly be the last time that the Tigers had to go looking for Boots.

Poffenberger quickly gained a reputation as an excellent fielder and, according to the *Daily Mail* "managers under whom he has played state that he is without a doubt the greatest fielding hurler they have directed. In fact, Dixie Parker stated that with Poffenberger on the mound the Charleroi team had ten fielders."[9]

Parker, who appeared in four major league games with the Philadelphia Phillies in 1923 was Boots' manager at Charleroi and again in 1935 in Fieldale, Virginia where he played for the Fieldale Towelers of the Class D Bi-State League. Parker was a catcher and it was he who converted Boots into a full-time pitcher. Boots began to gain real notice when he won both ends of a double-header versus Mt. Airy, and ended 1935 with a 16-15 record in 241 innings (to go along with a .288 batting average.) According to a 1938 *Colliers* magazine article, Boots' salary jumped from $50.00 a month to $70.00 a month once it was discovered that he could, indeed, pitch.[10]

Working his way up the Tigers' farm system, Boots was assigned to the Charleston Senators of the Class C Middle Atlantic League for the

1936 season. It was in Charleston, West Virginia that Boots solidified his reputation as a top-notch pitching prospect and also began his reputation as good-time loving, girl-chasing guy who might disappear at the drop of a baseball cap.

His salary was now $125.00 a month "which was high for the Mid-Atlantic," according to the *Collier's* article. Boots so impressed Iggy Walters, Charleston's manager in spring training that he was given the starting assignment on Opening Day. Boots won 16 games against 12 defeats, while pitching 255 innings. At one point in the season, Boots, who would also be christened with the nickname, "the Baron," lost a couple of close games and then was hit hard in his next two starts. The close losses followed by the poor performances

> *sort of got the Baron's goat and he didn't show up one night at the ball park for a double-header. Then he went A.W.O.L. when the team left on a six-day road trip. Maybe he went back home to sharpen up his control . . .*
>
> *At any rate, Iggy Walters, Charleston manager, needed some pitching strength right then, so instead of firing the Baron he coaxed him back and only docked his pay so he would remember not to go running off that way.*
>
> *The Baron not only remembered, but performed so faithfully his "fine" was returned to him.*[11]

The *Daily Mail* of Hagerstown stated in a September 9th article that the season ended on Labor Day and that "Boots Poffenberger, play boy of the Mid-Atlantic League and the outstanding hurler for the Charleston Senators," would be pitching for the Wildcats on Sunday the 13th against the Rosemont Club of Martinsburg at which time fans could witness some of his "peculiar antics." Noting that he had provided Charleston sports writers with excellent copy, the article also discusses Boots' accomplishments, pointing out that his 2.75 earned run average would likely lead the league once all numbers had been tabulated. It was predicted that Boots would be promoted to Beaumont of the Texas League for 1937 as "baseball followers [credit] him with more natural ability than any other hurler in the loop." It was also noted that Boots led all pitchers in total chances, an indication of his fielding skill.[12]

Boots was indeed assigned to Beaumont of the Class A1 Texas League for the 1937 season (although he apparently felt that he was ready to go straight to Detroit.) Class A1 was the equivalent of modern AA baseball, which is two steps below the major leagues. According to Crichton, Boots did not report to Beaumont on time because of a salary dispute.[13]

Thus, the pattern for Boots' major league career was set before he ever left the minors: he thought nothing—quite literally—about exhibiting his eccentricities, he never felt he was paid what he was worth, and if his performance or the results of the game made him mad or there was a good time to be had somewhere else, he simply left.

Notes

1. *Detroit Free Press*, July 16, 1937.
2. *Detroit Free Press*, July 19, 1937.
3. Bob Fleenor, "Old-Timers' Night," *Herald-Mail*, August 23, 1986.
4. John Steadman, "Meet One and Only Boots Poffenberger," *The Sporting News*, August 19, 1967, p 5, 6.
5. Frank Colley, "Detroit Recalls Local Moundsman To Help Out," *Morning Herald*, June 5, 1937.
6. Dick Hudson, *Charleston Daily Mail,* June 29, 1941.
7. John Steadman, "Meet One and Only Boots Poffenberger," *The Sporting News*, August 19, 1967, p 5, 6.
8. *Ibid.*
9. "Country Boy is Headed to Detroit," *Daily Mail*, June 5, 1937.
10. Kyle Crichton "Poffenberger Pitching," *Colliers*, August 6, 1938, p 20, 49.
11. Unattributed, undated, but clearly from 1937 after Boots was called up to the Tigers. Probably from a Charleston newspaper in a scan I made during the first read of this material. The original is now missing or, more likely, misplaced.
12. *Daily Mail*, "Cats To Use Star Hurler," August 9, 1936.
13. Kyle Crichton "Poffenberger Pitching," *Colliers*, August 6, 1938, p 20, 49.

CHAPTER 2

Rookie Phenom

Any dispute Boots may have had with the Beaumont Exporters' ownership over money did not affect his performance on the field. He won nine of his first ten decisions and by early June the home town papers in Hagerstown were speculating on how soon he would be called up to the Tigers.

A June 2nd *Daily Mail* headline proclaimed, "Texas Sports Writers Continue to Sing Praises of County Boy" with a subhead of "Boots Poffenberger Now Virtually Assured of Chance With Detroit Tigers—Rated As Leading Hurler in Texas Circuit." The accompanying article read in part,

> He writes home that he is feeling tip-top and honestly believes he is twice as good today at pitching as he was when he tossed 'em over for the Williamsport Wildcats.
>
> Sports writers over the Texas circuit are of one opinion that Boots is the best in the league. Pop Boone, one of the veteran scribes of the section recently wrote of the high regard in which Manager Jack Zellers [sic] holds Boots and of there being little doubt that the Washington County boy will go up the ladder to the big time.[1]

Three days later, the *Daily Mail* sports pages announced in a headline, "Country Boy Is Ordered To Detroit." Pride in the local product is evident, despite the fact that the paper reported Boots' given name incorrectly:

Cletus Edward [sic] (Boots) Poffenberger is a full-fledged member of the Detroit Tigers today, having been ordered to report from the Beaumont club of the Texas league for immediate hurling duty. Boots' climb to the big time was predicted in these columns a few days ago because of his sensational hurling this spring with the Texas club, a Detroit farm.

In all probability Boots will get his chance with Detroit in a day or two, as the Tigers are in need of pitching strength.

"Boots" wired to his sister in Williamsport that he will report in Detroit tomorrow, and be ready for action whenever called upon.[2]

The Tigers were very much "in need of pitching strength." Lynwood "Schoolboy" Rowe, who had won 62 games the previous three years for a Detroit team that won the American League pennant in 1934 and the World Series in 1935, had come down with a sore arm. Rowe's self-diagnosis was that "a ligament had slipped out of place," and now the Tigers searched their farm system looking for a replacement.[3] Stan Corbett, a 25-year-old-right hander was to be called up from Beaumont but Corbett was on the "casualty list" and so his Beaumont teammate was summoned instead.[4]

Then, as now, businesses sought the endorsements of popular athletes and now that he had made the big time, Hoffer's Sportswear of 474 Pearl Street in Beaumont sent Boots a letter, dated that same June 5th asking to use Boots' likeness in their advertising. Noting that a local column had commented upon Boots' "taste in snappy toggery," the letter concluded with a post script: "Remember that pair of classy sport trousers that you ordered? They'll be mailed to you free if you sign and mail the letter now." (Boots was constantly characterized by friends as a well-groomed, well-dressed man. "Even in his work clothes, he looked good," said Jack Rupp.)

Upon his arrival in Detroit in early June, Cletus Elwood Poffenberger, declared to his teammates, "Just call me 'Boots' and on time for meals. I'm here to stay. I am just a young punk from a small town and I don't know what the hell it is all about, but boy I can blow that apple in there and when I get smartened up a bit, I'll give those batters plenty to worry about."[5]

It's hard to imagine that this declaration was well-received at a time when brash rookies were held in contempt, and in a clubhouse that included future Hall of Famers Hank Greenberg, Charlie Gehringer, and Goose Goslin. Player-manager Mickey Cochrane was a future Hall of Famer as well, but he was not present when Boots arrived having suffered a severe beaning by Bump Hadley in Yankee Stadium on May 25th. The resulting fractured skull ultimately ended his playing career and Coach Del Baker was managing in Cochrane's absence.

Regardless of what the Tiger veterans might have thought of the brash rookie upon his arrival, they must have been impressed when, in his first major league appearance on June 11th, Boots defeated another future Hall of Famer, and a fellow Marylander, Lefty Grove.

The Tigers already trailed the Boston Red Sox 4-2 with only one out in the third and the bases loaded, when Del Baker, summoned Boots from the bullpen to relieve starter George Gill, who had made his major league debut only the month before. Boots induced a double play grounder off the bat of catcher Gene Desautels to get out of the inning and the Tigers took the lead in their half of the third, scoring three runs. Boots held Boston to only one additional tally while pitching the final 6.2 innings and Detroit won 6-5. *Sporting News* columnist Richard Farrington noted the victory in his column, adding that Poffenberger "had never seen a major league park before joining the Tigers a few days before."[6]

In an interview with *Detroit Times* reporter Leo Macdonnel, Baker tried to describe the secret to Boots' success stating that Poffenberger's fastball

> *is what you call a live fast ball. It jumps—breaks fast. And it comes from the box like a shot. Boots uses no windup—he just shoots it out startling like. Hell, I can't just explain it. But, he's got what it takes or else I'm a poor prophet.*[7]

"Just as smooth as silk," states Laco Anderson regarding Boots' delivery. Anderson caught Boots in practice sessions several times back in Williamsport and himself played professionally for two years in the Class D minor leagues.

According to Anderson,

> *Boots short armed and he quick pitched. When he was ready he just chucked her on. He never had a big windup—he was faster than anything in Washington County! They had no [speed] guns, but I would say he was definitely in the 90s [miles per hour]. Some might say much more than that; some might say, "Well, I'm not so sure."*

Boots simply said, "Oh, I don't know. I just pitch like any kid. I like to pitch—I like to play baseball."[8]

The Detroit press loved Boots' irrepressible, boyish nature, which meant that he was always good for a quote, often a colorful one. Almost immediately they began calling him "The Baron" because, "Cletus Elwood Poffenberger" sounded like a royal moniker as far as the scribes were concerned.

He was certainly regarded as royalty back in Williamsport. Not only were his neighbors and former amateur teammates proud of his victory, word had begun to circulate that Boots would stop off in his home town when the Tigers traveled from Detroit to Washington to play the Senators. The June 12th *Daily Mail* exuberantly proclaimed in a headline, " There'll Be Toots For 'Boots' In The Old Home Town Monday: Exultant Williamsport Baseball Fans Plan Reception For Former Wildcat Player, If He Pays Expected Visit":

> *There will be more handshaking and backslapping in Williamsport on Monday, when "Boots" Poffenberger stops off on his way to Washington with the Detroit Tigers than the town has witnessed since George Washington visited there a century ago seeking a site for the national capital.*
>
> *And there may be a band to play "See the Conquering Hero Comes," if the jubilation over "Boots" busting into the big time stuff on the sports pages today keeps on growing.*
>
> *If you are up on baseball it is not necessary to state that "Boots" went into yesterday's game for Detroit against the Boston Red Sox as a relief pitcher in the third inning with the score against him, and emerged a victor by 6 to 5.*

Getting back to the hometown stuff and pride, it is recalled that Cletus, alias "Boots," (he prefers his alias,) has gone from the Wildcats to the major league in about three years, and that's something to cause home town pride to swell to the bustin' point.

Brown's barbershop, where "Pickle" Betts' Wildcats foregather and is the scene of baseball activity in Williamsport, seethed last night from the time news of the Detroit game came in. "Let's get a band," snapped Johnny Whittington, who has umpired behind "Boots" in the local games and admitted he fired the ball in so fast he could not tell whether they were strikes or balls.

So, there may be a band and what else no wildeyed Williamsport fan could tell if "Boots" can get time off on the trip from Detroit to Washington. Anyhow, every baseball minded fan from kids to 70-year olds in Williamsport are in a state of preparation and jubilation to show "Boots" what they think of him in this first successful break into big time baseball. They all said he could do it, and "Boots" showed 'em, they exultantly proclaim.[9]

The box score from the game was tagged, "No. 1 For Boots." Boots did not pay his expected visit, however; instead, the *Daily Mail* reported on the 15th that fans from Williamsport had hired a bus to take them to Griffith Stadium in Washington and had even wired ahead to find out if Boots was scheduled to pitch. The paper noted that Boots' fans "will have the pleasure of meeting their pitching idol even if he does not get into the game."[10]

That busload did, in fact, get to see Boots pitch, again in relief and again pick up a victory when the Tigers rallied for a run in the fifteenth inning to defeat the Senators 9-8. The next day, the *Daily Mail* reported that

The highest praise is being heaped today by the sports writers of the country on the broad shoulders of Williamsport's own Boots Poffenberger as a result of his second victory yesterday in as many starts in major league baseball.

Going to the mound after three older and more experienced Detroit hurlers were unable to stop the Senators, Boots handed

the fighting Griffith outfit six zeros in a row and then supplied the ground ball in the fifteenth which Myers muffed to later permit the winning run to score, giving the Tigers the game.

Needless to say Boots was the real hero of the day and the bouquets being tossed to him today are well deserved. Among the nice things being said about the former Williamsport Wildcat is the following from the typewriter of Vincent X. Flaherty, staff writer of the Washington Herald:

"A fresh, young novice from Williamsport, Md. whose name is Cletus Elwood Poffenberger came in and completed the old master's Tommy Bridges unfinished symphony yesterday afternoon at Griffith Stadium. He came in with his chin up when the Nats had smudged Bridges' superb portrait with six hits and seven runs in the ninth inning.

"And he went on from there, this raw neophyte, shading the Nat's cause with fierce, bold strokes for five flawless innings— for he painted the Detroit Tigers back into the game they finally won in the fifteenth inning, 9 to 8."[11]

The "raw neophyte" did travel to Williamsport after the game and when it rained all the next day, Boots remained at home, not leaving until the following morning. According to an interview Boots gave in 1940, he neglected to inform Del Baker that he was staying the extra day. He joined the team in Philadelphia, but the Tigers gave Boots "a fit, said it was against the rules. I didn't know any better."[12] This claim was certainly conceivable and in any case, the Tigers imposed no punishment. In retrospect, they might have wished they had, for this would hardly be the last time that Boots would operate on his own schedule.

None of that mattered to the local press, if they even knew of the situation. Had a local boy been elected President, it is not likely that the *Daily Mail* could have waxed more exuberant:

Nobody observed any peculiar bumps on the cranium of "Boots" Poffenberger when he blew into his home town yesterday to receive congratulations of Wildcat players and a host of admiring friends and fans for his performance in the Tiger-Senator game in Washington.

If anything, "Boots" was mellower and a little reserved. Of course, he felt "good," as he expressed it, but his sudden elevation to prominence as a pitcher in the big league apparently has not upset his equilibrium. That's a good beginning. Swollen heads have spoiled the chances of many men and women in all walks of life.

"Boots" wanted to come to Williamsport to see his family and friends, and Del Baker, acting manager of the Tigers, said he could have the day off because of his good work against the Senators and the Boston Red Sox.

The good right arm of the young twirler that has been mowing 'em down had to take some punishment yesterday and last night. "Boots" circulated in Hagerstown and got a big hand here as he did in Williamsport.

He said he is getting fine coaching and expects a pitching assignment when the Tigers go to Philadelphia this week. He returned to the capital this morning to get into batting practice, and what else he could not predict.

"Boots" said pitching to the swat smiths of the big league does not give him any more concern than pitching against a sandlot team.[13]

It's not likely that Boots knew what *braggadocios* meant anymore than he knew what a *neophyte* was. Certainly he was becoming more of the former and less of the latter already.

Boots again pitched well on the 23rd against Boston, giving up only one run in 7.2 innings of relief, but that lone run was enough to saddle him with his first defeat.

Making his first start on July 1st, his twenty-second birthday, Boots suffered his first poor outing, a 15-8 shellacking at the hands of the White Sox in Chicago. Boots never made it out of the third inning while giving up four runs. Perhaps, however, Boots was a bit distracted as he was about to take on a major league responsibility. Boots announced that he was getting married to Miss Josephine Brown of Charleston, West Virginia whom he had met the year before while pitching there. At 5'2" and less than 100 pounds, Jo was a brown-eyed, brown-haired bride who would not turn 20 until October 17th of that year. Jo was not even a baseball fan until she met Boots.[14] It was a sudden decision, although *decision* may be too strong a word to use in the case of Boots Poffenberger. Boots acted as he saw fit at any given moment as the future would amply demonstrate and the following newspaper account indicates:

> *Cletus (Boots) Poffenberger, rookie Tiger pitcher, today is far more nervous than he ever was in facing the "wrecking crew" of an opposing team, and for a good reason. "All I know is that it'll be some time within the week," Poffenberger said, running nervous fingers through his hair. "Gosh, but I'm all nervous. I wanted to be married right away, but there is some five-day law or something, and I don't know just when it'll be. I guess it was love at first sight," he said grinning. "Anyhow, we kept up a steady correspondence when I came to Detroit, and when she came to Flat Rock to visit friends, we just decided to get married."[15]*

Whatever nervousness Boots might have had about getting married, certainly did not surface the day before the ceremony when he faced future Hall of Famer Bob Feller and the Cleveland Indians in Detroit. Feller was coming off a sensational rookie season, but was experiencing arm trouble in his sophomore year.

Pitching against the 18-year-old Feller, and with Jo seated behind the Tigers' dugout[16] and keeping score, Boots fell behind 1-0 on a home run by Moose Solters in the fourth inning only to have the Tigers tie it in the bottom of the fourth. Boots again gave up a homer in the top of the sixth, this time to Hal Trosky, but again the Tigers tied the game in the bottom of the same inning. Feller surrendered only two hits in the game, but walks and a wild pitch had contributed to the Tigers' runs. In the bottom of the ninth the Cleveland hurler issued another walk, his sixth on the day, to Charlie Gehringer who eventually scored the winning run when Tiger left-fielder Gee Walker went into second base standing in order to break up a potential inning-ending double play.

"I coulda kissed that Gee Walker out there when that run scored. He mighta got his brains knocked out," Boots told Charles P. Ward, sports editor of the *Detroit Free Press*, who wrote that Boots' teammates "wanted to present him with a victory as a wedding gift."[17]

The *Morning Herald* in Hagerstown noted that the game had been "billed as the battle of the juveniles, because of the youthfulness of the two moundsmen" and that it had "turned out to be one of the best hurling duels of the season at Navin Field, according to sports writers." The paper went on to state that Boots "also gave a classy exhibition of fielding that brought the fans up out of their seats."[18]

In the same article, the *Morning Herald* added that,

> *Although Boots has been with Detroit for a comparatively short time, he has already become a heavy favorite with the fans. After he defeated the White Sox 8 to 4 on July 5 and after his win over Cleveland, baseball followers jammed the doors of the Detroit dressing room to secure his autograph.*[19]

The following day, July 12th, Boots and Jo were married at a friend's house in Flat Rock, Michigan some 25 miles south of Detroit. Reverend W. S. Smith of the First Methodist Episcopal Church performed the ceremony. According to one newspaper account, "Only a very few close friends attended. Mrs. James Hudson, sister of the bride was the matron of honor, while Abner Kaplan of Williamsport, MD was the best man."[20] While "a very few close friends" were present, the *Daily Mail* reported that "several hundred citizens of Flat Rock braved a heavy rain to watch the ceremony from the outside" as several newspaper photographers recorded the event.[21] Boots received a letter from J. R. Burchnell, the President of the Village Commission of Flat Rock that proclaimed it an honor "that a member of the Detroit Baseball Club and his bride should choose Flat Rock for such an auspicious occasion." The letter went on to state,

> *Words cannot properly express our sincerity, but we are wishing you both, health, wealth, happiness, all the luck in the world, and a long happily married life.*
>
> *We also extend to you and your party the freedom of the Village, the Key is yours, and we want you to know that should you at any time feel like returning to the scene of your wedding, we will do our best to make you welcome.*

One of the photographers in attendance snapped a shot of Boots and Jo leaving the ceremony. Boots is nattily attired in a three piece suit with white shoes, his hair is slicked back and he is holding an umbrella, his coat tails flapping in the wind of a sudden shower. The most noticeable thing about the bride is a giant, happy smile.[22]

The *Daily Mail* observed coyly that

> *Boots, whose latest pitching feat was a 3 to 2 victory over Bob Feller and the Cleveland Indians last Sunday, was a great favorite with the fair sex in the automobile city and his venture in the field of matrimony came as a complete surprise.*[23]

Jo immediately began to keep a scrapbook of her husband's exploits and she would dutifully cut and paste anything and everything, positive and negative in a succession of scrapbooks for the next 10 years. One of the initial pages in the first scrapbook contains a program, scored in her handwriting, and a ticket stub from the July 11th game as well as a ribbon from the wedding bouquet. It also contains a napkin from the lounge at the Wolverine Hotel, where Boots and Jo took up residence.[24]

Despite the fact that his record now stood at 4-2 and that he had defeated two of the league's stellar pitchers, Boots was fast gaining the reputation for being one of baseball's true characters rather than for being one of its best pitchers. Charles P. Ward wrote on July 16th:

> *Two weeks ago Baron Poffenberger, discussing the interesting subject of himself and his future said very frankly, 'I ain't so very damn smart but I know how to blow that old apple in there.' Yesterday the Yankees furnished the proof of this statement when they worked the hidden ball trick on the Baron to break up a budding Tiger rally in the third inning.*[25]

Boots picked up his fifth victory in that game, going six innings and giving up five runs in a 14-7 romp over New York, but not before almost committing another blunder on the base paths. With teammate Birdie Tebbetts on first, The Baron hit a pop up to short where Frank Crosetti, seeing that Boots was not running, trapped the ball in an attempt to start a double play. First base coach Cy Perkins yelled for Boots to run hard and Boots barely beat the relay to first. It was Crosetti who had pulled the hidden ball trick on The Baron.

Boots received a note dated July 23rd from Reverend Smith who playfully informed him that since the day that he and Jo were married, he had officiated two more weddings and Boots had notched two more victories. Ever playful himself and always ready to please the press and entertain the fans, Boots was photographed wearing a monocle as befitting his new regal nickname. The photo appeared in the Detroit papers on July 25th with the caption, "'The Baron,' Cletus Elwood Poffenberger who will try for victory number 7 today."[26]

He did not get it. Lasting only an inning and two-thirds against the Philadelphia Athletics, Boots walked four and gave up three hits and four runs. His teammates bailed him out, however, scoring 12 runs and knocked off the A's in a rain-shortened contest, 12-9.

In late July, Boots' friends and neighbors in Williamsport decided to honor him with a "Boots Poffenberger Day" at Griffith Stadium when the Tigers came to play the Senators in early August. Williamsport's Mayor, Richard Hawken, served as chairman of the nine-man committee, with Boots' best man, Abner Kaplan serving as the secretary. They chose Sunday, August 8th—the three year anniversary of Boots' professional debut with Charleroi—and sold tickets for $1.25 which was $.15 more than the actual price printed on the ticket. The committee explained that the extra money would "go toward a suitable and appropriate gift for Poffenberger to be presented on that day."[27]

A block of three hundred tickets for seating behind the Detroit dugout was procured from the Senators and sold by several outlets in Hagerstown and Williamsport. People were urged to carpool. The Washington County League called off all of its games because so many players were headed to Washington to see Boots. Clark Griffith, the Senators' owner had pledged his cooperation and when the initial block of tickets sold out, he was more than happy to forward two hundred more. Tiger manager Del Baker assured the committee that Boots would indeed pitch.[28]

The day was a great success as the *Daily Mail* reported:

> *That Boots Poffenberger is in the majors to stay until Father Time exacts his toll is the consensus of opinion of those 750 Washington Countians who journeyed to Washington yesterday to honor the former Williamsport boy and to see him in action.*

Boots rewarded his many admirers 500 of whom were from Williamsport, by allowing the Washington Senators four bingles in the five innings the game lasted to score a 5 to 1 victory. Boots was presented a big traveling bag made out of Byron Tannery leather and a fine shotgun while his attractive bride was presented a huge bouquet of flowers.[29]

The fans applauded wildly at the conclusion of a "thank you" from "Boots" and the ball game was on.

The former local youth was given a big hand on each trip to the dugout and at his appearances at bat. Although he struck out twice nobody not even "Boots" seemed to care, for the ball game appeared in the bag from the very first inning.[30]

The *Washington Herald* ran a photo of Mayor Hawken presenting a variety of gifts to Boots. Reporter Vincent X. Flaherty wrote:

Mayor Hawken on behalf of Poffenberger's Williamsport admirers presented a handbag and a fancy shooting 'arn which Poffy shall use this off season when the quail get to flying around his front porch. On hand for the occasion was the Detroit thrower's brand new bride who beamed approvingly as her illustrious spouse stepped up, shook hands and muttered a few words of appreciation.

Then came the game and there was a sneaking suspicion whispering its way through the stands that Poffenberger was using his shooting 'arn out there in the pitcher's box, because his fast one—whee!—your guys didn't see it.[31]

As for Boots' "new bride," Jo was not only presented a large basket of flowers she was also presented with her first opportunity to meet Boots' family. One reporter noted that Jo

talks with mock indignation in her slight southern accent about the way her husband has a yen to break training rules, but says she keeps him towing the mark."I looked out for him last year," she says, "and here I am this year—looking out for him more than ever."[32]

"Looking out for Boots," however, was a full-time occupation. Bud Shaver, a writer with the *Detroit Times* penned a column on Poffenberger's fastball, as well as his reputation for eccentricity. The headlines read in part, "Poffenberger Has It . . . He's Three-Ring Circus."

Shaver wrote that he had talked about Boots' "sneaky fastball" with Harry Heilmann, a former Tiger who would also make the Hall of Fame, and who at the time was broadcasting Detroit's games on the radio. Heilmann replied that there's

> nothing sneaky about it. It's just hopping fast, a lot better than a good many of the so called fastball pitchers in the league. And he not only has control, but knows how to pitch. He's one of those guys who doesn't care if he is pitching in Beaumont or the big town. Nothing bothers him, I mean. The ideal pitching temperament—there's a little bit of Dizzy Dean and Buck Newsom in him. He likes to stop those fancy hitters.[33]

Shaver then noted, "When I carried the research a little further I discovered that Boots has more than a little of Dizzy Dean in him. There's a dash of Rube Waddell in him, too."[34]

More than one baseball player has walked the fine line between colorful and crazy; the comparison to Dean suggested the former, while the comparison to Waddell suggested the later. Dizzy Dean, who once remarked "It ain't braggin' if you can back it up," did so. The charismatic Dean pitched for 12 seasons and entered the Hall of Fame in the minimum five years after retirement, eventually becoming a popular baseball broadcaster. George Edward "Rube" Waddell pitched for 13 years in what was also a Hall of Fame career, but was known to miss starts because he was off fishing or playing marbles with kids. He would disappear during spring training and disappear during the season. He was fined, suspended, and unable to play in Massachusetts during the 1908 and 1909 seasons because his in-laws had sworn out a warrant for his arrest on assault and battery charges. Alcohol certainly influenced some of Waddell's behavior but he clearly had what we might now label a personality disorder.[35] This would not be the last time Poffenberger would be compared to Waddell, both in terms of being a "rube" and in his robust appetite for alcohol, the latter trait becoming more apparent all the time. The Detroit writers added "Prince of Pilsner" to Boots' growing list of nicknames. No one was quite sure at this point whether Boots Poffenberger would be more like Dizzy Dean, which is to say brash and colorful, but ultimately in control of himself, or more like Rube Waddell, which is to say eccentric to the point of unmanageable.

Shaver was more than happy to contribute to Boots' budding legend as a true character:

> Down in Williamsport, for instance, the 'big fair' won't seem the same this year without Boots. He is in the habit of sneaking back there every Fall and breaking up the show by knocking the paint off all the baby dolls in those throwing contests. Maybe that's the way he acquired his control.
>
> At any rate he picks up a lot of cigars and prizes and has a lot of fun until the concessions close up to save their stock.[36]

Shaver ended the column by listing Boots' peculiar habits which included "talks in his sleep, carries good luck charms all over his person, won't go near telephones, sleeps through team meetings, talks with bleacher fans and goes on buying sprees."[37] While this list of eccentricities may sound like the result of a sports writer's imagination, a sports writer short on copy and long on an audience who had no other means of getting to know their favorite players except through newspaper accounts, Shaver's description sounded accurate to Laco Anderson particularly concerning the strangest habit on the list. "I never ever seen him use a telephone," says Anderson.

Jerry Knode observed the same thing. "He'd let it ring or he'd just get up and walk out. I have no idea [why he did that.] Boots was Boots." The Tigers were beginning to find out what that meant.

One habit that annoyed Tigers' management was Boots' penchant for giving baseballs to kids in the stands. "I never had nothing as a kid and figured it made 'em happy to get an old ball," Boots told Baltimore reporter John Steadman in a 1967 interview. "But Spike Briggs, who was the owner's son, didn't like me giving away those $1.25 balls."[38]

Back on the diamond, Boots garnered another victory with two innings of relief against the St. Louis Browns on August 22nd, his ninth win against only two losses. He was feeling his oats on the field during the day (the first game under the lights in Detroit was not played until 1948) and spreading them all over Detroit at night. "What's so tough about this American League? I've won nine games already and I ain't even started thinking yet," he remarked.[39]

At least one anonymous fan was decidedly unimpressed and took the time to write Boots a letter expressing his disgust at The Baron's childishness. Addressed to "Mr. Cletus Poffenberger" and signed, "A frequent spectator," the letter read:

> During the time (two hours) of batting practice before yesterdays [sic] game with New York we were very interested watching the workout, as we always are.

> Every man on both teams during that two hours behaved like a man and used the intelligence of a man excepting yourself. Me, and those about us, could not understand why you acted so childish, trying to be cute, attracting attention before all sections. It was most disgusting all agreed.

> Act like a person of normal intelligence if you expect to be at all popular with Detroit fans.

What Boots did to elicit such a letter can only be imagined. Had the "frequent spectator" known Boots, he would have realized that the rookie was not "trying" to be cute or attract attention, he was simply being himself. "Boots was Boots" as Jerry Knode said; this was a phrase repeated in one form or another by everyone in Williamsport who knew him. In any case, Boots' "eccentricities" came as no surprise to the Tigers' ownership, or at least, they shouldn't have. Conrad Hardman, a columnist for the *Charleston Daily Mail* wrote,

> Last year, when 'Boots' was playing the part of 'bad boy' with the Senators and failed to show up at the park several times, [President of Charleston, Watt] Powell slapped a fine on him but promised to refund the dough if he behaved until the end of the schedule. Detroit bosses advised Watt to send the boy home, but the Senator skipper hung on. Now look where 'Boots' is.[40]

In an early September column in the *Detroit Free Press*, sports editor Charles P. Ward wrote about Boots' call to Detroit, noting that owner Walter Briggs' attention

> *was called to the Baron, who had won nine and lost two [sic]*
> *for Beaumont even though he wasn't "really serious about his*
> *work down there" because he thought he belonged in the Big*
> *Time. He came to the Big Time and has been doing very nicely,*
> *thank you.* [41]

There's little doubt that the quote in Ward's piece regarding Boots' lack of seriousness is from Briggs who would have a detective following Boots before the 1937 season was finished in an attempt to discover where the Baron spent all his free time.

In his article on Boots for *Collier's* penned the following year, author Kyle Crichton chronicled some of Boots' 1937 adventures: The Baron never showed up at the ballpark and missed a start against the Yankees at the end of July, then some three weeks later went missing again in Chicago where he was finally found leading a swing band long past sundown. The band, wrote Crichton "was indisputably dizzy from swinging to the Poffenberger tempo." [42] A clipping from an unknown newspaper pasted into one of Jo's scrapbooks provided greater detail—or simply elaborated the stories:

> *Among the more serious charges against Poffy were: That he*
> *once was found leading a swing band at 4 a.m. on a day he*
> *was due to pitch; that he detoured an up-by-9:30 rule by load-*
> *ing him ham and eggs and then snoozing again until an hour*
> *before game time; that he failed to keep a pitching date with the*
> *Yankees, prematurely celebrating his success before reaching*
> *Yankee stadium; that he consistently revolted against pitching*
> *against the Browns and Athletics, preferring opposition to the*
> *top-ranking clubs, etc. ,etc., to mention a few.* [43]

Boots had always made it known that he indeed, preferred to pitch against the best competition such as the Yankees and Red Sox and disdained pitching against the Senators and St. Louis Browns. Boots reasoned that there was no glory in defeating second rate clubs.

By September 6th, Boots had run his record to an impressive 10-3 with a "save" as well, but Mickey Cochrane, returned from his beaning and managing the club again, was quickly tiring of The Baron's almost nightly escapades; therefore, Cochrane began to pitch Boots less often. On September 21st at Fenway Park, the Tiger skipper sent Boots to the mound for the first game of a double header to face Lefty Grove once more.

Cruising along in a 1-1 contest, Boots retired the first two batters in the bottom of the fifth, when Joe Cronin, the Red Sox shortstop stepped to the plate.

"Hello, showboat!" Boots yelled to the future Hall of Famer. In a 1996 interview with John Steadman, Boots claimed that Cronin smirked at him after fouling one off and then Boots laughed at Cronin after getting him to pop out; all this apparently in an earlier at-bat.[44] That the hard-nosed Cronin would try to embarrass a rookie who had the gall not only to be seen but also be heard—and frequently—would not be surprising. Indeed, this game was a rematch of an August 28th contest in which Lefty Grove had defeated Poffenberger 3-0 and in which Joe Cronin was two-for-four with a double. Perhaps a word or look had already been exchanged in that game. In any case, Cronin's response was long and loud and probably cleaned up in translation by a *Detroit Free Press* reporter:

> *Listen you big busher. Take a good look at this ball park. Take a good look at the rest of 'em you see before the season closes and get your eyes fixed up during the winter because you're going to be pitching under electric lights down there in the Texas League next year. This is your last look at the big time, you busher.*[45]

A *busher,* in the parlance of the day, was a "bush leaguer," the "bush leagues" being a nickname for the minors. Being a *busher* had more to do with the manner in which a player conducted himself than with his physical talent.

Boots quickly got ahead of Cronin 0-2 and then tried to throw a fastball as hard as he could.[46] He promptly drilled Cronin in the hip, and that started an incredible 10 run rally of which Boots was responsible for seven of those runs. The Tigers made it respectable, but lost by a final score of 12-7 and Boots' final line was not a pretty one. In 4.2 innings he had given up eight runs, all earned, nine hits, four walks and hit four batters. He had allowed 17 total base runners while recording only 14 outs.

Unlike his first start, against the White Sox in which he might have lost focus because of his impending marriage, Boots might have lost his focus against the Red Sox because of his impending divorce.

In a story dated that same September 21st, Leo Macdonnel of the *Detroit Times* quoted Boots as saying,

> "She has asked for a divorce and can have it if she wants it. We just haven't been getting along. We were too young to marry, I guess. She seems to think my baseball career means more to me than she does."[47]

Jo cited too much competition as the reason for their troubles. "You mean from baseball?" she was asked by a reporter. "No, I mean other competition," she replied.[48]

The next day, the *Detroit Free Press* addressed both the game and the divorce:

> Cletus Elwood (Boots) Poffenberger may be a bust as a husband to his bride, but he certainly was a sweetheart to the Red Sox in the fifth inning of the first game of the double-header at Boston. Ten runs! Zowie! That's almost grounds for divorce in itself.[49]

That same day, the sports editor of the *Charleston Daily Mail*, Dick Hudson devoted his entire "Warming Up" column to the ballplayer who had married the local girl.

> Boots didn't make the headlines this time because of his stocky right arm. It's because he has had a hard time walking the straight and narrow since becoming a big leaguer early in June.
>
> As a result—he will be sued for divorce in the near future by the former Miss Jo Brown of Charleston, who is now at home. It seems that Boots' escapades, which became well known in Charleston last season, have been carried on in Detroit and other American league cities. They have been blown to larger proportions, however, what with more money to throw away.

Boots' marriage ran smoothly for just about one month. Then he began to step out. When informed by his young wife that she planned a divorce, he told newspaper men in Boston about it. He admitted in a letter to Jo that he had not acted right. But he went much too far and she plans to go to Detroit within a week to file divorce proceedings. It's a sad situation for both of them.

Boots is a peculiar fellow. He doesn't deny his faults, but he persists in them. He's in the 'dog house' with Detroit officials and the other Tigers who like Jo and resent his treatment of her. We feel sorry for him. He's just a kid who doesn't know how to handle himself. He is his worst enemy. Boots should never have married so soon—and he knows it.

His wife is taking her disappointment with her chin up. As strange as it seems, we really believe Boots likes Jo. The parting of the ways may wake up the carefree rookie. If so, he can go ahead to become one of the stars of the game. If not he's headed back to the minor leagues—branded as a small towner who was blinded by the bright lights and bold headlines.[50]

Dick Hudson knew what he was talking about, but it would take the Tigers more than a year to finally come to the same conclusion.

Notes

1   "Texas Sports Writers Continue To Sing Praises Of County Boy," *Daily Mail*, June 2, 1937.
2   "County Boy Is Ordered To Detroit," *Daily Mail*, June 5, 1937.
3   Sam Greene, "Tigers Try X-Rays on Rowe Mystery," *The Sporting News*, November 4, 1937.
4   Leo Macdonnel, "Poffenberger Slated to Go to Minors," *Detroit Times*, July 21, 1938. Corbett never did play in the major leagues.
5   Charles P. Ward, *Detroit Free Press*, March 30, 1938.
6   Richard Farrington, "Fanning With Farrington," *The Sporting News*, June 17, 1937.
7   Leo Macdonnel, "Boots Earns Place as Starting Hurler," *Detroit Times*, undated in SB 37-40.
8   *Ibid.*
9   "There'll Be Toots For 'Boots' In The Old Home Town Monday," *Daily Mail*, June 12, 1937.
10   "Many Fans Plan Trip To Capital To Greet 'Boots'," *Daily Mail*, June 15, 1937.

11   "Sports Writers Again Sing Praises of County Boy," *Daily Mail*, June 16, 1937.

12   Fred Russell, "Sideline Sidelights: Poffenberger's Side of It," dateline March 20, 1940.

13   "Same Old Boots Claim Admirers; Hurler Spends Day With Mother," *Daily Mail*, June 17, 1937.

14   Unattributed, "Bride's Prophecy Made On Saturday At Swimming Pool Proves To Be Valid," undated in SB 37-40.

15   Unattributed, "Boots, Ace Tiger Rookie To Wed; Fiancee Will Set Date," undated but probably July 9, 1937 in SB 37-40.

16   "'Boots' Idol Of Tiger Fans," *Morning Herald*, July 16, 1937.

17   Charles P. Ward, *Detroit Free Press*, July 11, 1937.

18   "'Boots' Idol Of Tiger Fans, *Morning Herald*, July 16, 1937.

19   *Ibid.*

20   Unattributed, "Boots Married In Flat Rock," obviously from July 13, 1943 in SB 37-40.

21   "'Boots' Poffenberger Takes Bride In Detroit On Monday," *Daily Mail*, July 15, 1937.

22   Unattributed, undated photo that appeared in the July 13, 1937 editions of Detroit's newspapers according to the *Daily Mail* story of the 15th.

23   "'Boots' Poffenberger Takes Bride In Detroit On Monday," *Daily Mail*, July 15, 1937.

24   I have no direct proof that this is where they lived, but the napkin, along with a 1938 letter addressed to Boots at the Wolverine makes it highly probable. Jo stated in a 1940 interview that they had always lived in hotels until they arrived in Nashville.

25   Charles P. Ward, *Detroit Free Press*, July 16, 1937.

26   Unattributed, undated in SB 37-40.

27   "'Poffenberger Day' Fixed For Sunday, Aug. 8, In Washington," *Daily Mail*, July 22, 1937.

28   "Tickets Ready For Boots Day," *Daily Mail*, July 30, 1937.

29   Boots told John Steadman in a 1996 interview that he still had the suitcase, but had hocked the shotgun when he was "short of money." http://articles.baltimoresun.com/1996-06-30/sports/1996182039_1_beer-williamsport-tavern

30   "County Fans Certain Boots Is In Major League To Stay," *Daily Mail*, August 9, 1937.

31   Vincent X. Flaherty, "Tigers Thump Nats 5-1 In 5 Innings," *Washington Herald,* August 8, 1937.

32   Unattributed, "Bride's Prophecy Made On Saturday At Swimming Pool Proves To Be Valid," undated in SB 37-40.

33   Bud Shaver, "Shavings—" *Detroit Times,* undated.

34   *Ibid.*

35   Dan O'Brien, "Rube Waddell," www.sabr.org (O'Brien's excellent piece is part of SABR's biography project.)

36   Bud Shaver, "Shavings—" *Detroit Times,* undated.

37   *Ibid.*
38   John Steadman, "Meet One and Only Boots Poffenberger," *The Sporting News*, August 19, 1967, p 5, 6.
39   Charles P. Ward, *Detroit Free Press*, March 30, 1938.
40   Conrad Hardman, "Just in Sport," *Charleston Daily Mail*, undated.
41   Charles P. Ward, *Detroit Free Press*, undated, but contextual evidence strongly suggest early September, 1937.
42   Kyle Crichton "Poffenberger Pitching," *Colliers*, August 6, 1938, p 20, 49.
43   Unattributed and undated in SB 38, possibly in a Toledo, Ohio newspaper.
44   John Steadman, "'Boots' was made for walking onto list of great characters," http://articles.baltimoresun.com/1996-06-30/sports/1996182039_1_beer-williamsport-tavern, June 20, 1996.
45   *Detroit Free Press*, September 22, 1937.
46   H. G. Salsinger, "Boots Poffenberger Decides To Be Good To Be Better," *The Sporting News*, February 10, 1938.
47   Leo Macdonnel, *Detroit Times*, September 21, 1937.
48   A badly torn entry in SB 37-40, it is nevertheless discernible that it is an AP story with a hand-written date of September 21, 1937.
49   *Detroit Free Press*, September 22, 1937.
50   Dick Hudson, "Warming Up," *Charleston Daily Mail*, September 22, 1937.

CHAPTER 3

Problem Child

Only Josephine Brown Poffenberger could say for sure why they did, but for whatever reason, Boots and Jo reconciled. Perhaps now that the season was over and Boots was home regularly he settled down into a domestic routine. Most likely, she just couldn't stay mad at Boots regardless of what he had done. Few people could. The couple was not only reconciled and living back in Charleston, but Jo negotiated a $150.00 promotional fee with Wheaties breakfast cereal for Boots to appear in a magazine ad. A Wheaties representative initially offered $100.00, the same fee that Bob Feller received. Jo countered, however, with the fact that Feller was hurt half the year and she received the additional $50.00.[1] The copy reads, "Spectacular young Tiger pitcher, Boots Poffenberger, is out to beat his 1937 record. The 'Baron' is one of a whole flock of Wheaties-eating Bengals. He says, 'You'd be surprised how many Tigers put 'em away every morning!'" However, when called upon to do so by the Wheaties folks on live radio one day during the season, Boots didn't say so. Jerry Knode tells the story:

> The way I understood it, he come down there in Detroit [to the hotel lobby] and he was getting breakfast and it was live then; they didn't have recordings. The Wheaties man paid him the night before and when he come down [he was] to tell 'em he was going to have Wheaties for breakfast. When they asked him what he was going to have for breakfast he told 'em "A beer and a steak!"

31

Boots denied this story to John Steadman saying that, "Anybody who knows me knows that isn't true. I'd either be icing a case of beer in the bathtub or be out at a bar," but Jerry believes the story to be accurate.[2] Articles throughout the scrapbooks reveal that Boots would admit to an adventure on one occasion and then deny it on another occasion.

In any case, while Jo was negotiating Boots' Wheaties fee, Boots' was keeping in shape by the training standards of the day: hunting, bowling, and playing billiards. He was also busy rejecting the contract that the Tigers sent him, claiming that he wouldn't play major league ball for "a minor league salary." According to the Associated Press, Boots

> said he got a raise but claimed a promised bonus for good work was not paid because of a love for the "bright lights." But he said he still thinks this year's salary should be based on his 10 and 5 record. The Tiger rookie said he got his contract last week and spent '32 good cents' to send it back.[3]

It was not at all unusual for players to hold out. It was the only leverage they had in the days long before the Major League Players' Association was formed. In fact, Joe DiMaggio, Ducky Medwick, and Dizzy Dean were also on the list of players who refused to sign their initial contract offers for 1938.

Sports editor of the *Charleston Gazette* Frank A. Knight reported on Boots' holdout, quoting him as saying,

> I was promised a bonus. But do you think I got it? No sir! And they wouldn't pay me what I'm worth this year either. So—what do I do? I send the contract back. No, I haven't heard from them yet.
>
> I am 21 years old [Boots was 22, but The Baron never hesitated to change his story when it suited] and I am a married man and I need more money than I used to need. What is more they told me when I was pitching for Charleston and Beaumont that I would have to wait until I got into the majors before I could start making real money. I am a patient sort of a mug—and so I wait.
>
> Now I am losing patience. If I'm in the big time I think I deserve one of the big time salaries. Oh, I don't say I should get as much

as the guys who have been up there for a long time and have been turning in good records, but I'm worth more than what the Tigers offered me.

Everything was swell as long as I was winning. I chalked up nine victories and had only two defeats. Then I lost three games in a row. And did they hop on me? Wow! Yet I came back to win another as a relief pitcher the day the Yankees clinched the pennant.

But no more night clubs and running around for me. I'm watching my step from now on. I've been keeping myself in shape, too, here in Charleston. Last fall I went hunting every chance I got and now I'm keeping limbered up by bowling. I expect to be down to 182 pounds when we go into training at Lakeland.

So I ask you—if I can win for the Tigers when I'm not in shape what can I do when I am?[4]

Tiger manager Mickey Cochrane probably did not read that article, but he couldn't have missed the blaring headlines that appeared in *The Sporting News* of February 10th, which read, "Boots Poffenberger Decides to Be Good to Be Better: 'If I Can Win Ten Staying Up at Nights, What Can I Do in Shape?' He Asks." H. G. Salsinger, the sports editor of the *Detroit News* who wrote the story, reported that Boots had ended his holdout. Clearly, Salsinger sided with Boots, writing that the contract dispute was resolved

> *in a few days when the club adjusted the matter satisfactorily. He returned to the bowling alleys and the billiard tables and continued his training program.*
>
> *He says they promised him a bonus, but he didn't get it. They substituted a lecture for the bonus. By that time, Mr. Poffenberger regarded lectures as a dime-a-dozen product. He gathered enough, or heard enough, for an entire career.*

Salsinger also expresses admiration for Boots freely admitting he went out on the town. "There are many other gents here and there in the big leagues who keep no better hours than Mr. Poffenberger, but who would deny it under oath."

Boots embellished the statement that he made to Knight, saying, "If I can win ten games in four months in the major leagues while staying out at night, how many games can I win in five and one-half months if I keep in perfect condition?"

Salsinger then moves from admiration to full-fledged adoration bordering on idolatry.

> *Mr. Poffenberger has a strong arm and strong opinions, particularly regarding his own ability. He believes completely in himself and that is not a liability in baseball. No player ever got to the top unless he did believe completely in his own ability. The difference between Mr. Poffenberger and the others is that he is more frank about his opinions. He is open and above-board with them. He does not resort to pretenses or hide his estimates under a mask of false modesty. He tells you right out how good he thinks he is, but he does not say these things in a spirit of boastfulness; he is just as frank about his faults as he is about his virtues. His confessions establish his honesty.*
>
> *Baseball needs men like Mr. Poffenberger. He is a character out of the game's past. When he arrived last June, they called him a 'fresh busher.' We remember when they were all that in baseball; if they were not like that they did not last long.*
>
> *He struts to the pitching mound, adopts a Napoleonic pose, rears back and cuts loose. He throws his body behind the pitch. He rarely wastes one. His fast ball is deceptive, his curve average, but it will improve. His control is good.[5]*

Upon reaching the conclusion of Salsinger's piece, one can only imagine that Cochrane must have instinctively rubbed his head and wondered if it was Poffenberger or last year's beaning that produced a bigger headache. There could not have been on the Tigers' roster or anywhere else on earth for that matter, a personality more opposite Boots' Poffenberger's than that of his skipper, Mickey Cochrane. Friendly and a great handler of pitchers, Cochrane was also intense to the extent that he suffered a breakdown in 1936 after he was named General Manager. That duty was removed from him and he returned in 1937 again as a player-manager before being beaned in May.

There is a telling photo in one of Jo's scrapbooks marked from a "Chicago paper" showing Boots and his manager along with several other pitchers and catchers. Everyone is smiling or laughing except Cochrane who is pointing his finger at Boots, who doesn't look particularly happy, either.

United Press was reporting from the Tigers' spring training home in Lakeland, Florida that Cochrane might use Boots in relief, while the Associated Press reported that Boots might be the fourth starter behind Tommy Bridges, Eldon Auker, and Vern Kennedy, the latter of whom had joined the Tigers via a December trade with the White Sox. Meanwhile the Detroit writers were lamenting the Tigers' ongoing shortage of pitching. Taken together, these reports indicate that despite Boots' impressive record, Cochrane had some serious reservations about The Baron.

No such doubts existed for *Detroit Free Press* sports editor Charles P. Ward who was not about to stand second in line to the *Times'* Salsinger in praising Boots:

> *The Baron has determined to be a good boy this year and has reduced his beer consumption to two bottles in the evenings after games.*
>
> *The Baron seems too good to be true, and certainly too natural for big league baseball. We have a fear that the Tigers will attempt to make him conform to the standard young businessman pattern of the major leagues even if he wins. That would be sad. Too many of baseball's young businessmen are full of dignity. And tripe.*
>
> *If we had to choose between the two, we'd take the Baron as he is and, if necessary, with beer. It isn't every day that you find a ball player as naïve, as honest, as likeable and as human as Cletus Elwood Poffenberger, the first Baron of Sauerkraut. So here's to him as he is.*[6]

Ward also reported that Tiger owner Walter Briggs had "bawled out [Boots] for his transgressions." The incident was recalled by Fred Haney in the October 8, 1958 edition of *The Sporting News*. At the time, Haney was the manager of Detroit's top minor league affiliate, the Toledo Mud

Hens. Haney stated that Briggs called Poffenberger into his office and revealed to Boots a list of his transgressions from the previous year.

"Where did you get that dope?" asked a surprised Poffenberger.

"I had a private detective follow you."

"Well, that shows you're not so smart for a millionaire. If you were, you'd have the detective follow the other guys on the club. You know what I'm going to do."[7]

The story is sometimes repeated with the added line, "I'll be in the bar nearest to the ballpark," or words to that effect.

Mickey Cochrane would never have thought to say such a thing to his boss. Boots Poffenberger would never have thought not to. This was also the same Boots Poffenberger who was telling everyone that he had reformed, explaining to Charles Ward,

> I was just a young kid making more money than I ever made before in my life and I figured I had to spend it quick. I spent a lot of it on beer. A pitcher can't spend a lot of money on beer and be happy. Especially on this club. You know that Del Baker watches the pitchers closely and whenever he sees one sweating a lot, he decides he's been drinking too much beer and he makes him chase fungoes until he is kicking his tongue around. He liked to kill me a couple of times last year.[8]

As for his actual work on the diamond at Henley Field where the Tigers trained, Boots was working on a "ghost pitch" according to Eddie Brietz's "Short Shots" column in the *Charleston Daily Mail*. Brietz noted, however, that the "only thing wrong is that he doesn't know where it's going when he heaves it."[9] In September of the previous season, Coach Del Baker was trying to teach Boots how to throw a curveball, but with apparently no more mastery than Boots had of his "ghost pitch." About his curve ball he would tell Crichton of *Collier's,* "I can't make it out nohow. Sometimes I grab her and she's there; other times she ain't."[10]

Whether he was reformed or had control of his curve ball or struck a "Napoleonic pose," Boots won his first start, a 5-1, complete game victory over the White Sox on April 29th. Five days later, Boots gained a measure of revenge on Joe Cronin and his Red Sox by defeating Boston 4-1 in another complete game effort. According to Charles Ward, Boots had predicted the victory, although he was uncertain about the score:

> *"I'll charge those people and mow them down," he said last night while holding forth in the lobby of the Tigers' hotel. "That Joe Cronin once made a monkey of me and now I'll make monkeys of his monkeys. I'll charge them tomorrow and I'll win that ball game." Chalk up No. 2 for Baron Popoff of Sauerkrat.[11]*

Boots again defeated Boston on May 22nd by a 4-3 score when left fielder Rudy York hit a grand slam in the first and Boots made those four runs stand with another complete game. Cronin did homer this time but Boots actually garnered two singles of his own.

A clipping in the 1938 scrapbook noted that his Tiger teammates enjoyed playing behind Boots. Indeed, he must have been a quick worker. His three victories so far took all of 1:58, 2:00, and 1:54 to play:

> *The Baron is a business-like person. He likes to go out there on the hill, throw the ball up to the batter and let the batter hit it into the ground or pop up to become a putout victim. The Baron doesn't believe in fussing around all afternoon, throwing three balls and two strikes to every batter. He doesn't believe in doing a lot of landscaping on the pitching mound, nor in stopping the ball game to gaze at airplanes, no matter how big they might be. The Baron gets his ball games over in a hurry.[12]*

The national press was beginning to take note of the eccentric pitcher who was at home on a mound or in a saloon. Paul Mickelson, an Associated Press writer filed this report on June 2nd:

> *An up to date report on Mr. Cletus Elwood Poffenberger of the Maryland, West Virginia, Iowa and Detroit Poffenbergers:*
>
> *His pals on the Detroit Tiger ball club call their eccentric rookie pitcher everything from "Boots" to "Baron" to just "Pop-Off-Poff." Like Manager Mickey Cochrane, they think he's as delightful as a raise in salary. His escapades so far have been as harmless, funny and jammed with as many chuckles as the best pie-tossing comedy.*

Because this is the Baron's first full season with the Tigers, you won't find him in the current edition of Who's Who in Baseball but you can find him occasionally in the nearest tavern. There are numerous times when you can't find the Baron at all because he has a habit of making strange disappearances. He's a big, chunky guy but he always dresses in jet black clothes, which makes it all the harder for Mickey Cochrane and his scouts to locate him.

Cochrane thinks the Baron is refreshing because he has a great future as a pitcher and because, like George Washington, he never tells a lie. Once Mickey challenged the Baron when he failed to show up for a game. "Where were you" demanded Mickey.

"Oh, I just got cockeyed," said the Baron.

So Mickey wants to know how anyone can get really sore at a ball player like that. "The Baron," says Mickey, "is just a happy-go-lucky guy who likes to relax now and then. He's harmless and honest. He'll make a great pitcher."

The Baron's weakness is big talk. He loves to win his ball game and then talk it over with a flock of beer-quaffing fans. But if it's a second division club he's just licked, why, the Baron goes off by himself in rather dejected mood. He doesn't get a kick out of beating second-raters.

"I always tell Mickey I don't want to pitch against clubs like Philadelphia, St. Louis and Washington," says the Baron. "Beating those guys don't mean anything. Nobody ever gives you credit for it. I want to beat those good clubs like the Yankees and Indians 'cause that means something.'"

The Baron! A very aristocratic gent with piercing black eyes and dark hair, was born almost 23 years ago at Williamsport, Maryland, but he honors many communities with his residence. He is married. The ceremony took place in Michigan. The Baron isn't exactly sure where but he says it was at "Bad News, Michigan." His wife is from Charleston, W. Va., where Boots once played with the Mid-Atlantic League Senators.

"We Poffenbergers are restless folks," he says. "We're divided up into either preachers or wanderers. I'm the wandering type but

I sure hope I stay with Detroit for a spell because we're going to win some pennants."

Like most strange young athletes, the Baron is a great competitor whether on that mound or in a tavern swinging the baton for an orchestra. In many ways he's just like Babe Ruth—fun-loving, capable and free and easy with his dough. He's got a good fast ball and a snap delivery.

"What's the best way to pitch," he was asked.

"Just charge 'em," replied the Baron. "That's the only way, charge 'em. Let 'em have all you got but charge 'em."

Until last fall, Cochrane was puzzled over the Baron's habit of disappearing. Then, one day at Cleveland, Mickey decided the Baron had inherited his fault from his father. It was the Baron's turn to pitch that afternoon so he got his father up to Cleveland and bought him a ticket for the game. But when noon came, the Baron hunted up Cochrane and asked where he could get his money back for the ticket.

"Pop has disappeared," the Baron explained.[13]

By the end of May, Boots' record stood at 4-1, but the beginning of June was the beginning of trouble for The Baron. On the same day that Mickelson's article appeared, he lost to the Yankees 5-4, giving up 11 hits in eight innings. Four days later on Monday the 6th, he started against the Red Sox, but asked to be relieved because he was suffering the effects of a hangover.

"His uniform was soaked with perspiration and he plainly showed the effects of over-indulgence. I had told him to get to bed early Sunday night because he would pitch Monday but he apparently didn't hear me or forgot what I told him," related Mickey Cochrane to the *Detroit News*.[14]

Boots actually left the game with a 5-2 lead, having pitched six innings, and had even contributed an RBI single, but his replacement, Slick Coffman, surrendered six runs over the final three innings. In modern terms, Boots had turned in a "quality start," but in 1938 asking to come out of a game after pitching "only" six innings was viewed as anything but quality work.

With the Tigers in fifth place in the eight-team American League, and already trailing Cleveland by 8 ½ games, Cochrane felt the need to impose some discipline on his underachieving squad. The game in Boston, in which his starter quit and his reliever coughed up the lead in the final three innings seems to have set Cochrane in action. On Tuesday morning before the first of a three game series against the Athletics in Philadelphia, Cochrane called a team meeting at which he told the players:

> From now on this is going to be a cold turkey ball club. You produce or else. You will co-operate with each other or you will have to begin thinking about paying off a fine.
>
> Furthermore, the privileges that a champion ball club enjoys are herewith withdrawn. You fellows have proved that you don't appreciate them and so you can't have them. Therefore, every man on this club will have to be in his room at midnight every night and will have to register with the night clerk when he does come in. And every man will have to report in the dining room for breakfast not later than 9:45 every morning. Those who report after that time will have to pay for their own meals.[15]

Boots Poffenberger was the first Tiger to break Cochrane's new curfew—that night. The Detroit papers indicated that he had been out on the town all night, a charge that the Baron denied insisting that he had just missed the midnight curfew by 15 minutes. "I tried to bargain with the hotel clerk about those 15 minutes, but he said, 'You can't argue with a timeclock,' so I told him I wouldn't sign," said Boots, referring to the hotel registry which Cochrane had ordered each player to sign each night upon his return to the hotel.[16]

A fine was in the offing and Cochrane was apparently contemplating sending Boots back to Detroit under suspension. The next day, an enraged Cochrane found Boots in the locker room and demanded to know where Boots had been. According to some accounts, Boots was suffering from a hangover. There is no way to know Cochrane's exact question which may have been "Why didn't you sign the register last night?" In any case, Boots' reply must have blunted his manager's anger if for no other reason than to figure out what Boots was talking about.

The Baron rose from his chair, looked at Cochrane and said, "I refuse to reveal my identity."

John Steadman interviewed second baseman Charlie Gehringer who recalled that Cochrane had screamed at Boots,

> *"I want to know your whereabouts!" Boots looked up at Cochrane from one of those little stools we used to sit on in dressing rooms. We all listened for his answer. Then Boots, after a long wait, replied, `I refuse to reveal my identity.' It was so funny, even Cochrane had to laugh.*[17]

Cochrane fined The Baron $100.00 and "had a talk with the young man," according to Leo Macdonnel.[18] Interestingly, Macdonnel also noted that Boots had turned up missing in spring training for a "couple of days" and had almost been sent back to Beaumont as a result of that infraction.

"Mickey's the manager. Maybe I had it coming—I guess," Boots told Macdonnel in a June 9th story. Cochrane told Macdonnel, "I couldn't let Poffenberger get away with it," but the *Detroit Times* reporter reassured Tiger fans that Cochrane "has a genuine affection for the young pitcher as well as a high regard for his pitching."[19] In addition, Cochrane was short on pitching; The Baron remained with the Tigers.

Perhaps the Senators had read Boots' comments about pitching against second division clubs because in the Baron's next start on June 12th, Washington scored 11 runs on 11 hits in only three innings against Boots. His teammates, however, scored 10 runs in the sixth and seven runs in the ninth to defeat the Senators 18-12.

One of Boots' teammates assumed the task of trying to reform the Baron. Ray Hayworth, the Tigers' third string catcher (he would appear in only eight games before being selected off waivers by the Dodgers in September) lectured Boots whenever the two of them were together in the bullpen.

"You are the biggest busher I ever saw," said the 34-year-old Hayworth who was in his 11th season with the Tigers. "Your name ought to be Joe Bush."

Apparently, Boots endured his would-be reformer in good-natured silence until Hayworth missed the train that would take the Tigers to Cleveland.

"The manager of the Bush Ball club," Boots reportedly told Hayworth, adding "Don't you give me any more lectures."[20]

Naturally, Boots didn't require any more lectures because he had now reformed. Again. Leo Macdonnel wrote in the *Detroit Times* on July 20th:

> *Baron Cletus Elwood (Boots) Poffenberger has reformed. He isn't going to play hookey any more.*
>
> *"Naw, I'm through with that disappearing stuff," the Baron announced solemnly on his return from the ancestral estate at Williamsport, Md., where he visited with his mother and friends.*
>
> *"I got special permission from Mr. Mickey Cochrane to go down there," Baron Poffenberger explained. "That's the best way. I'm growing up now. I can't afford to be running away like I did before. Besides, it worries Mr. Cochrane. And I don't want to worry Mr. Cochrane. He has plenty of worries as it is."*
>
> *The Baron recalled his disappearance from Washington a year ago.*
>
> *"I wasn't exactly playing hookey," Poffenberger explained. "I just forgot to tell Mr. Cochrane about it. It was a mistake—like Corrigan made going to Ireland instead of California. Then I overstayed a day—another mistake."*
>
> *The Baron didn't care to go into his disappearing act in Lakeland, Fla., during Spring training or the one in Philadelphia earlier this season. Anyway, he thinks folks should forget those things now that he has reformed.*[21]

That same day, however, in the first inning of a game in Washington, Boots failed to cover first base on a ball that Hank Greenberg fielded, well behind the bag. Greenberg waited for Boots to break toward first, but The Baron never moved and the play was scored as a single. It had been raining in the nation's capital and yet another of Boots' peculiarities was that he never liked to pitch when it was wet; rather than taking a chance on slipping, he anchored himself to the mound. In any case, he walked the next batter on four pitches and, disgusted at his performance, he promptly headed for the clubhouse. Boots had faced four batters, giving up two hits and walking two while allowing two runs. Boots had lost the game and Mickey Cochrane had lost all patience with Boots. The next day, Cochrane suspended Boots and sent him back to Detroit where his fate, which probably included a fine and a trip down to the minors, would be determined.

"I am through with him," Mickey told Leo Macdonnel. "That exhibition yesterday was enough for me. A pitcher who won't even step out of the box to cover first base doesn't want to play in the major leagues."[22]

When informed that Boots was being sent back to Detroit, Jo told Macdonnel,

> "I will not believe anything until I talk to Boots. Sometimes they get things confused. Boots has been working so hard this year, and trying so hard, I don't believe they'll send him back.
>
> "He's a good boy. What they don't understand is that he's really grown up this year. He'll do all right."[23]

Growth is relative and Boots never learned how to deal with his own failures on the field. He would pout or sulk or in this case, when things weren't going right, he simply quit. Teammate Slick Coffman, a fellow righthander who was five years older than Poffenberger sympathized, telling Charles P. Ward,

> "I'm sorry for Boots, I really am. I think he can win up here and now I'll bet they send him out to the minors. That kid has a lot of stuff. Every ball he throws is alive. Hayworth was telling me the other day in the bullpen.
>
> "He has a lot on the ball in the bullpen, but he loses it when he gets in the game. Things go wrong and he gets sore at himself and doesn't try. You shouldn't do that."[24]

Ward found Boots at breakfast the next morning and Boots spoke like a child who realizes too late that pouting has only compounded his problem. The *Detroit Free Press* editor wrote,

> *Poffy is not his usual cheerful self. The incidents of the day before when he was batted out of the box by the Griffs still rankle.*

"Boy," he says with a frown, "I'm a lousy pitcher. I didn't hit the plate with a single curve yesterday. That's terrible."

Poffy reflects awhile.

"Baseball is a funny thing," he says presently. "Last year I came up just a dumb kid who didn't know anything but to try to throw the ball past the batters. So I go right out and win nine games while losing only one. This year I try to be a little smart and I can't get anybody out. I don't know what's the matter.

"I think maybe I came up too fast. Maybe I need another year in the minors. Sometimes I wish they would ship me to Toledo. Maybe I could get started there and get myself straightened out again."[25]

It was during this breakfast that Cochrane informed Boots that he was being sent to Detroit. Boots accepted the news "gracefully," then promptly asked his manager for $10.00.

"Well, I gotta eat on the train and I gotta tip the porter," said Boots who as always had moved on to the situation at hand.[26]

Tipping the porter became a moot point when Boots refused to accept the train ticket to Detroit offered to him by Tiger traveling secretary Arthur Sheehan, after which he promptly disappeared. The Baron turned up in Williamsport, where he announced that "The salary I'm getting is not enough," and that he would refuse to report to the minors. He informed the Tigers that he would return to Detroit on Monday, the 26th.[27] As unbelievable as it sounds, his outrageous actions were not meet with outrage, but with sympathy; and not just from the Detroit press, but from Tiger management as well.

"Poffy isn't such a problem child," said Walter O. Briggs, Jr. "He's a likeable kid and I think this may be worked out."[28] The consensus among Briggs, Jr. and Sr. as well as Mickey Cochrane and Jack Zeller who was now in charge of the Tiger's farm system and who had served as what amounted to the general manager of Beaumont the previous season, seemed to be that the Tiger organization had a better chance of reforming Boots at the major league level and with major league resources than by sending him back to Beaumont or to their top farm club in Toledo.

Edward A. Batchelor wrote that "the inner working of the Poffenberger mind would probably extend the most learned Viennese psychiatrist." He then quoted Zeller who gave a very perceptive analysis:

> Poffenberger is a sort of Topsy. He seems to have just grown up wild as a boy. His first encounter with discipline apparently came when he entered organized base ball. Never having known discipline, he refused to recognize authority.
>
> "Even his drinking seems more a desire to defy rules than a craving. He likes to be the center of a group and it's easy to do that in a bar.
>
> "It's a question of immaturity. If the boy is ever going to grow up he ought to be able to learn just as easily up here."[29]

Zeller noted that there were also a couple of flaws in Boots' delivery that if corrected, would make him a better pitcher, but The Baron had refused to take any advice.

Charles P. Ward believed that the root of Boots' problem was money. That is to say, if he had it, he disappeared in search of a good time and if he didn't, The Baron disappeared until he was paid what he thought he was worth. According to Ward, the Tigers hit on the strategy while Boots was still with Charleston of paying his salary in small increments figuring that the faster the money ran out, the more likely it was that Boots would stay at home, both literally and figuratively.[30] Once he got to Detroit, they figured that he would get serious about his craft. Once he got married, they figured that he would become more serious. They should have stopped figuring.

Even without the aid of a "Viennese psychiatrist," the Tigers were understandably guilty of over-analyzing their eccentric young pitcher: For Boots, it was all about the fun to be had during the moment at hand and Ward's description of "the friendly battle" that Boots waged with Mickey Cochrane over the breakfast rule reveals Boots' outlook. At first, Boots would arise at 7:30 or 8:00, eat breakfast, and then go back to bed, but when The Baron realized that Cochrane approved of this maneuver, he changed tactics. Poffenberger took to sleeping all morning, "ordered breakfast food at noon and called it lunch. He made up for the lost meal

at dinner." Interestingly, Ward stated that during this "war" on the breakfast rule, "no angry words had been spoken by either [Boots or Cochrane]."

Ward wrote a now familiar refrain:

> *Those who have to chronicle the doings of the Tigers hope that
> Poffy's suspension is not final. With all his faults he is as like-
> able, as amusing and as unpredictable as a pet monkey.*

> *There are not many Poffys or Waddells in baseball nowadays,
> and more's the pity. They come in handy when a guy has to dig
> up a color story on a club that is sadly lacking in color. And the
> Tigers are getting more colorless by the year.*

> *But Poffy probably will receive another stay of sentence. He is a
> hard guy to turn loose. And a harder guy to hang on to. In base-
> ball today there is nobody quite like Poffy. Which is one reason
> his bosses are puzzled.*[31]

For whatever reason, most likely because Zeller felt that he had no
one better in the minors with whom to replace Boots, his suspension was
lifted and he was not sent out. Mickey Cochrane gave him a stern talking
to and Boots promised that he had learned his lesson.

A photo of Boots and Mickey appeared in the Detroit papers as proof
that this had taken place, although the sarcastic tone of the caption-writer
certainly indicated that he and others, probably 99% of Detroit had their
doubts. The caption read, "Cochrane Lays Down the Law to the Baron
Before Officially Announcing the Great One's Reinstatement" and the
photo showed Cochrane in a wooden swivel chair leaning in to Boots who
wears a glum expression. Boots is looking down at his hands; he seems
to be fiddling with a nail and appears to be working hard at looking con-
trite. Both are in uniform.[32]

Tod Rockwell, the quarterback of Michigan's 1923 national championship team, who was now a sports writer for the *Detroit Free Press*
reported on Boots' unauthorized trip to Williamsport:

> *Poffy showed up at his home town apparently to get away
> from it all.*

> *"But it rained all the time and I couldn't go fishing," the Baron
> complained. "And otherwise I couldn't relax because they were*

burning up the telephone and telegraph wires. I guess every-thing will be all right now."

Poffy requested that it be publicized that he had learned a vital and valuable lesson. He put it this way: "The Baron now is himself."[33]

And that was exactly the problem; The Baron was *always* himself. As Charles P. Ward wrote, Boots "will tell how he promised to be a better boy and how he stepped out of the office and promptly forgot the promise. Poffy is not to be blamed for forgetting. That is the kind of guy that Nature made him. Poffy didn't have any say in the matter."[34]

Boots finally returned to the playing field in a game against the Athletics on July 30, starting the second game of a Sunday double header. Whether it was the recent lack of work, the drama, a flawed delivery, too much beer, or a combination of everything, Boots stunk up Briggs Stadium as it was now called. (Walter Briggs had added double-decking down the foul lines and across the outfield to Navin Field during the off-season, giving Detroit's ballpark the look it would have until it was replaced by Comerica Park in 2000.) Lasting only four innings, The Baron surrendered eight hits, including two home runs, six runs (five earned) and three walks. The Tigers came back to win the game 8-7 for their eighth straight victory, but despite the win, they were still only a .500 team and stuck in fourth place, nine games in back of third place Boston and 12.5 games back of front-running New York. Time was running out on the season and, needing to change things around and no doubt weary of Boots' behavior, the Tigers sent The Baron down to the Toledo Mud Hens then of the American Association. They recalled right-hander Al Benton who pitched previously for Detroit and who would enjoy a 14 year big-league career.

Dated August 2, 1938 and signed by Walter O. Briggs, Jr., Boots' "Notice to Player of Release or Transfer" noted that the Tigers retained the right of "24 hours' recall." In those days, a player could be recalled from the minors within 24 hours of being sent down, which meant that teams were shuffling rosters without any player actually having to report to the minors. The rule was amended in the early 1950s and is still in effect so that a player has to stay at least 10 days on a minor league roster unless replacing an injured major league player.

Starting the second game of a double-header for Toledo in Indianapolis on the 3rd, Boots notched a 12-2 victory and enjoyed a stellar day at the plate going two-for-four with two RBI and two runs scored.

In a remarkable stroke of bad timing, a feature article on Boots appeared in the August 6th edition of *Collier's*. Author Kyle Crichton detailed Boots life in Williamsport as well as his signing and rise to the majors. Crichton also chronicled the colorful parts of Boots' brief career including the incident with Joe Cronin in Boston and Boots proclivity to "step out" as the saying was. Crichton concluded thusly:

> *Young Boots is a throwback to something. He is likable, he is dead game and he is independent. If he looks on the flowing beaker, it is out of no evil design—it means merely that he has met congenial companions. If the boss wants him to pitch to the hitters in batting practice, warm up for eight innings and pitch the remainder of a sixteen inning game, he'll be in there doing it. He can field; he can hit; he will take the leg off anybody who attempts to halt him in mid-flight. If he can stick in the big leagues, he will come out better than most players, for the club only pays him spending money, keeping the rest in trust for him.*
>
> *The other players can't buy him anything and can't lend him money, under penalty of execution by Cochrane in person. The gentleman is a mystery to himself, just as he is a mystery to Mickey. In a way he is a philosopher. About the New York Yankees he says: "Just when you think you've got them they've got you."*[35]

Boots continued to pile up victories for manager Fred Haney in Toledo and he was pitching a large number of innings, which was his wish. Frank Buckley of the *Toledo News-Bee* reported:

> *A fellow cannot work a game today, then labor in the bullpen for another 10 days in Poffenberger's opinion. He got a good start with the Tigers this year, then bogged and in his words had "his ears pinned back.*
>
> *"It was my own fault," the Baron said, "I was wild and got behind the batters too much. When a pitcher gets behind like that he's got to have something to catch up, I'm going to get*

that something with the Mud Hens. I want to pitch and after my regular turn, I'll take a relief role the next day, if the boss needs me," Poffenberger concluded.

Haney will see to it that Poffenberger gets plenty of work as a Mud Hen. The Baron is one of nine pitchers the boss has at his call for a parade of double headers on the road in the waning weeks.[36]

Boots' attitude runs directly opposite the modern game's obsession with five man rotations and pitch counts, but how to keep pitchers healthy is a question almost as old as the game. In his *Mirrors of Sport* column entitled "Let's Feel Sorry for Pitchers," *Toledo Blade* sports editor Bob French wrote

Pitchers, the most valuable animals in the baseball menagerie, are getting a great deal of attention and much sympathy these days. They are bogging down under the strain so rapidly that the best place to get an action photograph of a hurler is in a hospital. All concerned—fans, managers, club owners and big league officials—are wondering what can be done to keep the species from becoming extinct.[37]

Boots piled up an 8-3 record in month and a half pitching for the Mud Hens, which was twice the number of victories he had accumulated in his three and a half months in the majors that season. Detroit recalled The Baron in mid-September and Boots defeated the Athletics 3-0 in a rain-shortened contest on the 21st. He won his next start on the 25th against Cleveland, recording a complete game, but not pitching particularly well, giving up 10 hits and five runs while striking out only two. In his final start on October 1st, this time in Cleveland, he absorbed a 5-0 loss, giving up all five runs in six innings while walking six. His final major league record for 1938 stood at 6-7. Detroit had come on strong during the final third of the season, going 37-19 under Del Baker who was named Tiger's manager after Mickey Cochrane was fired on August 6th, shortly after Boots was sent to Toledo (and adding an even greater sense of bad timing to Crichton's article). Based on their late season run and an outstanding lineup, Detroit had hopes of overtaking the Yankees in

1939. The question for the Tigers as it is for most teams every season was would they have enough pitching? Part of the answer to that question was in the form of another question: Would Boots Poffenberger report to Spring Training, on time, in shape, and ready to consistently apply himself to his craft?

Notes

1   Charles P. Ward, "Ward to the Wise," *Detroit Free Press*, undated.

2   John Steadman, "In character-rich game, Poffenberger was a jewel," http://articles.baltimoresun.com/1999-09-05/sports/9909040420_1_poffenberger-gehringer-cochrane, September 5, 1999.

3   Associated Press, "Boots Poffenberger Is Tiger Holdout; Contract Returned," undated, but probably late January, 1938 in SB 37-40.

4   Frank A. Knight, "Boots Determined Tigers Must Pay—And Pay," *Charleston Gazette*, undated.

5   H. G. Salsinger, "Boots Poffenberger Decides To Be Good To Be Better," *The Sporting News*, February 10, 1938.

6   Charles P. Ward, *Detroit Free Press*, undated, but probably from March 30, 1938.

7   Dick Young, "Young Ideas," *The Sporting News*, October 8, 1958.

8   Charles P. Ward, *Detroit Free Press*, undated, but probably from March 30, 1938.

9   Eddie Brietz, "Short Shots," *Charleston Daily Mail*, March 28, 1938.

10   Kyle Crichton "Poffenberger Pitching," *Colliers*, August 6, 1938, p 20, 49.

11   Charles P. Ward, "Poffenberger's Boast Fulfilled As Tigers Win," *Detroit Free Press*, May 4, 1938.

12   Unattributed, "Tigers Like to Play Behind Poffenberger," undated.

13   Paul Mickelson, AP report appearing in Frank Colley's "The Colley-See-Um of Sports" column in the *Morning Herald*, June 8, 1938.

14   H. G. Salsinger, "Cochrane Assesses Him $100," *Detroit News*, June 8, 1938.

15   Charles P. Ward, *Detroit Free Press*, June 8, 1938.

16   Charles P. Ward, *Detroit Free Press*, undated.

17   John Steadman, "In character-rich game, Poffenberger was a jewel," http://articles.baltimoresun.com/1999-09-05/sports/9909040420_1_poffenberger-gehringer-cochrane September 5, 1999.

18   Leo Macdonnel, "Baron Breaks Tigers Curfew Law," *Detroit Times*, June 8, 1938.

19   Leo Macdonnel, "Poffenberger Silent After $100 Fine," *Detroit Times*, June 9, 1938.

20   Unattributed, undated in SB38.

21   Leo Macdonnel, "Poffenberger Admits He Has Reformed," *Detroit Times*, July 20, 1938.

22 Leo Macdonnel, "Poffenberger Slated to Go to Minors," *Detroit Times*, July 21, 1938.

23 *Ibid.*

24 Charles P. Ward, *Detroit Free Press*, July 21, 1938.

25 *Ibid.*

26 H. G. Salsinger, "The Umpire: Poffenberger Boots Another Chance," *Detroit News*, undated, sometime after July 15, 1946 when Boots was suspended by San Diego. Borrowing $10.00 is reported by Charles P. Ward in a March 8, 1939 story, but he does not include the reason, i.e. tipping the porter, etc.

27 *Detroit Times*, "Boots Demands More Money," July 22, 1938.

28 E. A. Batchelor, Jr., "Poffy Hears Fate Today," *Detroit News*, undated.

29 *Ibid.*

30 Charles P. Ward, *Detroit Free Press*, July 23, 1938.

31 *Ibid.*

32 Unattributed, undated in SB 37-40.

33 Tod Rockwell, "Baron Learns Lesson from His Suspension," *Detroit Free Press*, undated.

34 Charles P. Ward, *Detroit Free Press*, undated, but sometime around July 24, 1938.

35 Kyle Crichton "Poffenberger Pitching," *Colliers*, August 6, 1938, p 20, 49.

36 Frank Buckley, "Baron Poffenberger Craves Regular Work," *Toledo News-Bee*, most likely August 4, 1938.

37 Bob French, "Mirrors of Sport: Let's Feel Sorry For Pitchers," *Toledo Blade*, undated.

CHAPTER 4

The Dodgers, Down, and Out

Boots and Jo returned to Williamsport for the offseason. Unlike any other major league ballplayer at the time, Boots Poffenberger received a check from his team throughout the entire year as the Tigers thought it better to ration out Boots' pay so that he wouldn't have too much of it at once. Jack Zeller, the Tigers' General Manager "found that money disappears from Poffenberger even more quickly than Sir Poff can disappear from the ball club."[1]

Of course, the problem for Jo was that even if Boots had just a little money, he was going to spend it, and spend it on a good time. This did not make for a calm winter. One of the first clippings pasted in the scrapbook for 1939 is an undated blurb that reads, "Ho, Hum, the Boots Poffenbergers have made up again although the Mrs. did file for divorce last week. Boots has been given more last chances than the cat with nine lives. Someone should tell Poffy about the foolish shepherd boy who cried, 'wolf, wolf' too often."[2]

As for his off-season training regimen, Boots was playing fullback for the Williamsport Wildcats town soccer team. A Detroit writer noted this fact, adding, "His bosses are hopeful that he will report at Lakeland in fair physical condition."[3]

He did not. In fact, he didn't even report on time, despite his off-season pledge to do so. Detroit's first official workout occurred at 10:30 a.m. on February 27th and according to Charles P. Ward, every Tiger reported on time, "with one exception. He was—yep, you guessed it—Cletus Elwood Poffenberger, first Baron of Sauerkraut, first Duke of Weinerschnitzel, Lord of the Liverwurst and Earl of the Pretzel. Without a word of warning, the Baron turned up missing. Again."[4]

On March 1st, Ward wrote an entire column dedicated to Boots' absence:

> *New and more interesting rumors drifted into Lakeland today concerning the whereabouts of Cletus Elwood Poffenberger, the Tigers' missing pitcher. They were:*
>
> *1—That Poffenberger had decided to abandon baseball to become a snake oil salesman with a carnival.*
>
> *2—That Poffenberger had become an orchestra leader and was acting as master of ceremonies in a Maryland night club.*
>
> *3—That Poffenberger had lost his advance expense money and ticket and was waiting at home until Secretary Arthur T. Sheehan sends him another order of the same.*
>
> *4—That Poffenberger had lost his calendar and therefore didn't know he was supposed to be in camp.*
>
> *"I haven't heard a word from him," laughed [Manager Del] Baker today between swings of a fungo stick, except the report that he had bought himself a hurdy-gurdy and a monkey and was working his way south. But I'm not worried about him. I know he'll be in. He will probably report with the second squad of pitchers Monday."[5]*

The third rumor on Ward's list proved to be most accurate, although Boots did not "lose" his advance money since Boots always spent money much faster than he could lose it. Del Baker did state on March 3rd that he had heard from the Baron who said that he would "report later."[6] The next day the Associated Press reported that Baker had received a telegram from Boots stating that he "had been detained" in Williamsport "because of business."[7] Boots finally arrived in Lakeland on the 7th stating, "I received some expense money and also a railroad ticket. But when I got through paying my bills, I didn't have any expense money left. So I had to wait until the club sent me more. I couldn't fast all the way to Lakeland."[8]

Baker, who had consulted with team owner Walter Briggs on the matter, told Ward

> *"Oh, he's been on some kind of a sit-down strike over expense money," said Baker impatiently when asked whether it were true that Poffy had eaten his railroad ticket as reported. "He didn't eat it and he didn't hock it; he has the ticket. But he didn't have the expense money he was supposed to have. So he refused to come to camp until we sent him some more."*

> *"The guy could be a 20-game pitcher if he wanted to be," he said, "and we're going along with him in the hope that he will get some sense. Maybe this will be the year."*

> *Baker fled when it was recalled that Rube Waddell never got any sense, even with advancing years.[9]*

A photo by Dan Sanborn that appeared in the *Lakeland Ledger* shows an unhappy looking Boots shaking hands upon his arrival with a wary Del Baker. The caption reads in part:

> *The good Baron put in a belated arrival yesterday after waiting a week in his Williamsport, Md., home for the club to send him some additional expense money. While he was 20 pounds overweight, he stunned onlookers by winning a foot race which was put on the practice program for his special benefit—or embarrassment.[10]*

Baker no doubt thought the foot race represented a "teachable moment," but the incorrigible pupil ruined the lesson when he beat rookie pitcher Jim Lynn in a race from home to second by way of first for Boots and by way of third for Lynn.[11] As for being overweight, Boots had a very logical explanation. "Boots Poffenberger says he's overweight because the Tigers made him get up too early . . . Instead of letting him snooze, the Baron pointed out, they rolled him out at 8 a.m., and he had to eat breakfast, luncheon and dinner . . . By sleeping until 1 in the afternoon he would require only one meal."[12]

Fellow right-hander Roxie Lawson, who had attended Iowa Wesleyan College explained his theory regarding Boots to Charles P. Ward:

Roxie Lawson, who says that Baron Poffenberger is the best young pitcher on the Detroit ball club, insists that he is being demoralized by listening to the conversation of such persons as Charley Gehringer and Hank Greenberg. "Those guys use too many big words," said Lawson, "Why last year when Mickey Cochrane asked Poffy where he had been the night before, he replied, 'I refuse to reveal my identity.' That isn't what he meant. He was just trying to use words that Gehringer and Greenberg use."[13]

Another Tiger teammate, shortstop Billy Rogell asked to be Boots' roommate during spring camp on the chance that he could help Boots find that straight and narrow path that the latter was always pledging to walk. Rogell told Charles P. Ward:

> Poffy is not a bad guy to have for a roommate, but he talks too much. He sort of hypnotizes you with his constant chatter. Why, last night he gave me such an ear-beating that instead of taking my shoes off to go to bed, I put them on. Maybe I'll get used to him after awhile. He'll only pop off when I tell him to. At least that is part of the agreement. But you can't always tell about Poffy.[14]

Indeed, now that he was actually in Lakeland, The Baron was telling everyone, "I'll be in there winning games for the Tigers. I mean it this time when I say that I'm going to cut out all the playboy stuff. I'm beginning to think it doesn't pay."[15]

H. G. Salsinger applied an old baseball saw to Boots in an article headlined, "Poffy Again Resolves to Sin No More," describing him as a pitcher with a million dollar arm and a ten cent head. "Well, I didn't put that price on my arm; it was somebody else. Maybe I ain't overrated as a thinker," Salsinger reported Boots as saying. "And maybe they're right. Here I am, 24 years old, and still doing childish things. When a man reaches the age of 24 he ought to be acting sensibly, shouldn't he? Well, I guess it's about time I got some sense." Boots assured Salsinger that "they'll find me walking the straight and narrow" especially knowing that the Tigers were keeping an eye on him. Salsinger's conclusion was rather philosophical and definitely insightful:

*He is sincere in his promise and his prophecy but he has been
making the same promises and the same prophecies ever since
he joined the Detroit club and we're pretty sure that he isn't
going to keep any of them because he never has. Not that it
is his fault, any more than it was the fault of George Edward
Waddell when that left-hander used to behave much like the
right-handed Mr. Poffenberger behaves today. The spirit is willing but the flesh is weak and, as Baker says: "You can't help but
love the guy for his faults."[16]*

The flesh was not only weak after three weeks in training camp,
there was still too much of it. Regardless of how hard he worked, Boots
could not shed his excess weight. In fact, some reports indicate that Boots
actually gained weight as March wore on. One newspaper photo in the
1937-40 scrapbook contains a photo of Boots running in a windbreaker
in an obvious effort to lose weight. On the same page, and under the
headline of "A Guy Can't Be Working All the Time," another photo shows
Boots napping on a bench. Boots definitely worked while being watched,
but apparently he wasn't watched too often.[17]

In a game on March 28th, Boots relieved rookie Fred Hutchinson,
facing only two batters one of whom he walked before he pulled himself
from the game with a sore arm. A clipping in the scrapbook described
the injury as "stiffness in the elbow," adding, "The Tigers are figuring on
Boots as a starting hurler and when the soreness leaves his arm he will be
right out there tossing in his regular turn. Let Boots stick close to Baker
and follow his instructions and he will be a 20 game winner this year and
you can put that down in your book."[18]

The only thing that was "put down," however was Boots when the
Tigers sent him out to Toledo just a couple of days later. In a March 31st
article, Charles P. Ward wrote:

*One of the saddest men in camp over the scheduled departure
of the Baron was Manager Del Baker. In fact he seemed sadder
than the Baron himself.*

*"The boy could be a starting pitcher on our club if he only tried,"
said Baker, "And I was counting on him because I thought he
would. I'm as sorry for his sake as for my own."*

The Baron worked hard, they agreed, but they insisted that he did so only in spurts and that he fattened up on fun between workouts.

The Baron himself seemed unremorseful at the news of his release.

"I knew I was going a week ago," he said with customary frankness, "but didn't say anything because I was told to keep my mouth shut when newspaper men were around."

The Baron's act was a severe blow to Willie Rogell, the good Samaritan, who had asked to be made the Baron's roommate this season in the hope of getting him interested in the straight and narrow path. The morning before the Baron walked off the mound [referring to the March 28ᵗʰ game] Rogell had sat up with him until 3 o'clock, giving him a pep talk. When he went to bed, he finally thought that he had talked the Baron into being serious.[19]

On April 1ˢᵗ, the Associated Press reported that General Manager Jack Zeller "said yesterday the Detroit organization was definitely through with the eccentric Poffenberger and that if no major or minor league club wanted to buy him, he would be given an unconditional release."[20] The AP also reported that Detroit had offered Poffenberger to the Browns where Fred Haney, his manager the previous year in Toledo, was now the skipper. Haney had no desire to reunite with Boots and explained his reasoning to Bob Murphy a columnist with the *Detroit News*:

"One of the most unusual characters I ever met in baseball," said Haney. "The Tigers ordered him to Toledo. He reported on schedule.

"I knew I had something on my hands. I decided to see if I couldn't find a way to handle him. The day he reported I called the whole squad together.

"I gave them a little routine talk about the day's game, about certain batters and their supposed weakness. Then I directed some remarks toward Poffenberger.

"Poffy," I said, "you had Cochrane half crazy up at Detroit. But you're not going to do this to me. It's up to you. Go out and do what you please. I'm not going to bother about you. If you are willing to work, you are going to get your regular turn. If you are not willing to work, I'm going to forget about you."

"The funniest thing of all happened in Milwaukee. 'Poffy' had been watching the veteran Fred Johnson pitch with that easy motion of his. 'Poffy' decided this was the way to pitch.

"I put him in a game on Sunday in Milwaukee and he started to imitate Johnson. I walked out to the mound and talked to him. I told him Johnson had to pitch that way because he had no fast ball . . . that Johnson had to depend on control and brains. I told Poffenberger his only chance was to fire the ball at the batter. Everything I said went over his head. He tossed them in and they blasted the ball all over the lot. I took him out in the second inning."

Haney recounted how "Poffy" refused to come to the bench when he left the mound.

"I followed him to the dressing room," continued Haney, "I told him that I had taken him out only because a Sunday crowd was there and I couldn't see them pay their money and see such an exhibition as he was giving.

"I told him he was going back on the mound the next day—on Monday. I told him he was going to stay nine innings even if they scored 100 runs. Once more I told him he couldn't imitate Johnson . . . that he had to fire the ball toward the batters.

"Well, I started him the next day. But, by goodness, he started the same thing all over. He was trying that pretty delivery. He was trying to show off fancy. The first two balls he served up were hit back at him, and one struck his shin. 'Boots' went down. I walked out to the box, and he was groaning.

"Git up," I said to him. "Git up from there and pitch. You are going to stay, even if you pitch on one leg.

"Poffenberger got up as mad as a wild boar. He grabbed the ball and started firing away. They didn't touch him the rest of the game and we won a shutout victory.

"After the game I sent the clubhouse boy out for a bottle of beer. I took it over to 'Boots' and said: 'Well, here is something you deserve. I know now how to make you pitch. I'll hit you on the shins.'

"He's a good kid," concluded Haney "and I would have claimed him off the Tigers by the waiver route, but for one reason. He's always going to do things his own way off the ballfield. I've got a lot of young kids on my club. Every one of those kids has a chance to make good. If one of them happened to turn out like 'Poffy' I would always blame myself.

"But I still like him. He's a grand guy."[21]

In a rambling interview with Leo Macdonnel, published April 1st, Boots acknowledged that being sent down might "be a good thing," then stated he didn't know if he would report to Beaumont where the Toledo club was training. He threatened to return to Williamsport and play soccer and semi-pro ball. He threatened to quit altogether. He wondered why Detroit didn't trade him to another club. He blamed the Tigers for giving up on him and blamed Baker and Zeller for not liking him. He complained that his salary wasn't high enough and that the Tigers didn't give him enough expense money while he was in spring training. Boots characterized his money situation this way: "They say, Boots you'll only spend the money anyway. Sure what in h—- is money made for. And all I get from them wouldn't give me much of a time." Most of all Boots was hurt by the demotion and seemed genuinely unaware, at least at this moment, that he may have earned it.

I take it when they laugh at me and tell me I'm a playboy. You know some things hurt—hurt even a playboy. Well, I'll take it. I'll go back. But I'm still a good pitcher and if they would let me go to

some other big league club I would have fun beating the Tigers.
Though I would hate to do it. The Tigers are great fellows.[22]

Just as with money, bruised feelings didn't last long with Boots who quickly reported to Beaumont where the Mud Hens were training. In an interview with a local Beaumont reporter Boots stated, "I feel fine. I tried hard to work off some pounds at Lakeland. I worked early and late. I backed away from potatoes and steak and didn't drink a single bottle of beer the first week I was in camp, but those pounds just wouldn't come off. It's hard to whittle 'em off a guy like me." He stated that his arm soreness was in a "muscular spot just above the wrist," adding that the Tigers thought he was "jaking it."[23]

Within a week, however, Boots was gone from Beaumont, but this time his departure was legitimate. The Tigers had sold him to the Brooklyn Dodgers who were enduring a rash of injuries to their pitching staff.

Stanley Frank, a staff correspondent for the *New York Post* wrote that Dodger General Manager Larry MacPhail had asked Tiger broadcaster Harry Heilmann his opinion of Boots before making the deal. Heilmann, the future Hall of Famer told MacPhail that The Baron had the best pure stuff on the Tiger staff. MacPhail then asked his manager, Leo Durocher if he wanted Boots on the team. According to Frank, Durocher replied, "Sure. Everybody tells me he can pitch. Dean gave Frisch plenty of headaches, but he won ballgames. I'll take the headaches if wins go with them."[24]

The Dodgers were already known as a team full of flakes and the acquisition of Boots and his eccentricities was gleefully reported as more than appropriate.

United Press (UP) reporter Henry McLemore, wrote:

When Cletus Elwood Poffenberger was named Cletus Elwood Poffenberger, his fate was sealed.

When his parents gave him that name 24 years ago, they might just as well have tied a tag around his chubby wrist marked: "Destined for the Brooklyn Dodgers."

Training rules were just something to take up on the wall to cover a spot on the wallpaper. He could break 'em faster than

*three managers could think them up. He always found sched-
ules a nuisance, too. This business of being at a certain spot
at a certain time was beyond him. He liked to eat, too. He was
particularly fond of breakfast, lunch and dinner, and often had
three or four of each during the day.*

*It will be interesting to see how Leo the Lip and Cletus the Pip
get along. It would make good listening too.*[25]

Jack Miley, a columnist for the *New York News*, left no doubt what
he thought of the Dodgers' acquisition:

*Well, this is all the Dodgers need. They have now got Cletus
Elwood Poffenberger, intimately known as Boots, and he should
be a great help to Van Lingle Mungo in the daffodil department.
For they are kindred spirits. Both of them are nuttier than a
fruit cake, both love to look upon the wine when it is red, and
if they decide to go at the same time, God forbid, Brooklyn will
have no pitching staff left unless it is Larry MacPhail, who has
more brass than a Salvation Army band. Cletus Elwood, otherwise known as Boots, pitches too well for Brooklyn, but his
behavior is so bad that the Dodger club is the only one who will
take a gamble on him on his sheer alcoholic content, which is
about 110 proof net.*

*Cletus is a Grade A tippler. He will also drive several other people
to drink, including Leo Durocher and MacPhail. If he doesn't, I
will give him their money back. Cletus is about a size and a half
larger at the moment than Babe Phelps. They will both have to
be deflated or they will be sent up as World's Fair balloons.*[26]

(Given the acerbic nature of his comments, it is little surprise that
this is the same Jack Miley who was involved in a brawl in a Tampa hotel
lobby two springs before when he was confronted by Dizzy Dean over one
of his columns. Ultimately, over a dozen fellow Cardinals and another
sports writer got into the scuffle which resulted in a lacerated scalp for
Miley when someone hit him in the head with a pair of cleats.)

The Associated Press reported, "Extremely helpful in seeing that the
Brooklyn Dodgers maintain their reputation as baseball's gift to comedy,

the Detroit Tigers sold them Cletus Elwood (Boots) Poffenberger, their oft-suspended, oft-fined, and oft-missing pitcher." The story also noted that "unconfirmed reports said Brooklyn paid $20,000 for the right-hander."[27] Other sources said the price was $12,500. In reality, the Dodgers paid $7,500 which was the cost of the waiver claim.

Another UP story read in part, "The Dodgers like 'em wacky, and Poffy is dependable in that respect. When he doesn't feel like pitching, he doesn't pitch. He should be royally welcomed in Flatbush park where Babe Herman made history by banking fly-balls off his head."[28]

Before they were the "Boys of Summer" in the 1950s, the Dodgers of the 1930s were the "Daffiness Boys." Babe Herman, for example, was a hard hitting outfielder but whose "misadventures in the field and on the basepaths" were so legendary that they were noted in his *New York Times* obituary. Herman once famously doubled into a double play when with the bases loaded, he hit a long fly ball that fell in. The Dodger third base coach yelled at Herman to go back to second because Chick Fewster, the runner ahead of him had not yet rounded third. Meanwhile, Dazzy Vance, the runner who had been on second had rounded third, but thought the coach was yelling at him. Vance listened to the coach, Herman didn't, and all three runners ended up on third. Vance was ruled safe, being entitled to the bag; Fewster and Herman were out. This gave rise to a long-standing joke in Brooklyn in which someone would exclaim, "The Dodgers have three men on base!" the reply to which was "Which one?" Herman had actually been a teammate of Boots' on the Tigers for two weeks before being released by Detroit on June 15, 1937.

Herman was no longer in major league baseball, but the lyrically named Van Lingle Mungo was a key part of the pitching staff and was a notorious drinker and womanizer. Indeed, Associated Press reporter Whitney Martin wrote, that the Dodgers "have Poffenberger to relieve Mungo, but will need aspirin to relieve Durocher if Boots and Van team up for extra-curricular activities."[29]

The 1939 Dodgers also featured Red Evans who would be their Opening Day starter, but who ended up 1-8 on the year, his final one in the big leagues. Also a first class carouser, Evans was having an interesting spring training as well. Missing a midnight curfew by a couple of hours on the night before he was to pitch, Leo Durocher called him out the next day in the clubhouse, stating that he would ask Evans team-mates what penalty should be applied. Coach Charley Dressen, testified on behalf of the "prosecution" that "Evans drinks eight or nine bottles of beer a night," to which Evans irately replied, "You can't belittle my beer drinking like that! I had twenty-six bottles last night!"[30]

Clearly, Leo Durocher had experience handling "daffiness boys" and entertained no doubt that he could handle Boots. Harvey Boyle, the sports editor of the *Pittsburgh Post-Gazette* wrote in his "Mirrors of Sport" column that

> *Durocher is confident that he can keep the unruly boy within the bounds and on the straight and narrow. But here [sic] what the Dodger chieftain has to say about his latest acquisition:*
>
> *"I've never met Boots, but in the last few days I've gathered a lot of information about him," said Durocher after he came in line for a citation for bravery when he agreed to take on the Tigers' problem child. "Some of the things I heard about him were bad and some were good. I found out he has a strong arm, is fast and can pitch. There is nothing wrong with his arm. If he is overweight, as everyone says, you can bet he will have to start doing a lot of leg work. I'm going to make him do everything I think he ought to do in order to get himself in proper shape. I believe I can handle him.*
>
> *"Boots is going to get a chance to be one of my starting pitch-ers. Maybe the fact Detroit sent him to Beaumont a few days ago to join the Toledo team has made the boy realize he was foolish and must pay more serious attention to baseball if he wants to stay in it."[31]*

Apparently, Durocher did not gather enough information about Boots. Boyle added a quote from Boots' previous manager Del Baker, who had obviously been convinced of something Durocher had yet to learn:

> *"[Boots] proved to me that his major interest was not cen-tered on his pitching and I had to get him off the team," said Baker when the Dodgers were negotiating for the services of Boots. "It would have been unfair to all of the other players on my team if I kept Boots. We tried to make him take a sensible*

view of things and behave but he wouldn't. Then we had to turn him loose."[32]

Boots himself was happy with the trade in part because of Brooklyn's excellent catchers. The *New York News* reported that "Boots Poffenberger says he is glad to be with the Brooklyns on account of their having a smart catching staff—[Al] Todd, [Ray] Hayworth and [Luke] Sewell. 'When I was with Detroit I had to work with [Rudy] York,' says Boots. 'That big, thick-headed, ignorant so and so! Why, he doesn't know any more than I do!'" Indeed, Hayworth the former teammate who had tried to reform Boots, until he missed a train himself, was not only to be Boots' battery mate, but his roommate as well.[33]

Boots also appreciated the fact that the Dodgers wanted him—and planned to increase his salary. Some reports said that The Baron's paycheck would double.

> *"Larry MacPhail is willing to gamble on me and I appreciate that. No, I never met him but heard a lot about him. I heard he treats ball players who deliver the goods liberally, and I'm going to do my best to make some money.*
>
> *"Sure I drink a bottle of beer now and then, but I'm not nearly as bad as the newspapers picture me."*[34]

Boots also stated that Jo was happy to be out of Detroit.[35]

Naturally, Brooklyn's fans were eager to see Boots make good. In a note dated April 12th and signed by one A. G. Smith, Boots was assured that he was coming to "a real baseball town where the fans eat, drink, talk, and sleep, baseball from morning to night." Smith exhorted Boots to "get off on the right foot," warning him that "this boy Mungo had a big chance, but pulled a few fast ones in recent years," adding that "he got in a sore head, sore arm" cycle.

The Baron made his debut with the Dodgers on April 16th in an exhibition game, hurling three scoreless innings against the Yankees as the two teams barnstormed their way back to New York. In typical fashion, Boots told reporters that he was happy to be facing the Yankees: "Well, if you beat the Yankees, you are hailed as a really great pitcher. If you lose, no one is surprised."[36]

Apparently, however, he managed to irritate Yankee manager Joe McCarthy. The Yanks and Dodgers were riding the train north from Florida together, playing exhibition games along the way. An undated clip from Baltimore's *The Sun* noted that Boots managed to hold up the train when before departure, he ordered a steak and then "got a toothache after a couple of bites, rushed out, had it pulled, came back and started finishing his meal.

"In the meantime, it is related the train was being held up while they waited for Cletus to finish and that when Manager McCarthy, Yank professor heard what was causing the delay he threw a fit."[37]

The story is most believable not only because it fits Boots' personality, but also because it fits his dental records. His Marine Corps physical notes that he had eight teeth missing at the time of induction.

It didn't take very long for Boots to irritate Leo Durocher as well. Brooklyn's very first road trip of the season was a three game set in Philadelphia over the weekend of April 21-23. The Dodgers were staying at the Bellevue-Stratford Hotel, which had a large clock on the wall behind the desk, surrounded by smaller clocks telling the time around the world. According to Leo Durocher in his 1947 book, *The Dodgers and Me*, Boots arrived back at the hotel 30 minutes past the midnight curfew on Friday night, walking right past Brooklyn's skipper who was seated in the lobby. The next day Durocher confronted Boots who claimed that he had returned at 11:00.

"I was right there," growled Durocher, "and the clock in the lobby said 12:30."

"Maybe," shrugged Boots, "Maybe the clock you looked at said that. But one of them little clocks said 11:00 and that was the one I went by."[38]

The next night Boots arrived back at the hotel at 1:00 a.m. at which point Durocher leveled a $200 fine. On Sunday night, Durocher and Larry MacPhail waited until 2:00 a.m. for Boots to show up at which point they gave up and headed to their rooms. Who else should appear in the elevator with them than Boots? They said nothing to The Baron, but MacPhail later lectured Durocher that he was being too lenient on the players.[39]

The next road trip which lasted almost two weeks began in Boston on May 12th. The Dodgers' sleeper train was to depart at 2:50 a.m. but Durocher had ordered everyone in their berths by midnight. Boots was seen in his pajamas, but now thoroughly suspicious, Brooklyn's skipper checked The Baron's compartment, finding Boots' suitcase tucked firmly under the covers. By the time Boots finally confessed to Durocher what time he had re-boarded the train, which was right before it left, The Baron was short another $300.[40]

The problem as Boots saw it was although he was seeing plenty of action off the field, he was seeing precious little action on it. Pitching two innings in relief in the first game at Cincinnati on Sunday, May 21st brought Boots' season total to a meager five innings.

On Tuesday, Boots was missing from the Dodger clubhouse and when Leo Durocher began to rant about yet another fine that he was imposing on his absent hurler, outfielder Dolf Camilli spoke up. The Baron had said it was too hot to come to the park, according to Camilli and had asked him to inform Durocher that he was tired of being kept "like a bird in a cage." Durocher immediately suspended Boots.[41]

Later that day, International Press correspondent Bob Considine, the same Bob Considine who would write *The Babe Ruth Story*, as well as *Thirty Seconds Over Tokyo*, wrote:

> *Cletus "The Baron" Poffenberger, one of the most eccentric right-handers on the Brooklyn pitching staff, was fined $400 and indefinitely suspended here today.*
>
> *The charges against him are that he stayed out until 3 a.m. this morning sampling this village's many brews and then failed to show up at Crosley Field this afternoon for the game between the Dodgers and the Reds. He was tagged $200 on each count. His pay automatically ceased with the suspension and it is possible that Larry MacPhail, president of the team will take further action.*
>
> *Poffenberger was up and about the hotel lobby before game time today. In answer to a reporter's query as to why he wasn't at the ball yard, the young pitcher replied, "I'm taking the day off."*
>
> *Manager Leo Durocher snorted when he heard this. "He's been having 'off' days ever since we got him Easter Sunday. That rabbit certainly brought us a bad egg."[42]*

Jack Miley, clearly no fan of Dodger management, took a sympathetic attitude towards Boots, essentially explaining The Baron in the way his surviving friends still do: Boots is just Boots.

> Now he is back pitching boulders at hoot owls, walking very few of them, and is probably a darned sight happier. All of which proves you can take the boy out of the country but you can't take the country out of the boy.

> Cletus Baron Boots Poffenberger once told me, "These big leagues are the bunk. Down home, I can get $15 for pitching a Sunday game. And for $5 I can raise hell all week!"[43]

Miley noted that Boots was simply different, and went on to discuss both Red Evans and Van Lingle Mungo, adding:

> The three admitted they were two-bottle men and made no bones of their favorite pastime. They are now one down and two to go. And I don't blame them. When a Brooklyn pitcher goes out there and pitches his heart out, only to have his game bobbled away behind him by a butter-fingered infield and an astigmatic outfield, what do you expect him to say?—"aw, gee whizz!"

> Poffenberger got set down for nipping at that amber fluid in Cincinnati. There's not much else to do there. When John McGraw was alive, he used to throw terrific parties every time he hit the town. And John won more pennants than Durocher and McPhail [sic] will ever see.[44]

In *The Dodgers and Me*, Durocher claims that he sent Boots home. Tommy Holmes, who covered the Dodgers for the *Brooklyn Eagle* reported in the June 1st edition of *The Sporting News* that when Boots received word of his suspension, he decided for himself to go home, sending word to Durocher in a telegram that read, "Never mind about the fines as I am retiring from baseball. Regards, Boots."[45]

Holmes who would in 1979 be named the J. G. Taylor Spink Award winner by the Baseball Hall of Fame, wrote that Boots had told him just a day or two before that he had never been treated better by any club than he had by the Dodgers, but "they can't coop me up. Maybe I ought to be back home in Maryland pitching a game every Sunday for $15. I can have a helluva time on $5 a week in my home town of Williamsport."[46]

Indeed, the *Washington Post* reported on the 28th that word from Winchester, a Virginia town some 40 miles south of Williamsport, was that Boots would pitch for the Winchester Park team.[47] Meanwhile, Boots was announcing that he would pitch for the Hagerstown Chevies of the Washington County Baseball League, but according to Durocher by the end of June, Boots was asking for another chance.[48] The Dodgers optioned him as part of a multi-player transaction to their top farm club in Montreal where former major league hurler Burleigh Grimes was the manager. Grimes, who had retired after the 1934 season, his 19th in the big leagues, and who would be elected to the Hall of Fame in 1964, admitted to *The Sporting News* of June 29th that Boots was a "problem child." *The Sporting News* reported that Grimes, "nevertheless, is convinced that he has been punished by a month's suspension by Brooklyn and that he will be ready to get down to business." Clearly Burleigh Grimes knew nothing about Boots Poffenberger.[49]

In fact, Boots never made it to Montreal, but this time he had a legitimate reason. The AP reported on June 30th that Boots would join Montreal the next day and quoted him as saying "My family life is all OK now. The fact is, we're expecting a little Poffenberger, and I've got a lot to work for. I'll win a lot of ball games, and I'm coming back."[50] He did not leave immediately, however, waiting until almost a week later and getting as far as New York when he received a telegram that Jo was "sick" back in Charleston. If indeed she was pregnant, this "illness" must have in reality been a miscarriage because Boots and Jo never had any children together. In any case, he asked Montreal for another ticket, but received no response.

An Associated Press story dated July 12th contained the Montreal Royals' response to the situation:

> The Royals president, Hector Racine, announced that Poffenberger is up to his old disappearing tricks, and that, as a result, the club feels the hurler "doesn't figure in its plans now."
>
> "On four occasions in the last fortnight," Racine explained, "Poffenberger has informed us he would report on a certain

date, and four times he has failed. It's quite obvious we can't depend on a man like that."

The Brooklyn Dodgers, who sent Poffenberger to Montreal in a player deal, also have been in touch with the pitcher, Racine added, but to date it hasn't done any good.

The Royals' managers have met his requests for another ticket with silence, Boots said.

"They just don't trust me," he added, "because of these other deeds in the past—they don't look so good, you know."

"But I'm ready to go if they'll send me a ticket. I'll be out of here the night I get it."[51]

Montreal never did, and Brooklyn went so far as to ask commissioner Kenesaw Mountain Landis to ban Boots from organized baseball, so frustrated were they by Boots' behavior and what they must have perceived as a complete lack of gratitude. Landis granted the Dodgers' request and declared Boots ineligible on August 15th. An AP story from Hagerstown dated August 16th explained Boots' perspective. The story was no doubt written by Dick Kelly of the *Daily Mail* because he invariably reversed Boots' first name with his middle moniker (although the 1930 Census lists Boots as Elwood Cletus for no known reason):

Elwood Cletus Poffenberger [sic], the crossroads husky who went out with hay in his hair to stand big league batters on their ears—when and if he felt like it— opined he was still young enough to get a job in the brickyard or the tannery and play a little sandlot baseball or go fishing.

The oversize Dutchman said he hoped he'd get back in baseball sometime—but admitted the blacklist hung on him by Commissioner K. M. Landis would probably keep him out for good.

Poffenberger, 25 years old, said he'd asked for a transfer to the minors all through the season before he jumped the club in Cincinnati. He jumped, he said, because his arm wasn't right and he felt he needed to work the kinks out against hitters in the lower league.

When they sent him to Montreal, he took his transportation and headed for Canada, he said, only to be recalled by a telegram in New York saying his wife was seriously ill at their home here.

He didn't show to play with the Royals. Moguls of baseball put it down as another Poffenberger escapade, and the threats they made got Boots angry. So he went fishing, and heaved a few to the boys on the vacant lot. When his wife got well, he was already marked for the skids. Confirmation came yesterday with formal notice of the blacklist issued by Landis at the request of the Dodgers.

Boots wrote to Landis today. He didn't beg for reinstatement. He only asked if it would be all right for him to play sandlot baseball here.

"I guess they got me to Brooklyn to cover up for Mungo and Evans and few more and now they put the 'bee' on me.

"I guess this finishes me in baseball, but I'm not to be classed with those Chicago Black Sox of 1919."[52]

Jack Miley weighed in the next day writing,

For pathetic penitence the prize goes to Cletus Elwood Poffenberger, roly-poly pitcher who synchronized his elbow to the 'Beer Barrel Polka' and merrily quaffed his way through three baseball assignments. Then, an ex-Tiger, ex-Dodger and ex Montreal Maple Leaf, sobriety and the situation simultaneously dawned as he found himself without funds and contract on the old Maryland farm.

"I can see where I done wrong," he belatedly confessed, "but I can get into shape if they'll let me. I think they still owe me that chance."

He didn't get it, so to our national pastime was thus lost a droll figure.[53]

Miley's story was accompanied by a photo of Boots in a horizontally striped tee shirt standing in a boat with his fishing pole and tackle box.

Frank Colley of the *Morning Herald* took a decidedly sympathetic view of Boots' self-created predicament. He interviewed the "thunder struck" Boots on August 15th and reported the following in his column the next day:

> *If the Associated Press report of Cletus "Boots" Poffenberger being declared ineligible from organized baseball means that he has been placed on the blacklist the same as members of that famed Chicago "Black Sox" team of 1919, then this column believes that the kid from Williamsport needs a little sympathy.*
>
> *"Well if that's the answer," said Boots, "I'm glad it didn't come when I was 50 years old. I still have a chance to get a job, but I can't figure whey they should put me in the same class with those Chicago boys. I never tossed a game and I never stole or gambled on a contest.*
>
> *"What's worrying me is how about these kids I'm playing with; will my being a member of the team hurt their chances of entering organized baseball if they should make the grade? At least I'll write Landis and ask my full status and the status of these kids. Sure it was Brooklyn's work, they were sore at me and just did that as a mean comeback. They could have sold me, Toronto would have taken me and in fact I believe that Toledo would have taken me outright. I guess they named that club right when they called them the 'Daffiness boys.'" Since he jumped the club Boots has appeared in the Washington County League with the Ruppert Bluebirds and at present is managing the Williamsport Wildcats. He is in fairly good shape and stated last night that his arm is coming around fine.[54]*

Boots' concern was that the amateur players with whom he was now playing in Williamsport might be tainted by appearing on the same diamond with him. It is not known if Landis ever answered Boots, but it is clear that his concern was unfounded.

Upon his banishment, Boots had filed for unemployment from the Michigan Unemployment Commission which would have granted him up to $16.00 a week for 13 weeks. On September 22nd, however, the Commission announced that "the papers are ready to be mailed," but that they couldn't find Boots. The Baron never cared about money even when it was being handed to him for *not* having a job.[55]

With his career seemingly at a dead end, and he and Jo at least physically separated—she was now living down in Washington, D. C.—Boots still maintained a sense of humor. On a "Limpin' Limerick" post-card printed to look like a beer coaster and postmarked October 18, 1939, Boots was instructed by the sender to supply the last line. It read:

The eighty-year-old Mr. Trout

Has taken to Ballantine's Stout.

Once anemic [yes] and pale,

He's grown hearty and hale!

Boots' handwritten last line: *And now the "Baron" is out.*

While never losing his sense of humor, Boots never gained a sense of responsibility, not even after being traded, fined, suspended, and finally banned from baseball. In a blurb from late November or early December, a newspaper photo of Boots appears in the 1937-1940 scrapbook with the following caption: "Cletus (Boots) (Disappearing) Poffenberger ran true to form and failed so show up at the Maryland All-Star-Baltimore Soccer Club game in Baltimore on Thanksgiving Day. It's an old act with the former big-league hurler, who performed the disappearing act both for the Detroit Tigers and the Brooklyn Dodgers."[56]

Notes

1   Dick Hudson, "Warming Up," *Charleston Daily Mail*, January 6, 1939.
2   Unattributed, undated in SB 37-40.
3   Unattributed, undated, but probably a Charles P. Ward column in SB 37-40.
4   Charles P. Ward, "Baker is Calm as Baron Fails to Reach Camp," *Detroit Free Press*, February 27, 1939.

5   Charles P. Ward, "Baker Certain Missing Baron Will Show Up," *Detroit Free Press*, March 1, 1939.

6   *United Press*, "Poffenberger to Report, He Wires," March 3, 1939.

7   Associated Press, "Business Detains Boots Poffenberger," March 4, 1939.

8   Charles P. Ward, "Baron Reveals He Was Busy Soccer Player," *Detroit Free Press*, March 8, 1939.

9   Charles P. Ward, "Baker Hopeful as Baron Ends Home Sit-Down Strike," *Detroit Free Press*, March 7, 1939.

10 *Lakeland Ledger*, "Baron Is Greeted By Boss," photo by Dan Sanborn, undated in SB 37-40.

11 Unattributed, March 9, 1939, in SB 37-40.

12 Unattributed, undated in SB 37-40.

13 Charles P. Ward, *Detroit Free Press*, undated.

14 Charles P. Ward, "Rogell, Rooming With Baron, Sees Sleepless Nights Ahead," *Detroit Free Press*, March 11, 1939.

15 Unattributed, undated in SB 37-40.

16 H. G. Salsinger, "Poffy Again Resolves To Sin No More," *Detroit News*, March 9, 1939.

17 Unattributed photos, "One Tiger Hurler Runs" and "A Guy Can't Be Working Al the Time," undated, but most likely mid to late March, in SB 37-40.

18 Undated, unattributed, but most likely from a Hagerstown paper in SB 37-40.

19 Charles P. Ward, "Club Is Trying To Sell Him at Waiver Price," *Detroit Free Press*, March 31, 1939.

20 Associated Press, "Six Tigers Shipped To Toledo Mud Hens; Poffy May Lose Job," April 1, 1939.

21 Bob Murphy, "Bob Tales," *Detroit News*, undated.

22 Leo Macdonnel, "I Asked For Money And They Gave Me $5' Poffy Wails," *Detroit Times*, April 1, 1939.

23 Unattributed, undated, but clearly from a Beaumont, TX newspaper in SB 37-40.

24 Stanley Frank, *New York Post*, April 10, 1939.

25 Henry McLemore, "Poffenberger Finally Lands In Right Spot," *United Press*, April 11, 1939.

26 Jack Miley, "Poffenberger in Right Spot With Dodgers," *New York News*, undated.

27 Associated Press, "Dodger Add Daffy Fuel," April 10, 1939.

28 *United Press*, "Brooklyn Buys Poffenberger," April 10, 1939.

29 Whitney Martin, *Associated Press*, as cited in an unattributed blurb, undated but clearly early April, 1939 in SB 37-40..

30 Leo Durocher, *The Dodgers and Me* (Chicago: Ziff Davis Publishing, Co., 1948) p 37. A slightly different version of this story appears in Durocher's *Nice Guys Finish Last*.

31 Harvey Boyle, "Mirrors of Sports: Poffenberger Gets His Big Chance," Pittsburgh Post-Gazette, April 12, 1939.

32 Ibid.

33 *New York News*, at least according to a hand-written note, undated but early April, 1939.

34 Unattributed, but signed, "E. T. M." entitled, "Baron Poffenberger Speaks Out," undated, but early April, 1939.

35 Ibid.

36 Charles Segar, "Hits—Runs—Errors," New York Sun Mirror, undated, but early April, 1939.

37 The Sun, "Poffenberger Eats Steak, Yanks Wait," undated, but some time before April 18, 1939 which was Brooklyn's opener.

38 Leo Durocher, *The Dodgers and Me* (Chicago: Ziff Davis Publishing, Co., 1948) pp 43-44.

39 Ibid, p 44.

40 Ibid, p 45.

41 Ibid, p 46.

42 Bob Considine, *International Press*, May 23, 1939.

43 Jack Miley, "Boots Is Happy Pitching Rocks at Hooty Owls," *New York News*, undated.

44 Ibid.

45 Tommy Holmes, "Dodger Turnabout Blow At Turnstiles," *The Sporting News*, June 1, 1939, p 3.

46 Ibid.

47 *The Washington Post*, "Once a Dodger—Cletus Scheduled To Do a Twin Act," May 28, 1939.

48 Ibid.

49 J. L. McGowan, "Royals Take 'Fair Exchange' View on Dodger Deal For Parks," *The Sporting News*, June 29, 1939, p 3.

50 Associated Press, "'Boots' Poffenberger To Join Montreal," Hartford Courant, July 1, 1939.

51 Associated Press, "Montreal Club Ready To 'Throw in Sponge' On Boots Poffenberger," July 12, 1939.

52 *Daily Mail*, "Poffenberger On Blacklist," August 16, 1939, unattributed, but no doubt by Dick Kelly. The clipping that Boots and Jo pasted into SB 37-40 is entitled, "Blacklisting Unfair—Thinks Poffenberger," and with the same date of August 16, 1939.

53 Jack Miley, "Poffy Cruelly Harassed," August 17, 1939.

54 Frank Colley, "The Colley-See-Um of Sports," Morning Herald, August 16, 1939.

55 Associated Press, "Cletus Poffenberger Again Among Missing," Hartford Courant, September 23, 1939.

56 Unattributed, undated in SB 37-40.

CHAPTER 5

Nashville

The Dodgers, wanting no more parts of Boots Poffenberger, but quite desirous of minimizing the loss on their investment, took the unprecedented step of assisting Boots in his quest for reinstatement to professional baseball during the winter of 1939-1940. Commissioner Kenesaw Mountain Landis granted the request and on March 2, 1940, Brooklyn sold Boots to one of their affiliates, the Nashville Volunteers for $5,000.00. Most minor league clubs in those days were independently owned and operated, signing their own players. A major league club might "affiliate" with such a minor league team, supplying it with some players and generally having the first opportunity to purchase players from that minor league team. The "Vols" belonged to the Southern Association, an A1 league that is the equivalent to AA today.

In many ways, the 1940 season would be Boots' finest in professional baseball both on and off the field. Once again, Boots and Jo were reconciled. Once again Boots was reported to be one of the hardest workers in spring training and once again he declared that he had learned his lesson, telling Fred Russell, writing for The Sporting News that, "I realize that all the things I have done wrong have hurt no one but me."[1] Indeed, Boots was apparently down to 182 pounds. His salary was down to $350.00 a month.

The Vols were skippered by Larry Gilbert, who had become part owner of the club after managing New Orleans for 15 seasons. There, Gilbert developed a reputation as an effective handler of eccentrics, flakes, and trouble-makers, including Red Evans who won 21 games for New Orleans in 1938.

The Nashville press was anxious to hear Boots' side of his troubled story and he was more than happy to talk about himself as usual. Boots gave an interview from the Vols spring training headquarters, the Mayfair Hotel along the shores of Lake Monroe in Sanford, Florida, which appeared on March 20. The unattributed article entitled simply "Poffenberger's Side of It" appears in the 1937-1940 scrapbook and in it, Boots claims that his troubles stemmed from his own innocence and ignorance.

> *"Yes, advancing too quick in this game hurt me. Things might have been different if I had come up gradually. The bright lights sorta' got to me.*
>
> *"You know, in 1937 when I was notified to leave Beaumont and report to Detroit, I never had been in a city that big. I was just 21 and a green kid who could hardly find the ball park."*[2]

Boots went on to regale the reporter with a description of how he pitched batting practice his first day in Detroit and of his first win, over Lefty Grove. He then spoke of his victory over the Washington Senators and of his trip home; the one during which he spent an extra rainy day without informing the Tigers. "That's when they began to hound me, began to suspect things and not believe what I would tell them."[3] Certainly, this was not the moment when the Tigers "began" to doubt Boots, not when they were fully aware that he had jumped the Charleston Senators in 1936, and had themselves recommended that Charleston management suspend Boots for that infraction. Nevertheless, the explanation made for great copy and it is hard to say whether Boots was consciously trying to improve his reputation with this tale of woe or whether it was simply the best sounding story that occurred to him at that moment.

Boots claimed that Tiger management said nothing when he was winning, "but the minute I was knocked out, even if I had spent the night before in a church, they would start cross-examining me and making up a lot of stuff on places I had been and things I had done. I was persecuted."[4]

Claiming persecution was a "stretcher" as Huck Finn would have said, even for Boots. There is some doubt that Boots would have even used that word and the sentiment could be the work of a reporter who was interested in telling a story whether the facts matched or not.

Be that as it may, Boots hit the truth squarely on the head, when he added that he had indeed done wrong but that was because he was either mad at himself or felt mistreated. Stating that he harmed no one but himself, he claimed that if had only been handled better, that he "would be in the majors now, making big money, and without the reputation of being a hard man to handle."[5]

Boots concluded the interview by reassuring the reporter and the fans that "I'm not as bad as they make out. I'm no worn-out old drunk trying to hold on to a job. I'm 23 years old and ready to go."[6]

Nashville fans got their visual introduction to Boots in a newspaper photo that demonstrated his ready willingness to laugh at himself. In the photo, which is juxtaposed with one of him in his Nashville uniform, Boots is proudly holding up a tiny fish. The caption read,

> My, what a fine catch you have there, "Boots" Poffenberger. Yes sir, it'll make a fine addition for your Aunt Tillie's window-seat aquarium. 'Boots' like Simple Simon, must have gone fishing in a pail of water to come up with a catch (indicated by arrow in above picture) like this. But on the serious side the eccentric hurler is really bearing down during daily conditioning drills at the Vol's Sanford, Fla., camp.[7]

The Nashville press clearly enjoyed Boots' sense of humor. An undated and unsigned clip in the 1937-1940 scrapbook reads in part,

> Poffenberger is genuinely funny in an effortless way. His humor is spontaneous.

> Umpire Paul Blackard revealed that when Boots hit a Milwaukee batsman in the head at Ocala the other day he walked in from the box to the momentarily stunned hitter and said:

> "Ain't I the wildest so-and-so you ever saw?"[8]

Larry Gilbert clearly enjoyed what Boots' could bring to the mound. Another scrapbook article notes that

> Larry Gilbert believes Poffenberger will help the Vols plenty.

Poffenberger likewise believes he will. Poffy, as he is known to intimates, like most players was reluctant to make a prediction about how many games he'd win. He said he thought he would have a good season and probably win "somewhere between 15 and 20."

His best pitch is what he calls a "sneaky fast ball." Gilbert says he had a good assortment of stuff and knows how to use it.[9]

The Vols were set to open the season in Atlanta on Friday, April 12th and there was a great deal of excitement in Nashville surrounding this edition of the club. The "experts" were saying that Nashville looked to be the team to beat in the Southern Association. *Nashville Banner* sports editor Fred Russell reported that the three game series versus the Crackers could draw as many as 20,000 and Atlanta was preparing to welcome the new season with style.[10] The city's Junior Chamber of Commerce was flying in actor, comedian, and baseball aficionado Joe E. Brown to throw out the ceremonial first pitch. Brown, whose son Joe L. Brown would one day serve as general manager of the Pittsburgh Pirates, starred in three baseball films made during the early 1930s and he could often be found playing baseball on a Hollywood back lot between takes.[11] While Brown was taking a plane to Atlanta, some 300 Nashvillians including Mayor Thomas Cummings and other city officials were traveling on a special train to the Vols opener.[12]

Larry Gilbert had been so impressed with Boots' spring training performance that he considered starting him against Atlanta in the opener, but opted not to when the temperatures dropped into the 30s. Apparently, Gilbert would take no chances on injuring Boots' arm, which had been tender the previous spring, by pitching him in such cold conditions. Atlanta may have been cold, but the Vols started hot, winning the opener 12-8 over the home town Crackers. The Vols took the next two games as well, sweeping the series before returning to Nashville and their home ballpark which was as an eccentric a piece of architecture as Boots was a ballplayer.

Sulphur Dell Park was so-named because it was very near a sulphur spring and Nashvillians had been playing baseball on the site since the Civil War.[13] It was bound by Fourth Avenue, Fifth Avenue, Jackson Street, and a railroad spur which resulted in rather strange dimensions.[14] A major league 334' to left and 421' to center, it was only 262' down the right field line. Furthermore, it was a mere 42' from the grandstand to first base and a miniscule 26' from the grandstand to third base. As if the dimensions weren't peculiar enough, the field itself was below grade, giving rise, quite literally, to an outfield embankment that ran from corner to corner and not just a run of the mill embankment, either. Beginning its rise in right field at a 45 degree angle precisely 224' from home plate, any right fielder standing against the wall was a full 22.5' above the infield.[15] In practical terms, the park was not at all favorable to a right-handed pitcher, but when Boots took a look at his new home, he wasn't worried. Raymond Johnson, sports editor of the *Nashville Tennessean* quoted Boots in a column as saying

> *This park isn't bad. They ain't gonna hit many out of here on me even if the right field fence is short. I'll curve 'em and you ain't gonna see many curve balls hit over that fence.*
>
> *A feller who knows how to pitch should shut out the opposition here as well as in any other park. Sure, I'd rather pitch in a larger one, but I'll show 'em something here. And besides, we've got plenty of guys who can hit the ball over that fence.*
>
> *Look at that mound out there. That's the kind for good pitching. I'm going to like it here. I know that.[16]*

Johnson predicted that the fans would like Boots as well writing, "He's got more color than a late June rainbow."[17]

Denying a ready-made excuse for failure before even throwing his first pitch, coupled with his sense of humor, had the Vols' beat reporters apologizing for Boots previous escapades before he had even appeared in his first game. One Nashville scribe was already engaging in the most modern practice of blaming Boots' troubles on the media:

> *My guess is that Boots Poffenberger will give Gilbert a minimum of trouble, if any. You know, I believe a big share of Boots' reputation can be charged to his name. Newspapermen like to write about someone named Cletus Elwood Poffenberger.*

If his name had been Jones or Smith or Brown, chances are we would have heard little about him. Still, Poffenberger is a less conspicuous name than—well, Poppemfurther, for instance.[18]

Selected to start the home opener on April 16th Boots predicted that he would knock off the Knoxville Smokies, which he did, pitching a complete game, 6-4 victory. The Vols scored 6 times in the fourth inning and Boots gave up only 2 unearned runs until the ninth, when he surrendered 2 earned runs. Boots' Nashville debut took place before an excellent crowd of 7,500 and lasted all of 2:00 hours.

In contrast to the game as it is played at this writing in 2013, complete games were expected from and by starting pitchers. In fact, after the Vols first 36 games, Raymond Johnson lamented in his column that Nashville had recorded only 14 complete games. Such "puny pitching" he stated, "doesn't seem like very good pitching and it isn't."[19] By way of comparison, the average number of complete games per major league team in 2012 was four. Cincinnati and Detroit led baseball with nine each. The combined totals of Milwaukee, Colorado, Oakland, Chicago Cubs, Baltimore, Pittsburgh, Los Angeles Dodgers, Kansas City, and Cleveland equaled 11 in 1,458 games.

One reason that complete games were expected was for the simple reason that there were very few relief specialists, and minor league rosters were not as large as they are today. The Vols carried only 17 players including seven pitchers and the latter might see action in the field. One Nashville right-hander, a spot starter and reliever named Johnny Sain, who would one day team with Warren Spahn on the Boston Braves to form a most successful pitching duo, also saw some duty in right field. There were no coaches to aid Manager Gilbert and trainers were unknown.

The 2:00 hour game time was not at all unusual either. There was no emphasis on taking pitches in order to drive up a starter's pitch count, because nobody was counting. Batters swung at the first good offering that they saw, and with no television commercials to further slow the pace, the games moved along with a steady rhythm.

The Vols were moving along at a steady rhythm as well, winning their first six contests, something they had not done for 25 years. Boots had a winning streak of his own, pitching two more complete game victories to go with his win against Knoxville. He bet teammates and sports writers alike that he would win four straight, which he did, adding a fifth straight before suffering his first defeat.[20]

Harold Harris, a sports writer for the *Knoxville News-Sentinel* wrote about the bets, about Boots being happy to play for Larry Gilbert whom Boots described as "one of the smartest and fairest minded men in baseball," and about the fact that Boots was a beer drinker only and never touched liquor. Boots, as did many in and out of baseball at the time, labored under the quaint notion that the alcohol in beer didn't do as much harm as the alcohol in whiskey or any of the other hard liquors. "Yeah, I like beer," Boots told Harris, "but I don't drink liquor because it doesn't mix with baseball. If a fellow gets plenty of hard work a few beers won't hurt him."

Boots went on to say,

> "Once you get the reputation of a beer-drinker as I have, you can never live it down, but it does get your goat to have the fans ride you about it constantly. They're all the time leaning down into the dugout wanting to know if I'll have a drink out of their bottle. Some day I'm going to smack one of those smart alecks like I've always wanted to."
>
> That "Boots" nickname is a hand-me-down, his father before him having gone by that moniker. The "Baron" tag was placed on him while he was a member of the Detroit Tigers by one of the sports writers.
>
> "They'd do almost anything to get some new kind of a gag in their papers in Detroit. Why, one fellow came to the ball park and took my picture wearing a monocle and all that sort of stuff. I didn't mind, though, because I realized that it might help me become popular with the fans."[21]

In the wide-ranging interview, Boots made no mention of Jo's pregnancy or her "illness" when explaining why he had refused to report to Montreal:

> Last year Detroit traded Boots to Brooklyn where he stayed for two months and pitched only two innings of ball. You'll recall

the story about him jumping the Dodger club late in the season, but for the first time he gives the real reason.

"Some players don't mind sitting on the bench as long as they draw their pay checks. Not me. The Dodgers use me but two innings and I got tired of sitting on the bench. They farmed me to Montreal. But I wouldn't report there because there was just a few weeks of the season left, so I just quit for the rest of the season."[22]

Boots' explanation for not reporting does not necessarily contradict Jo's possible pregnancy, and perhaps he simply didn't want to mention the miscarriage at the risk of conjuring up bad memories, especially for his wife. Boots' version of events was known to change, however, so it's also possible that he felt this was the best story to tell at the moment. It's quite debatable how accurate his statements to Harris were concerning Jo's reaction to his drinking, saying, "She doesn't believe half of the stories written about me because she knows I'll tell her the truth. She doesn't mind my drinking beer, either."[23] Jo was never interviewed to confirm or deny this, but there were plenty of occasions to this point that demonstrated that she clearly "minded."

Harris concluded the piece by explaining why the Vols were willing to take a chance on The Baron, which is that if Boots had a rebound season, then Gilbert and Fay Murray the principal owner of the Vols stood to make a handsome profit on their $5,000 investment by selling his contract to a big league club.[24] *The Sporting News* speculated that Nashville could receive $25,000 to $30,000 if Boots continued to behave and continued to win.[25]

Major league executives remained skeptical that Boots would do either. In a May 16th column for the *Washington Post*, Shirley Povich wrote, "[Manager Buck] Harris says the Nats are uninterested in Boots Poffenberger, who has won four games in a row for Nashville . . . "Any bet that Poffenberger would win for you would have to start with the presumption that he' show up for the game," cracked Harris.[26]

Nevertheless, both Boots and the Vols continued to win and at an amazing pace. Playing outstanding defense and with a powerful line up built to take advantage of the short dimensions in Sulphur Dell, Nashville won 20 of its first 24 games. They were never out of a game no matter how many runs they were behind, and they began to specialize in comeback victories. On May 2nd, for example, Boots was knocked out in the sixth inning, but first baseman Mickey "Socco" Rocco's homer won it in the twelfth. In a May 5th double header at Birmingham Rocco had the game winning homer in each contest as the Vols swept the Barons 4-3 and 6-3. These were seven inning games as minor league double headers often were, and still are, shortened by two innings. They again swept a double header from Birmingham, this time at "The Dell" on May 12th before 8,000 fans. Game one was Boots' fifth straight victory, a 5-1 affair in which he gave up 12 hits, including five infield hits, but garnered two hits of his own. Catcher Charley "Greek" George hit a three-run eighth inning homer to seal the win.

The Vols stumbled a bit during the second half of May, but a three game sweep of the Memphis Chicks at the end of the month ran their first place record to 25-10, five in front of the nearest competition. Boots' record stood at 7-2 after a 3-0 Memorial Day shutout of the Chattanooga Lookouts at Engel Field in the second game of a double header that was shortened to six innings because of darkness. Despite the fact that Southern Association ballparks had lights, they were not turned on if they weren't scheduled to be turned on.

Boots was the first hurler in the league to reach seven wins and the first to reach eight, with a 10-4 victory over Knoxville at The Dell. The game was the first of a double header and Boots got off to a rocky start, walking the first batter, giving up a bloop single, then throwing eight straight balls followed by another blooper resulting in a three-run first inning for the Smokies. His mound opponent Paul Smith had more than a rocky end to his start however, when Mickey Rocco smashed a line drive off Smith's head about one inch from his right ear. Smith was rushed to the hospital with a concussion and possible skull fracture.[27] The blow had no long-lasting effect as Smith is still living at this writing, having turned 102 in 2013.

The Vols lost the second game 5-3 when John Hubbell made his first start of the season. Expectations were no doubt high for John; his brother Carl, famous for fanning five future Hall of Famers in the 1933 All Star game, would himself make the Hall of Fame in 1947. John was in his fourth minor league season, but would pitch only two more and conclude his career with a 48-52 record.

Boots continued his winning ways whether he pitched well or not, thanks to the hard-hitting Nashville line up. He knocked off Chattanooga for win number nine, a 12-8 slugfest in which he surrendered nine hits, eight runs, and seven walks in eight innings. Boots had now garnered eight wins in nine tries during day games, but had won only once in five starts at night. Lights were still something of a novelty in 1940 and teammate and fellow pitcher Leo Twardy believed that Boots' record illustrated his theory that it was more difficult to pitch at night, a theory in direct contradiction to what most players believe today. Twardy told George K. Leonard of the *Nashville Banner*

> "No matter how powerful the lights are, you still cannot see the ball as well as you can in the daytime," he contends. "I consider myself much more effective in the afternoon.
>
> "Sometimes at night I get to thinking I'm faster than I really am. I breeze a ball or two past a batter, and I think they can't touch me. It's because I can't gauge my speed accurately. I find out quickly enough when I hear the fences rattling behind me, though.
>
> "It's a lesson that's sometimes hard to learn. Try to throw the ball past the hitter when you should be using your head occasionally is a mistake many pitchers are guilty of."[28]

The fact that Twardy, who would never reach the major leagues and Boots were together in Nashville demonstrates what a small world baseball can be. Twardy and The Baron were teammates in each's debut season with Charleroi in 1934.

Boots defeated the Birmingham Barons, 7-2, for victory number 10. The various beat writers around the league were eager to see the wild man who was also proving to be a winner. Zipp Newman, sports editor of the *Birmingham News* wrote how Larry Gilbert had a collection of hungry players "and a hungry athlete winds up a champion or close by." Newman then noted that Boots was belying his reputation:

[Boots] looked every inch a major league pitcher last night in giving up six hits. He had control, a great curve and was making a fast ball look like a lemon wafer.

He can't miss going back up.

Gilbert laid down no strict rules for Poffenberger. He appealed to his sense of judgment, merely telling him he was a major league pitcher if he wanted to be one—and why not be one. Poffenberger is no exception with Gilbert. He has been taking players with playboy tendencies and making ball players out of them.[29]

Then there was this unattributed article in the 1937-1940 scrapbook regarding Boots and his reputation:

Poffenberger, by the way, has been remarkably subdued during his stay with the Vols. He has a sense of humor and a prank-ish mind, but to date about the only thing to happen to him around the circuit is to be interviewed.

Boots fears that he earned his reputation as a screwball by obliging photographers. He has even posed wearing a mono-cle and carrying an umbrella at a game.

"Every time I see something about me in the papers now, they say I'm a screwball or an eccentric," moans the Baron. "I don't even know what that last thing means, but whatever it is, I got a hunch newspaper guys are that way."[30]

Nashville's fans were certainly warming to Boots who won a Longines watch by topping the second in a series of popularity contests sponsored by radio station WLAC. Perhaps the burglar who broke into the Poffenberger home was after this watch. Whatever he was after, he was thwarted by Jo:

Mrs. Boots Poffenberger and the wives of two other Vol play-ers heard a noise at the door the other night. Mrs. Boots, who weighs only about 90 pounds, grabbed a mild bottle and went

*to investigate . . . When she discovered it was a burglar, she
called the cops and the thief is now in the workhouse.*[31]

Raymond Johnson considered Boots' eleventh victory, a 5-1 defeat
of the New Orleans Pelicans to be his best of the season.[32] The Baron
again had trouble in the first, loading the bases on a hit and two walks
before completing a spectacular 3-6-1 double play to get out of the jam.
Nursing a 1-0 lead, Boots surrendered the tie run in the seventh only
to see his teammates get him four runs in the eighth, including two on
Mickey Rocco's fourteenth homer of the season.

Boots not only pitched a complete game 6-2 victory over the Little
Rock Travelers for win number 12, he also went two-for-three at the plate
with a run scored and an RBI. Shortly thereafter, a photo appeared in
the Nashville paper of Boots starting to look and act like comedian Lou
Costello. Wearing an expression that looks as if he is about to break into
a giant laugh while smelling something bad, Boots has his hands to his
hat, the brim of which is angled over his left ear. Despite what he had
told reporters earlier in the season, Boots couldn't resist hamming it up
for photographers.[33]

Boots was racking up so many wins and staying out of so much
trouble that Fred Russell, in his "Sideline Sidelights" column actually
wrote that the Tigers and Dodgers were responsible for Boots' behavior.

*If Poffenberger was a problem to Detroit and Brooklyn, both
clubs must have been looking for trouble. Lots of times that
happens.*

*Useless snooping, childish rules, amateur detectives. Most
players resent such tactics. Some openly rebel.*

*Poffenberger is going great now because Larry Gilbert treats
men the way he wanted to be treated as a player. He has but
one general rule and that is that every man be in shape to play
when it's time to play.*

*The Vols have no curfew law. If they want a bottle or two of
beer after a game, that's all right. On trips, they play poker and
bridge. Off the field, they lead their own lives.*

> *Larry hasn't had a minute's trouble with Poffenberger, who's a lamb compared to some others who have worn Vol livery in the last twenty years.*[34]

Boots headed into the All-Star break with a record 14 wins and much was made of the fact that he had completed 12 of his 14 victories. Looking at his numbers from a modern perspective, however, reveals that he wasn't pitching all that well in the purest sense. He had allowed 163 hits and 43 walks in 139 innings and Boots was not missing any bats, striking out only 29. Clearly, he was benefiting from the Vols outstanding defense. The perspective of the day, however, was simply whether you were good enough during any particular game to still be pitching at the end. One scribe wrote, "There is no better gauge of a pitcher's value than his record of complete games."[35] Interestingly, however, in an informal poll of fans taken by George Leonard of the *Nashville Banner,* no one named Boots as the best pitcher in the league.[36]

The All-Star game, scheduled for Monday, July 8th pitted the first place team against a squad comprised of the best players from the other seven teams. A player voted onto the All-Star team who was on the first place team was simply replaced. Players were voted onto the All-Star team by the league's beat writers and Boots received all but two votes, both from Knoxville writers who didn't think it reasonable to vote for a player who would only have to be replaced. Nashville had insured its first place standing with four games left before the break and would, therefore, host the contest which was to be held under the lights at 8:00 p.m. Larry Gilbert named Boots his starting pitcher.

The festivities started on Monday morning when the 20 sports writers who covered the Southern Association gathered for a golf tournament at the Belle Meade Country Club followed by a luncheon which was hosted by the two local papers, the *Banner* and the *Tennessean.* Following an afternoon business session the writers were scheduled to "then join league officials and club owners at a dinner at the Andrew Jackson Hotel at 5 o'clock at which [owner] Fay Murray will be official host."[37]

Governor Prentice Cooper and Mayor Tom Cummings would be attending the game and a dozen major league scouts were expected. As intermittent showers were forecast a "heavy tarpaulin" covered the field during the day, an event apparently so unusual that the fact of its presence prompted a headline in a Nashville newspaper.[38]

The game went on as scheduled, however, before some 5,500 fans including Captain W. E. Seat, 89, of Trenton, Tennessee who had personally asked Confederate General Nathan Bedford Forrest if he could enlist when he was 12-years-old.[39]

League president Trammell Scott presented each player a check for $25.00 for making the All-Star game during a pre-game ceremony. Boots and Charley George received the "most boisterous cheers during the presentation of the $25 checks to the players," according to George Leonard.[40] Despite a half hour delay in the sixth caused by one of those intermittent showers, the game was played to completion, resulting in a 6-1 victory for the All-Stars. The game featured homers by Alex Hooks and Atlanta catcher/manager Paul Richards who twenty years later as general manager, would transform the Baltimore Orioles into an American League powerhouse.

Boots pitched three innings giving up two runs and took the loss although he was again involved in a well-turned double play:

> If there's a better fielding pitcher in baseball than Boots Poffenberger, we'd like to see him. In the third inning when the All-Stars loaded the bases on two hits and a walk, Alex Hooks ground to Boots in front of the mound. Poffenberger snatched it up like a shortstop and rifled to George without a moment's hesitation, and the Greek in turn threw to Rocco to easily complete a double play. It was done so quickly that a triple play might have been possible, with a little luck, at second base.
>
> The opposing players like Poffenberger. They kid him a lot, because Boots talks a lot, but there's not one of them that doesn't respect his pitching arm. "He can throw that ball in there," remarked Chuck Aleno of Birmingham.
>
> By the way, you've possibly seen Boots rant and rave on the mound or in front of the dugout. Know who he's raving at? Boots Poffenberger. He chides himself constantly.[41]

When the season resumed, Boots was chiding himself again in Chattanooga. After tossing a seven-inning, three-hitter against Atlanta in the second game of a double header, Boots gave up seven runs in 4.1 innings in an 8-1 loss to the Lookouts in his following start, and "was so disgusted he kicked his glove from the mound to the bench when relieved."[42] A childish gesture to be sure, but there was no doubt that Boots had matured. Raymond Johnson wrote a lengthy column crediting Jo for Boots' new attitude. In his "One Man's Opinion" column and with a headline that read, "Mrs. Boots Playing Big Role in Successful Comeback of Poffenberger" Johnson wrote:

> Baron Boots Poffenberger, to the average fan, is a happy-go-lucky guy who doesn't care whether the sun rises or sets just as long as he gets his beer. His reputation as a suds sampler is known almost everywhere baseball is played.
>
> Cletus Elwood—that's his name in the family Bible, is an eccentric right-handed pitcher, who was a hero in Detroit three short years ago and who now brings joy to Sulphur Dell fans.
>
> While he likes his beer, he isn't the screwball some have painted him. His puffing and snorting when the going gets rough is his way of letting off steam while trying to calm himself inside.
>
> The Baron has his serious moments and not all of them are when he is on the mound trying to puzzle an opposing batter. He can be as serious as any ordinary human although he delights in razzing friend and foe at times.
>
> Poffenberger was a baseball outcast when Larry Gilbert got him this spring. Detroit gave up on him more than a year ago and Brooklyn did the same thing last summer. Larry MacPhail, Brooklyn prexy, got so mad at Boots that he had him placed on Judge Landis' suspended list. The Baron's future as late as last February looked very dark.
>
> When he received word early in March that Nashville had bought him and that he had been reinstated Boots was trying to get a job with a semi-pro team, pitching once a week. For a

young man who was a major league star two short years before that was like moving out of the presidential suite of the Waldorf-Astoria into a dingy, little room in some back street alley.

Boots' passing from the majors was largely his own fault, for he became peeved at the fines the Dodgers slapped on him and he jumped the club. They would not let him pitch regularly and he felt that he was a lot better than most of the Dodger hurlers. And, too, he liked his beer and being peeved at Leo Durocher and Charley Dressen, he tanked up on the suds and disappeared.

He welcomed the chance to get back into organized ball this spring, but there was doubt if he would succeed. Larry Gilbert, who has had unusual success with other players of the Poffenberger type, was one who had confidence in Boots. One of Larry's first moves after Poffenberger was in camp at Sanford, Fla., for a couple of weeks was to suggest that Mrs. Josephine Poffenberger, Boots' tiny wife, become a resident of Nashville for the summer. Larry helped to obtain them a furnished home.

Not since they married in July, 1937 had the Poffenbergers had a home of their own. They had lived in hotels during the baseball season and with his and her people during the winter. A home all to themselves was like a paradise.

"Our home has meant a world to Boots," Mrs. Poffenberger said the other day as she and the Baron reviewed his career which is depicted in pictures and stories in a gigantic scrapbook they have kept. "We've never had a home before and Boots gets a tremendous kick out of being out where it is quiet and we can rest. He spends a lot of time at home and seldom leaves during the day until it is time to go the ball park.

"I feel positive the home has been a major factor in his success and, if possible, wherever we may go in the future I am going to see that we have a home.

"I know it's hard to believe, but Boots sometimes goes three or four days now without even one glass of beer. We always keep it on hand for any friends who might stop by, but Boots seldom touches it. After he pitches, we frequently stop uptown and he has a couple of glasses."

When Poffenberger was with Detroit and Brooklyn it wasn't unusual for him to guzzle a half case of suds in one night. At least that's the stories that have been handed down and the Baron doesn't deny them.

"You know, I guess it was that I finally realized I felt a lot better when I woke up the next morning when I didn't have over one or two glasses," Poffenberger said of his change in beer drinking tactics. "I haven't had a hangover now in—well, it's been months, I believe last summer."

Poffenberger's comeback, whether it is due to Larry Gilbert, little Mrs. Boots, the combination of both, or his realization that he couldn't succeed under his old habits, means that he will go back to the majors this fall. Already several clubs have dangled bait before the Nashville owners in an effort to obtain him.[43]

The story was accompanied by three photos; one of Boots in the middle of his windup, the oft-referenced photo of Boots wearing a monocle, and the third of Jo smiling at Boots who in turn is looking at the scrapbook referenced by Johnson and in which they eventually pasted his column.[44]

On July 31st the United Press reported that Boots was, indeed, headed back to the majors. Eventually:

Baron Boots Poffenberger, husky right-hander whose screwball antics were too much even for the Brooklyn Dodgers, believes he is pitching himself back into the majors, and his Nashville teammates and thousands of Southern Association fans agree with him.

He still retains much of the color, crowd-pleasing eccentricities and horse-play that made his meteoric rise and fall in the majors sparkle, but the Baron has stopped being a playboy— the reason he slid out of the big time.

"He hasn't given me any trouble, and he's ready to go back up, "Larry Gilbert, Nashville manager and vice-president, said of Poffenberger. "He has everything he needs. There's a price tag on him, and I believe we'll have plenty of bidders—but we don't promise delivery until the season is over."

"I'm headed back up," Boots insisted. "I'm only 24 years old and ready to go. I was faster two years ago than I am now—I used to blow 'em in—but now I'm a smarter pitcher. I've got better control and can pitch to better spots."[45]

The *Nashville Banner* was disappointed in Boots, however, when he failed to show for a hole-in-one competition that was part of a golf tournament that the newspaper was sponsoring. He had been quoted as saying that he was looking forward to the competition in which "all players again will be given four shots at the green, and the tournament is open to any white person in the world, professional or amateur."[46] In light of Boots' absence, the *Banner* reported that "The crowd was disappointed at Poffenberger's failure to show up for the exhibition . . . Appearances of this sort heighten a ball player's popularity with the people who, after all, pay his salary."[47] This non-appearance seems to have been the only occasion on which Boots did not attend as scheduled during the entire season.

On the field, Boots lost two straight for the first time all year in early August, the second defeat a 10-4 loss to Memphis in the second game of a double header. Boots didn't even get out of the second inning and didn't wait to be lifted after walking the bases loaded. "He just walked off," read a newspaper blurb in the scrapbook.[48]

The Baron returned to the win column on August 8th defeating Little Rock 9-6 and pushing Nashville's lead back to 5.5 games over Atlanta. Giving up only one hit in the first five innings, but with an eight run lead "he appeared to let up and the Travelers got to him for three hits and as many runs in the sixth. They also tagged him for three blows in the eighth and two more in the ninth."[49] The game featured 11 walks (five by Boots), and 15 runs, and still only took 2:14 to complete.

Boots notched his nineteenth win August 12th on Men's Night at Sulphur Dell before 14,000 fans, the second largest crowd in Dell history.[50] "Greek" George hit a grand slam, center fielder Oris Hockett went five for five giving him 10 consecutive hits, and Boots allowed only three hits to Knoxville in a 12-0 whitewashing of the Smokies. Boots even stroked an RBI double himself as the Vols increased their lead to six games over the Crackers. Boots struck out eight, a season high and allowed only five balls to be hit out of the infield.

Twenty-three years later, Raymond Johnson, still writing for the *Tennessean* reflected on the game in a January 22, 1963 article on Boots:

> *Poffenberger pitched what Larry Gilbert always said was the finest game he ever saw in the Dell . . . That was on Aug. 12, 1940 when he limited Knoxville to three hits in winning a Men's Night game 12-0 before 12,000 fans who packed the right and left field dumps . . . He didn't permit a ball to be hit into the crowd, which would have been an automatic double.*[51]

Win number 20 came four days later against the Lookouts, a 4-3 victory in game one of a double header at Chattanooga. "Poffenberger celebrated in the proper manner after reaching the twenty mark . . . Friends brought gifts in large brown bottles . . . Others chose cans."[52] Anyone who witnessed Boots' milestone victory that night paid a bit more for his or her general admission ticket than they would have had the game been played at Sulphur Dell. Both Chattanooga and Knoxville charged $.83 per ticket compared to the rest of the league which charged $.75.[53]

The Vols were rolling once again as they had at the beginning of the season; in fact exactly as they had been, going on another 20-4 run. To show their appreciation to their fans for such great support, it was rumored that the players were planning a talent show to be held at the new Belle Meade Theater. Oris Hockett was part of a quartet, Mickey Rocco was reportedly "rehearsing daily" on his violin, and "natural comedian" Boots Poffenberger would function as one of the masters of ceremony.[54]

The Vols missed an opportunity to clinch the Southern Association pennant on August 18th when they failed to sweep a double header in Atlanta. In the eighth inning of the second game originally scheduled for seven innings, the Crackers loaded the bases on a swinging bunt, an error and a looper. With the Vols' outfield playing shallow the Atlanta batter hit a long single, but the runners on first and second failed to advance. Nashville's double play combo argued that the game should not be over:

> *The Vols, headed by Dick Culler and Johnny Mihalic, argued that since neither [runner] touched the next base that they*

would have been out had the Nashville club been able to retrieve the ball from a bunch of Negro fans who had congregated in centerfield.

A double play of this type would have eliminated the deciding run. But since they were unable to get possession of the ball, Manager Gilbert decided to drop the matter.[55]

Despite surrendering 16 hits and eight runs in 8.2 innings to Knoxville on the 20th, Boots won his twenty-first game thanks to the 11 runs his teammates put up, although Boots had a hand in the offense as well, going two for four with two runs scored.

Nashville was abuzz about Boots in two different ways. There was speculation regarding how good Boots would be in his role as Master of Ceremonies for the upcoming players' talent show and there was even more speculation regarding the major league club to which the Vols would sell him. Boots was featured in a Jack Sords illustration which was entitled, "One His Way Back,"[56] and it was known that Pat Monohan, a scout for the St. Louis Browns had seen him pitch.[57] Hopefully, Monohan hadn't seen Boots' performance against the Smokies on the 20th or one on the 24th against the Crackers in which Boots surrendered four hits and four runs in just one-third of an inning in what was eventually a 16-15 loss. The buzz was felt back in Hagerstown as Frank Colley wrote:

"Boots" is in line for a bonus from the Nashville team for winning 20 games but whether he takes it or not remains to be seen. He has already refused to take an increase in salary when offered figuring it was coming to the club for their efforts in getting him back on the eligible list but perhaps when the season is over "Boots" will be handed a neat check by the Vols and maybe a piece of change out of his sale price, for no big league club is going to pass up "Boots" if he can win that number of games in the Southern Association and he is still a young fellow.[58]

The *Atlanta Constitution* echoed the idea that Boots, as well as Charley George were headed back to the bigs. A Pete Roton photo showed Boots and George sitting on Larry Gilbert's knee with Gilbert perched on a beer crate. Part of the caption reads "The title for the above scene should be the 'Taming of the Screws.' To hear Larry tell it, these one-time trouble-shooters are now just a pair of adorable darlings. The averages prove that these lambie-pies are very definitely on their way back to the big show."[59]

"Big show" or not, Boots and his fellow Vols had a real show to perform at the Belle Meade, Nashville's newest theater, which had opened only four months earlier. An advertisement for the theater on Saturday, August 24th showed that *Those Were the Days* with William Holden and Bonita Granville was playing, along with a serial, a cartoon, and a comedy. The next line reads, "On our stage 7:15 & 9:15 Vol Baseball Follies Freddie Russell Master of Ceremonies." The performance was also scheduled for Sunday.

This was the same Freddie Russell who served as the *Banner's* sports editor and whose Monday review of the show focuses on what such a performance revealed about the spirit of the 1940 Vols, especially since Nashville endured ugly losses on Friday and Saturday:

> *The stuff of which champions are made can show itself in the most unexpected manner.*
>
> *Take Nashville's Vols, for instance. About two weeks ago when the pennant began to appear a certainty, they rigged themselves up a little stage act. It would click, they agreed, only if the club kept on winning.*
>
> *The boys rehearsed on the road and came back home in an excellent frame of mind after winning two out of three in Atlanta and four straight in Knoxville.*
>
> *Then that 15-13 thing Friday night. It was awful. Another loss, 16-15 on Saturday, was worse.*
>
> *Everybody was low. They would have paid money to have called off the act Saturday night, but there it was on the schedule just like a ball game. They felt more like hiding than going on exhibition.*
>
> *It was a bad spot, definitely.*

It would have been a perfect time for a fold-up, or if not that, a half-hearted performance that might even stir up a few "wolves."

Ball players think about those things. They don't like to look silly anymore than the next fellow.

"We asked for this," said the 'captain [second baseman Johnny Mihalic].' "Shake it off and let's bear down."

And I wish you could have seen the show those players put on and the way the capacity audience at the Belle Meade responded.

Tommy Tatum ran out of songs. So did the quartet. They brought Mickey Rocco back again and again. And Poffenberger and George, with their bit of an Oriental dance, had 'em screaming.

It impressed Larry Gilbert so much that he had to say something about it.

"These boys have shown you a lot of 'false pepper' up here tonight," he told the audience. "They don't feel this good. I don't either. We have lost two terrible games. I believe the club has what it takes, though, and while I'm not flatly promising a pennant, I'm hoping we can have the thing sewed up when we come back here Labor Day."

They have seen another side of the ballplayers, seen them close up out of uniform, heard them sing and talk, watched them clown.

There's many a convert among those who thought ball players were for the most part just a bunch of roughnecks.

And there's more reason to understand why the club is on top.[60]

Captain Johnny Mihalic claimed facetiously that Hollywood was calling Boots. "They want him as a stand-in for Basil Rathbone," said Mihalic of the actor best known for playing suave villains in addition to Sherlock Holmes.[61] As previously mentioned, however, Boots was increasingly taking on the appearance of Lou Costello.

Given the number of base runners that Boots was allowing, it was hard to keep track of who indeed was on first. On Monday, the 26th, Boots allowed a whopping total of 19 hits in 8.2 innings pitched, including 10 in his final two innings. Nevertheless, he picked up win number 22 over

Little Rock, 10-9 in a game which, despite all the hits and runs lasted only 2:28. In his twenty-third victory over Birmingham, Boots allowed nine hits, eight runs, and six walks in 7.1 innings.

Atlanta had gotten almost as hot as Nashville since their comeback victory over the Vols back on the 18th and had staved off elimination for almost two weeks, but finally, on September 2nd, Labor Day, the Vols clinched the Southern Association pennant on the exact schedule that Larry Gilbert had hoped. A sweep of Little Rock, coupled with Atlanta's split with New Orleans brought Nashville the flag. It was the first championship for the Vols since 1916 and they had won in impressive fashion, spending every single day of the season in first place. As if to accentuate the magic of the season, Boots had won both games of the double header. Relieving Johnny Sain in the tenth inning of game one, Boots threw six pitches to end the top half of the inning and picked up the victory when third baseman Bob Boken drilled a ball off the left field wall with the bases loaded in the bottom of the tenth. Boken had scored the tying run in the ninth on a Little Rock error. Starting game two, Boots gave up nine hits in a 10-2 victory which was called after 5.5 innings on account of darkness. As if two victories in a single day weren't enough, Boots went two-for-three at the plate including a double.

The fans, numbering some 6,500, the largest Labor Day crowd in Sulphur Dell history up to that time, witnessed what was described as a "fitting and proper climax" to the season.[62] "Straw hats sailed on the field from cheering fans" after the game.[63] A special flag fund was begun in order to purchase an actual pennant. Fans could send their donations to the *Nashville Banner* sports department or drop them in boxes at Sulphur Dell.[64]

The players reprised their August show, this time at the Princess Theater on Church Street. Owner Fay Murray went on stage before a packed house of 1,800 to announce that it was he who had won the pennant for Nashville because he had "talked Larry Gilbert into coming here from New Orleans. He's the best manager in the minor leagues." Gilbert appeared on stage and received a three minute ovation.[65]

The players put on their act one last time on September 8th, the final day of the season, between games of a double header with New Orleans. Charley George and Boots began with a waltz and then broke "into that hot stuff" according to one witness.[66] A newspaper photo the next day showed Boots and George, each with his outside hand in the air, his finger pointing upwards. Boots was kicking up his right leg. "The clowning act was the sensation of between game follies."

Larry Gilbert was also presented a new Chrysler "in appreciation for the 1940 season and for leading the Vols to their first Southern League pennant in twenty-four years."[67] While Gilbert was receiving the keys to a new car Fay Murray received a scroll which read

> To Fay L. Murray and Larry Gilbert for their efforts in bringing to Nashville in 1940 its first Southern Association pennant in twenty-four years we fans express our appreciation for the enjoyment of watching a great ball club.[68]

As for the games, Boots entered in the ninth inning of game one to protect a 7-5 lead, which he did not. Giving up two runs on four hits, Boots blew the save, not that anyone thought in those terms in 1940, but redeemed himself with a two out single off the right field fence to drive in Bob Boken who had doubled. It was Boots' twenty-sixth win and Nashville's 100th. The Vols took game two for victory number 101; it was their thirteenth win in a row and it knocked New Orleans out of the playoffs. One wonders with all that took place between games, how at least five innings of the second game was ever completed.

Boots credited Nashville's defense as a prime reason for their sensational season: "One of the greatest defensive infields I've ever seen. A perfect double play combination, a guy who always throws strikes in Boken [to first], one of the most underrated fielding first basemen in Rocco. I never had a better bunch behind me."[69] Indeed, George Leonard, a *Nashville Banner* reporter, placed in perspective the record-setting 208 double plays turned primarily by second baseman Johnny Mihalic and shortstop Dick Culler when he wrote, "The brilliance of the mark is all the more evident when one realized that the major league record for 154 games is 195 set by Cincinnati in 1931."[70] (The 1949 Philadelphia Athletics would eventually set what stands as the current record at 217 double plays.)

Joe Hatcher noted the team's lack of injuries, a fact highlighted by the September 12th edition of *The Sporting News* which carried a page-five summary of Nashville's success.[71] Indeed, the Vols sent out two pitchers and picked up two pitchers during the season, representing the only transactions that the club made all year. *The Sporting News* also cited Nashville's "tremendous hitting and fine defense" and the numbers illustrate the point.[72] Nashville led the Southern Association in average (.310), runs (960 or 6.27/game), doubles (343), home runs (89), walks, (630) and a .970 fielding average. Boken, George, Rocco, right fielder Gus Dugas, and left fielder Arnold Moser knocked in 100 runs or more accounting for five of the eight players to top the century mark in the Southern Association that season. Moser also led the loop with 216 hits, while Dugas' 22 home runs tied him for the league lead with Knoxville's Dutch Meyers. The Vols rang up these offensive totals in 153 games during which time they were shut out only once.

Boot Poffenberger, of course, lead the league in wins with 26 becoming the first Volunteer hurler to notch at least 25 in a season. Boots appeared in 37 games and remarkably, received a decision in all but two of them. His .743 win percentage was first in the league. Ace Adams (*Ace* was Adams' given name) was second at .722 to go along with a 13-5 record, while George Jeffcoat placed fourth in the league with a .700 winning percentage, the result of a 14-6 mark. Adams led the league in strikeouts with 122, while Jeffcoat fanned 121. The pitching staff compiled 62 complete games. At least one Southern Association observer thought that the pitching across the league had been stellar. On his September 4th broadcast of "Sports News and Views" which aired on WSB in Atlanta, sports editor Ernie Harwell, discussed the "great hurling" in the Southern Association, noting that Boots was the 20th pitcher since 1900 to win at least 25 games.[73] (Harwell went on to a Hall of Fame broadcasting career, primarily with the Detroit Tigers.)

One other statistic that especially concerned the players was the amount of bonus money that they earned for winning the pennant. The total was $2,000—not per player, but for the entire team. The Vols voted to split the money with a full share going to 17 players, Larry Gilbert, and traveling secretary Lillard; a half share went to late season arrival, pitcher Pearce Corley, and the other half was to be divided among the groundskeepers, clubhouse attendants, and other Sulphur Dell personnel.[74] It is interesting to speculate what the groundskeepers, et. al. did with their share of $50.00. Fred Russell noted that the Vols hoped to earn another $2,000 in playoff money and were disappointed that Birmingham did not earn the final playoff spot that went to Chattanooga because it was estimated that the Barons would draw four times the crowd as would the Lookouts.[75]

The Southern Association held what was then referred to as a Shaughnessy playoff, in which the top four teams were seeded in a best three-out-of-five format. It is a common playoff system today, but was widely known then as the "Shaughnessy playoffs" because it had been devised only seven years before in 1933, by Frank Shaughnessy, the general manager of the Montreal Royals, then a member of the International League. The winner of the Southern Association playoffs would face the winner of the Texas League playoffs in what was known as the Dixie Series.

The Vols opened the playoffs at Sulphur Dell on September 10th against the fourth seeded Chattanooga Lookouts, who proved no match for starter George Jeffcoat. The right hander gave up only four hits in a 6-1 win, but most notably struck out a league playoff record 18 batters. Gus Dugas hit a home run and knocked in four. Ace Adams started the next night and allowed five runs, but Mickey Rocco homered in an 11-5 Nashville victory. Back in Chattanooga for game three, Friday the 13th proved to be lucky for the Vols and Boots who hurled the clinching 12-3 victory. Seven of those runs scored in the second inning including four on Oris Hockett's grand slam and all seven were surrendered by Ken Ash, the pitcher who recorded the lone shut out of the Vols during the regular season back on August 17th. Boots had a shakey start himself, giving up hits to the first three batters he faced and allowing two runs in the first, but he settled down to collect a complete game victory before only 1,075 fans.

The low turnout at Chattanooga, coupled with unexpected low turnout in Nashville, was indeed a problem for the players and the club as Raymond Johnson pointed out in his "One Man's Opinion" column following Nashville's sweep:

> *The Vol-Lookout series was a wash-out as far as the front office was concerned.*

Twenty-seven hundred cash customers were on hand for the opener here. The second night's crowd was around 1,400 due to the unusually cool weather. Then in Chattanooga Friday night they drew 1,075.

Out of the receipts the league took 10 per cent for its office and $500 toward the players' fund for the Shaughnessy playoff. The transportation to and from Chattanooga, meals, hotel bill and the players' salary for the extra week left a deficit of slightly more than $300 for the Vols.[76]

Indeed, making the Dixie Series was not only a matter of pride, but also one of profit for both players and club ownership as Johnson explained:

The victor in the Dixie Series will get 60 percent of the gate for the first four engagements and the loser 40 per cent.

The champions are already figuring that they are going to pull down between $500 and $600 out of the clashes with the Texas League winner. Even if they should lose, they would get around $300 extra.

"If that's not worth fighting for in the final playoff," Johnny Mihalic said yesterday, "then we haven't any business in it." That's the attitude of the entire Vol squad.[77]

That possible $500 share cited by Johnson for players winning the Dixie Series in 1940 is the equivalent of $8,000 in 2012.

Before the Vols could think about playing the Texas League winner, however, they had to defeat Paul Richard's tough Atlanta Crackers that had finished second during the regular season. The final round was a best of seven series and the teams split the first two games, Nashville winning the opener behind George Jeffcoat, but losing the second contest 10-9 when Ace Adams surrendered six runs in six innings. Boots started the pivotal game three and in the words of the headline that appeared over Fred Russell's copy in the *Nashville Banner*, "Mr. Boots Is Elegant In 6-1 Win":

[A] mixture of timely hitting steady defense and some magnificent clutch pitching by His Majesty Baron Cletus Elwood

Poffenberger produced a well-earned 6-1 decision last night, and today the doughty Dellers are again one-up on their bitter rivals, the Crumbling Crackers.

In tattooing his twenty-eighth triumph of the campaign, Kid Boots was positively elegant. Never has he exhibited more mound mettle, more real courage in pitching himself out of numerous tough spots midway of the battle, then finished unusually strong.

Two walks and Tom Hafey's single gave Atlanta its lone run in the first inning, and they had many other chances, but Poffy's percolating pitching and some jam-up support snuffed out every threat.[78]

Boots surrendered 10 hits and collected one himself.

The game was played in 2:25 before 3,329 fans, but Atlanta's press bemoaned what they saw as poor fan support, noting that a high school football game between Boys High and Marist drew either 8,000 or 10,000 depending on the source.[79]

The Crackers came back to tie the series at two games apiece when Leo Twardy allowed four runs in 2.2 innings and the Vols fell 9-4. At some point during the game someone dumped "contents of a drink bottle on Poffenberger, who was seated against the stands near the dugout. He was bounced promptly."[80] Boots and Charley George, were "booed and jeered at" in every game in Atlanta's Ponce de Leon Park.[81] Boots would hoist a celebratory beer however, when Jeffcoat pitched an eight hit, complete game 11-2 victory in game number five and Boots won the game six clincher. Moved up ahead of Ace Adams who, thanks to two travel days and a rainout would be working on too much rest, Boots walked five and surrendered 10 hits, but came away a 7-5 winner before 4,232 fans.

Luman Harris, who would lead the American League in loses in 1943 with 21 for the Athletics and would one day manage the Houston Astros and Atlanta Braves surrendered five hits and four of the seven runs in only one inning of work.

In the meantime Baron Boots Poffenberger was hurling one of the most magnificent games of his career. He got into a couple of jams because of his wildness, but a pair of twin killings extracted him without any damage. The Crackers had been able to solve him for only one hit, a slow roller that Boots narrowly missed grabbing as it went to his left.

Poffenberger was extremely wild in the first inning, when he generally has trouble. He walked three men to load the bags with only one out. Then he grabbed Tom Hafey's roller and turned it into a double play.

The Crax got only three balls out of the infield until the seventh, so tight was Poffenberger.

The only solid blow off Poffenberger until the eighth was Besse's single in the seventh that drove in two mates. But Marshall, Bates and Hill smacked out liners in the eighth when Boots became quite peeved when he and Charley George thought the umpire had missed two strikes on Bates.[82]

Twardy relieved Boots in that eighth inning and the Crackers loaded the bases with one out in the ninth, but Twardy escaped the jam and preserved the win. The Nashville Vols were the Southern Association regular season and playoff champions. They would now face the powerful Houston Buffaloes who had won 105 games and finished 16 games ahead of the nearest competition, in the Dixie Series. This was Nashville's second consecutive appearance in the Series; the Vols lost to Fort Worth the year before.

The teams split the first two games which were played at Sulphur Dell, with Nashville winning 7-5 in the first contest and Houston taking the second game 6-4. Ace Adams and George Jeffcoat started those games for the Vols and it would once again be Boots' turn in a pivotal game three in Houston.

When asked by the Houston press the secret to his phenomenal success during the season, Boots responded, "Clean living and a great second base combination."[83] As usual, Boots was loose and ready for the occasion and when the Houston club greeted his arrival on the mound with the "Beer Barrel Polka," and played the tune throughout the first inning, "the music loving Baron thrived on it."[84] Indeed, whether it was a relatively dead ball—the Texas League baseball was said to be far less lively than the Southern Association baseball[85]—or musical accompaniment, Boots gave up only one run and that was unearned on six hits through seven innings. Removed for pinch-hitter Tommy Tatum in the eighth with the Vols trailing 1-0, Tatum tied the score with a single and the Vols won it 2-1 in the tenth.

Behind Ace Adams, Nashville took game four 6-0, and then took the series when George Jeffcoat hurled a 10 inning, complete game, 5-3 victory. Rocco and Hockett had home runs for the Dixie Series champion Nashville Vols who, by winning the series split $6,427.69 which amounted to $338.30 per share, including manager Gilbert and traveling secretary Lillard.[86] The Vols had hoped to earn more, but cold weather in both cities suppressed attendance.

After their clinching victory, the team boarded a midnight train on Sunday for the trip back to Nashville where they were scheduled to arrive at 6 a.m. on Wednesday. (Had a sixth game back in Nashville been necessary, an express train had been arranged.) Larry Gilbert had the foresight to have food placed on the train and his wife and friends served the hungry and deserving Vols sandwiches as they rode through the autumn night.[87]

Once home on Wednesday, October 2nd, Larry Gilbert threw a dinner that evening at 6:30 at Hettie Ray's Club on Nine Mile Hill west of Nashville. Hettie Ray's was one of several "supper clubs" that put the life in Nashville's night life.

Fred Russell waxed sentimental writing in that day's *Banner*:

> *Ten, Twenty, Fifty years from now, they still will be talking about Nashville's 1940 ball club.*
>
> *Sure, it's often soppy to write about the spirit and flame of athletes who play for pay, but the memory of the 1940 Dellers isn't a true one without inclusion of the personal player flavor.*
>
> *It was that kind of a club, dripping with color. To get to the bottom of the bucket, you have to go back to spring training.*
>
> *Boots Poffenberger, unwanted, tagged as impossible, thrown out of baseball. They laughed when Larry Gilbert said: "I'll take him."*
>
> *Poffy prospered to the extent of twenty-nine victories. That's just a part of the story. Proper handling showed the roly-poly Marylander to be a good-natured, fun-loving fellow who never*

sought trouble with anyone, never missed a drill, never missed a game, never gave Gilbert a moment's worry.

I mean it with the utmost sincerity when I say that Poffenberger's reputation is unfair to him, and, as this season has proved, he has been the victim of major league operators' and managers' own deficiencies in what should be a prime requisite of their job—handling men.

Model boy? No. Bad actor? I have known ten dozen ball players who were bigger problems than Poffenberger.

Next year they will be scattered, some advancing to the majors; a few traded, perhaps; several returning. But there'll never be another 1940.

Relishing his close association with players on the Dixie Series trip, President Fay Murray says: "It has been the happiest summer I've known in baseball, all because of Larry Gilbert and these boys."

And the Vols act like college football seniors after their last game. They don't want to part. Honestly, I've never seen anything like it in baseball. Tears may leak from more than one pair of eyes tonight.[88]

According to Raymond Johnson, only Arnold Moser and Johnny Sain had to depart for home before the banquet. Lots of wives and the entire Gilbert family including Charley Gilbert, Larry's son who had spent part of the year with the Brooklyn Dodgers were in attendance.[89] The players revived some of their talent show routines with Boots acting as master of ceremonies.[90]

Summarizing the series win for *The Sporting News*, George Leonard of the *Banner* wrote "fans, owners, players and managers who saw the Vols of 1940 perform, will always regard them as one of the most brilliant collections of minor leaguers in the annals of the game, certainly in Southern Association history."[91] He was right. Bill Weiss and Marshall Wright, baseball historians writing in 2001 for milb.com, minor league baseball's official website, ranked the 1940 Vols as the 47th greatest minor league team of all-time.[92]

Thanks to 29 total victories and making every scheduled start, train departure, and theater performance, Boots Poffenberger had reestablished his reputation. In fact, Dick Williams a "magazine writer, formerly of the *New York World*, long time major league sports reporter," wrote a letter to Frank Colley the *Morning Herald* sports editor back in Hagerstown, which he ran as a column and in which Williams defended Boots by castigating all those who had taken part in his "ruination," particularly Larry MacPhail:

> *There is something about the comeback of Boots that is an indictment of a game that should need no indictments and it isn't the Boots Poffenbergers of the game that need first look into themselves.*
>
> *You know, and I have learned, that Boots Poffenberger had a pretty hard boyhood. He had no schooling, he had little of the attractive, comradely association with father that a boy, rich or poor, must have. Sometimes, I am led to believe, he hardly had enough to eat and his pistol pocket was missing, I am told, more frequently than it was present. Or perhaps we should say the piazza of his pantaloons.*
>
> *He didn't get much schooling. He had to work. He probably wasn't an ideal boy, but I haven't found anybody around here willing to call him a bad, or vicious boy. Mischievous and earthly, perhaps, but not vicious. His boyhood was constricted, his contact with the beauties that are still fairly abundant in this dizzy world were decidedly limited. Physically complementing these shortcomings, God, or nature, gave him a remarkable physique and a shrewd and cunning wit.*
>
> *He turned his talents to athletics, to baseball. He became a professional. He loved the game, perhaps, but above all, he needed money. He was a sandlotter, not a collegian; a poor boy, not an educated one. He needed money, but he needed work of the type for which he was best fitted. So baseball put him to work at the cheapest figure for which it could acquire his talents— because he had to take that figure to relieve the burden on his hard working mother.*

He saw lesser athletes about him getting more money and he resented it. He became unruly, difficult. Greedy men were taking from him the dollars that would buy comforts at home. Somebody told him he should be colorful—and he had heard there was color in a beer glass, so he became colorful and at the same time a problem because he had been treated with niggardly deceit in the first place.

Now there still were men in baseball who could have saved Boots Poffenberger the woes that beset him for two or three of his youthful years. Mickey Cochrane was a good manager, a splendid, manly fellow, but he was high strung and he was shackled by a front office situation that trammeled his natural capacities and deprived him of the sympathetic touch that could have salvaged Boots.

When Boots left Detroit, he had a certain odium attached to the name of Boots Poffenberger. And where did he go? Not to a gentle kindly, understanding, patient man like Bill McKechnie, or jollying Jimmy Dykes or kidding, forgiving Casey Stengel. Or even reasonable, encouraging Bucky Harris or patient, far seeing Joe Cronin.

He went instead, to baseball's foremost sensationalist—CALL IT EXHIBITIONIST, IF YOU WILL—Larry McPhail [sic], at Brooklyn. McPhail took Boots Poffenberger to exploit him. He would break him, bend him to his will, make a star of him. A swashbuckling, overbearing, impudent clod, McPhail completed the bulldozing ruination of Boots Poffenberger because he didn't understand that a poor boy had rebelled against a cheap deal in the beginning and needed help, not criticism, to find his way out of the labyrinth he had gotten into.

What a shame it was Boots Poffenberger couldn't have developed and prospered in the day of, and come to know and work for, the late Wilbert Robinson? He would have been a great star, as Dazzy Vance was a great star and Babe Herman was a star and Glenn Wright was a star. All these were rugged, individual, quondam confused men and he set them on the trail to fame and wealth.[93]

While not everyone was willing to view the Baron as a poor victim of an oppressive system, there was little doubt in most minds that Boots would soon be headed back to the big time.

Notes

1   Fred Russell, "Poffenberger Proffers Own Chapter of Story," *The Sporting News*, March 21, 1940, p1.
2   Fred Russell, "Sideline Sidelights: Poffenberger's Side of It," *Nashville Banner*, March 20, 1940.
3   *Ibid.*
4   *Ibid.*
5   *Ibid.*
6   *Ibid.*
7   Unattributed photo, "Boots Proudly Shows Catch, Slab Form," undated , but most likely early March, 1940, in SB 37-40.
8   Unattributed, undated in SB 37-40.
9   Tom McRae, "Poffenberger Says He'll Go Back Up Again," undated in SB 37-40.
10 Fred Russell, "Crowd of 20,000 May See Vols' Opener in Atlanta, *Nashville Banner*, April 8, 1940.
11 *Ibid.*
12 Bill Traughber, "Looking Back: The 1940 Nashville Vols," http://www.milb.com/news/article.jsp?ymd=20110703&content_id=21379308&vkey=news_t556&fext=.jsp&sid=t556
13 www.sulphurdell.com
14 *Ibid.*
15 *Ibid.*
16 Raymond Johnson, "One Man's Opinion: Poffenberger Announces He'll Shut Out Rivals Here Despite Short Fences," *Nashville Tennessean*, undated.
17 *Ibid.*
18 Unattributed, undated in SB 37-40. Perhaps from a Fred Russell, "Sideline Sidelight" column.
19 Raymond Johnson, "One Man's Opinion," *Nashville Tennessean*, undated.
20 Harold Harris, "Cletus Elwood Poffenberger, Bad Boy No Longer (He Has Won 3 Straight), Is Off Hard Stuff, Hopes to Go Up Again, "*Knoxville News-Sentinel*, undated.
21 *Ibid.*
22 *Ibid.*
23 *Ibid.*
24 *Ibid.*

25 *The Sporting News*, caption to photo entitled, "Boots Gets On His Feet Again," May 16, 1940, p 16.

26 Shirley Povich, "Postscripts," *Washington Post*, May 16, 1940.

27 Raymond Johnson, "Poffenberger Bags Decision," *Nashville Tennessean*, undated.

28 George K. Leonard, "Poffenberger Is Best At Hurling Afternoon Games," *Nashville Banner*, undated.

29 Zipp Newman, "Dusting 'Em Off: Gilbert Is Riding Fast and Furious," *Birmingham News*, undated.

30 Unattributed, undated in SB 37-40, but it certainly appears to be snipped from a Fred Russell, "Sideline Sidelights" column.

31 Unattributed, undated in SB 37-40.

32 Raymond Johnson, "Poffenberger Racks Up 11th," *Nashville Tennessean*, undated, but most likely June 18 or 19, 1940.

33 Unattributed and undated photo in SB 37-40.

34 Fred Russell, "Sideline Sidelights," *Nashville Banner*, undated.

35 Unattributed, undated in SB 37-40; appears to be clipped from a Fred Russell, "Sideline Sidelights" column.

36 George K. Leonard, "Fans Offer Opinions On Vols, Race, Fans, Umpires," *Nashville Banner*, undated.

37 Fred Russell, "Many Scouts, Scribes Will See Classic," *Nashville Banner*, undated but most likely from July 5-7, 1940.

38 Obviously either the *Banner* or the *Tennessean*. Full headline reads: "Heavy Tarpaulin Will Cover Playing Field Until Late Afternoon: Many Notables Here."

39 George K. Leonard, "Boots, George Are Proven Most Popular," *Nashville Banner*, July 8, 1940.

40 *Ibid.*

41 *Ibid.*

42 Unattributed, undated in SB 37-40.

43 Raymond Johnson, "One Man's Opinion: Mrs. Boots Playing Big Role In Successful Comeback of Poffenberger," *Nashville Tennessean*, undated.

44 *Ibid.* Photos by Ed Clark, a staff photographer on the *Tennessean* who would gain renown as a photographer for *Life* magazine.

45 United Press, "Poffenberger on Road Back," July 31, 1940.

46 Bob Rule, "Local Heroes To Compete In Afternoon," *Nashville Banner*, undated.

47 Unattributed, undated, but probably from the *Banner* in SB 37-40.

48 Unattributed, undated in SB 37-40.

49 Unattributed, "Boots Bags 18 As Moser Aids," August 8, 1940.

50 Raymond Johnson, *Nashville Tennessean* undated but more than likely August 13, 1940.

51 Raymond Johnson, "One Man's Opinion: After 22 Years, Boots Admits He Did Wrong," *Nashville Tennessean*, January 22, 1963.

52 Unattributed, undated but probably August 16, 1940 in SB 37-40.

53 Unattributed, but most likely a Fred Russell, "Sideline Sidelights" column, undated in SB 37-40.

54 Unattributed, "Vols On Stage," undated, but around August 13, 1940 in SB 37-40.

55 Raymond Johnson, "Chance Kicked to Sew Up Flag," *Nashville Tennessean*, August 18, 1940.

56 Jack Sords, "On His Way Back." Sords' illustration appeared in the August 9, 1940 edition of an unidentified Charleston newspaper as well as the August 12, 1940 *Morning Herald*. Boots had been featured in a 1937 Sords' illustration, which read in part, "Boots Poffenberger: Young pitching sensation of the Detroit Tigers."

57 Unattributed, but most likely a Fred Russell "Sideline Sidelights" column, undated in SB 37-40.

58 Frank Colley, "The Colley-See-Um Of Sports," *Morning Herald*, August 21, 1940.

59 Pete Roton photo, *Atlanta Constitution*, undated.

60 Fred Russell, "Sideline Sidelights," *Nashville Banner*, undated, but had to be August 25 or 26, 1940.

61 Unattributed, but most likely from a Fred Russell, "Sideline Sidelights" column, undated but definitely before, probably some time during, the week leading up to the show at the Belle Meade on August 25, 1940, in SB 37-40.

62 Fred Russell, "Larry Rests Regs, Rooks Get Chance," *Nashville Banner*, undated.

63 *Ibid.*

64 *Ibid.*

65 Unattributed, "Murray Pays a Tribute To the 'Gamest Club,'" undated, but probably September 3, 1940, in SB 37-40.

66 The witness was John Price Jones a comedian and actor from the 1920s as cited in what is surely a Fred Russell, "Sideline Sidelights" column, undated, but some time before the final game of the season on Sunday, September 8, 1940.

67 George K. Leonard, "Seasonal Marks," *Nashville Banner*, undated, but most likely September 9, 1940.

68 *Ibid.*

69 Unattributed, "Vols Clinch Southern Flag," but clearly a Fred Russell column. Undated, but obviously in the days following the Vols clinching the pennant on Septembre 2, 1940.

70 George K. Leonard, "Seasonal Marks," *Nashville Banner*, undated, but most likely September 9, 1940.

71 Joe Hatcher, "Vols On Top Everyday of Southern Loop Race," *The Sporting News*, September 12, 1940, p 5.

72 *Ibid.*

73 Unattributed, "History of Southern Pitching," undated in SB 37-40.

74 Fred Russell, "Sideline Sidelights," *Nashville Banner*, undated.

75 *Ibid.*

76 Raymond Johnson, "One Man's Opinion," *Nashville Tennessean*, undated, but clearly before the final round of the Southern League finals, which began September 16, 1940.

77 *Ibid.*

78 Fred Russell, "Mr. Boots Is Elegant In 6-1 Win," *Nashville Banner*, September 19, 1940.

79 *Ibid.*

80 Unattributed, but probably from a Fred Russell "Sideline Sidelights" column, undated but probably from September 15, 1940, in SB 37-40.

81 *Ibid.*

82 Raymond Johnson, "Vols Trounce Crax, 7 To 5; To Play Buffs," *Nashville Tennessean*, September 24, 1940.

83 Unattributed, undated in SB 37-40.

84 *Ibid.*

85 Raymond Johnson, "Vols Win, 2-1 From Houston In 10 Rounds," *Nashville Tennessean*, September 28, 1940.

86 Unattributed, "What Vols Get," September 30, 1940.

87 Unattributed, October 2, 1940.

88 Fred Russell, *Nashville Banner*, undated, but clearly October 2, 1940.

89 Raymond Johnson, *Nashville Tennessean*, October 3, 1940.

90 Unattributed, "Dixie Kings Dock Today At 6:30 A. M.," October 2, 1940.

91 George K. Leonard, "Dixie Series Win Of Nashville Brings Once-In-25-Years Thrill In Nashville," *The Sporting News*, October 10, 1940, p 12.

92 Bill Weiss and Marshall Wright, www.MiLB.com

93 Dick Williams, "First Of Feature Writers Sets Out On Trail of 'Boots' Poffenberger," *Morning Herald*, August 28, 1940.

CHAPTER 6

It All Comes Undone

Since August when Boots garnered his 20th win of the season, Nashville newspapers had been reporting that The Baron would inevitably be sold to a major league club. Indeed, catcher Charley George had been sold to the Cubs during the first round of playoffs against Chattanooga, although he continued to play with the Vols. In Hagerstown, Frank Colley reported a rumor that no less than the New York Yankees might obtain Boots.[1] The November 21st edition of *The Sporting News* noted, however, that despite his great year, Boots' contract had not yet been purchased.[2] There was speculation that the Washington Senators were interested in Boots, especially given their 64-90 record and 7th place finish in 1940. Clark Griffith, the Senators owner, demonstrated either an attempt at humor or a total ignorance of feline markings when he said of Boots, "A Tiger doesn't change his spots. I've had some good reports on Poffenberger and I just can't use him. He isn't the kind of a fellow you want in building up a team, although I'll admit he's a pretty good pitcher."[3] In a separate article in the 1941 scrapbook, Griffith stated:

"If he played in Washington he would live too close to his old home town (Williamsport) in nearby Maryland," said Griff.

"Some of those 'friends' of his might take notions to drop around and talk about old times, and when our train left, Poffenberger might forget to catch it."[4]

Perhaps, Boots had not shed his reputation as a bad boy, after all, but more than likely, Griffith and other major league executives and scouts were wary of Boots' numbers. Modern sabrmetrics tells us that wins are not necessarily a good indicator of good pitching. Indeed, not only the sabrmetric definition, but also the most common sense definition of *good pitching* is missing bats or at least missing the good part of the bat. A pitcher can win many games regardless of his own efforts if his team scores him many runs. Boots had a high earned run average at 4.58 and a high walks and hits per innings pitched (WHIP) rate at 1.655 with a low strikeout rate. Opponents hit a resounding .307 against him. In short, he didn't miss many bats in 1940, despite his 26 wins. Fred Russell would quote Boots as saying during the following spring training that he was going for the strike out more in 1941 because "Clark Griffith says a fellow who don't strike out but fifty-nine like I did last year ain't no good, so just figure on Boots bearin' down from now on on those third strikes."[5]

Granted, Boots was pitching in a tiny home ballpark that inflated the numbers against right-handed pitchers, but the fact that Ace Adams and George Jeffcoat started ahead of Boots in both rounds of the Southern Association playoffs as well as in the Dixie Series, indicates that manager Larry Gilbert felt that he had two pitchers on his own staff who were better than Boots.

Shortly before spring training opened for Nashville on March 10th, 1941 Raymond Johnson noted that Boots' hopes of going to Washington remained. In his "One Man's Opinion" column, Johnson interviewed Gilbert who made several interesting observations:

"His strikeout record wasn't impressive and neither was his earned run average," Gilbert declared yesterday in talking about Poffenberger. "But he can pitch. Don't you think he ain't smart. He's bearing down every time he's out there.

"I don't know whether he'll have as good a season as he did last year but he'll win us a lot of games. When we got him, I'd have been tickled with 15 or 20 wins. He might do better'n that this year. The felllas like him and he's always trying. I'm plenty willing to string along with him again.

"I gave him permission to try to make a deal, for I had promised him I would give him every chance to go back to the majors. I wanted him to see for himself. It wasn't a case of wanting to get rid of him."[6]

As part of the same column, Johnson also quoted a letter which he had received from Boots. The Baron wrote in part:

Anyhow, if I am back with Nashville, and I probably will be, I'll really bear down and repeat with a real record. Then maybe I can make some club see me for another year.

I've been in fine shape since coming home, hunting every day possible and playing soccer as in other years. I was manager of our club and we are now playing off a three-game series for the championship. We're one up at present. I worked in the tannery the first six weeks I was back home but quit since I didn't have any chance to hunt or to get out in the open. I'm also doing a little bowling to keep in condition.[7]

Boots was indeed, back with Nashville for the 1941 season, one that would prove to be bizarre even by Boots' standards.

The Vols held their spring training that year in Baton Rouge, Louisiana and on March 13th, the Associated Press once again reported Boots as saying, "I'm through with that bad boy stuff."[8] At least Boots did have an entire season of good behavior to back up this latest claim. Indeed, only five days before, Van Lingle Mungo had been smuggled out of Cuba because the police and the male half of a hotel dance team were seeking to restore the honor of the female half of the dance team with whom Mungo had carried on a notorious affair.[9]

In an interview with Dewey Holden of the *State-Times*, a Baton Rouge newspaper, Boots reiterated his claim that he was through breaking the rules:

"Aw, that bad boy stuff," snorted Boots. "Yeah! It's true. All of it up to last season. But I showed 'em last season and that's the way it's gonna be from now on out."

"I made my mistakes," explains Boots. "I was through with baseball . . . or rather baseball was through with me . . . until Larry gave me another chance. No other manager would take that chance but Larry and I'm out to stick with Larry. He'll get me back in the majors.

"It's up to them (the majors) now," Boots states calmly. "I proved to 'em last season I really mean to stay on the right track and I'll prove it to 'em again this season. After that, if they still refuse me, I guess my chances will be pretty well washed up."

"Larry Gilbert!" exclaims Boots. "Without a doubt, Larry is the best. Boy, he can really handle players. Why, I'm just learning how to pitch, and when you pitch for Larry . . . well, you just go out there to win for that guy."[10]

Thanks to cold and rain, the Vols spent very little time actually working out during the first week in Baton Rouge. Raymond Johnson noted on the 17th that they used the live stock arena at Louisiana State University with its tan bark floor in which to practice. Boots and Oris Hockett took grounders on the basketball court. Boots was reportedly 15 pounds heavier than he had been the previous spring, but in better condition, the weight being distributed through his arms, legs, and hips.[11] The poor weather continued into the second week of training camp and Johnson filed a story detailing how the players were spending their time:

If there are many more days as cold as Monday and Tuesday were and Larry Gilbert can prevail on Boots Poffenberger to remain in the hotel lobby, the Baron will be in great shape by opening day.

The reason is simple. The door that opens on the main street doesn't close properly and Boots spent at least five hours each of those two days closing it. He was on the move so much that Leo Twardy was all for getting him a doorman's uniform. The only hitch was the fact that there are no tent firms in Baton Rouge and the way the Baron has spread out, it would require an enormous amount of cloth to make him the proper type uniform.

When Tommy Tatum joined the Nashville squad at Sanford last spring, he was called a scatter arm. One day at short gave him the name, for he made five wild throws, including hitting Leo Twardy in the head on a throw to home plate on an attempted double steal.

Tommy apparently has mastered control. At least, judging from the way he has been tossing around Little Dickie Culler, 2 1/2 year old son of the Vol shortstop. Culler and Tatum have been using Little Dickie for a medicine ball in the hotel lobby in the mornings. They both should be getting into excellent condition. Little Dickie enjoys flying through the air, for he bawls whenever they stop.[12]

The bad weather never did let up and the Vols headed into the season without even working on cutoff plays; they were severely behind in their conditioning.[13] In fact, Boots was experiencing some arm soreness.[14] Once again, the Vols would feature a seven man pitching staff that besides Boots included holdovers George Jeffcoat, John Sain, Leo Twardy, Tom Drake, and Russ Meers, as well as newcomer Julian Tubb, a right hander who was nearing the end of a nine year minor league career. The departed Ace Adams would make his major league debut on April 15th for the New York Giants and spend the next six seasons in the big leagues.

The Volunteers got off to a mediocre start in 1941 largely due to the ineffectiveness of their hurlers who were giving up eight runs per nine innings over the first 14 games. A robust offense allowed Nashville to win six of those contests. One early highlight was an Easter Sunday duel between Boots and former Dodger teammate Red Evans who was now pitching for Chattanooga. One newspaper blurb noted that the "liveliest inter-jockeying in the league now is between Red Evans and Boots Poffenberger. If only it could be printed."[15]

Boots told Baltimore writer John Steadman that one time he and Evans had "held a beer-drinking contest. The loser was determined by the first man to head for the men's room, and the loser had to pay the bar bill. I won."[16]

Buss Walker, a sports columnist whose work appeared in the *Chattanooga Times* as well as other southeastern newspapers wrote:

The volcanic Evans, contacted on the phone Saturday morning, stated that he was ready for the battle and that when he got through with Boots he wouldn't be able to sleep any more.

"To tell you the truth, I'm going out there today and work on that guy so hard he'll be mentally unbalanced before game time Sunday. I'll have him so steamed up he won't be able to pitch a lick.

"He's not fooling anybody with that phony record of his. He walked almost 100 men and struck out less than sixty. That's almost twice as many walks as strikeouts in a whole flock of innings, and if that's good pitching I should go back to the farm.

"I'm glad Larry is giving him to me to pitch against. I'd rather beat that guy than anybody in baseball. Why he's just a big bag of wind."[17]

Whether this banter was all in fun or there was genuine animosity between Poffenberger and Evans is unknown. Walker thought it was the latter, writing, that the former Dodger teammates "learned to dislike each other so thoroughly that their personal rivalry has taken on the form of a perpetual duel."[18] Evans certainly struck right at the heart of Boots' pitching weakness when he commented on Boots' walk to strikeout ratio. Regardless, it was Boots who bested Evans in the first game of a double-header in which he gave up 11 hits, two walks, and struck out none in a complete game effort. For his part, Evans gave up six runs in five innings. Scoring 15 runs in the seventh inning of game two, the Vols won the nightcap by an incredible 25-1 score in an even more incredible time of two hours which comes out to a run about every four minutes and 40 seconds.

An undated, unsigned blurb in the 1941 scrapbook was the first public mention of the fact that Boots Poffenberger now looked almost exactly like comedian Lou Costello, a resemblance that would be noted throughout the rest of Boots' career.[19] Costello, of Abbott and Costello fame was appearing along with his partner in a movie entitled *Buck Privates,* a comedy about life in the American military and in which the song, "Boogie Woogie Bugle Boy" first appeared.

The Vols were staging their own comedies of sorts. Against the Crackers in Atlanta, George Jeffcoat came on in relief of Boots in an attempt to preserve a 5-4 lead. With two out in the bottom of the ninth, second baseman Johnny Mihalic commited an error that seemed to unnerve Jeffcoat who walked three straight batters to tie the score. At this point, Larry Gilbert emerged from the Vols' dugout for a mound visit, but Jeffcoat didn't see him coming and Gilbert didn't ask for time. In the middle of his windup, Jeffcoat finally saw Gilbert, stopped his motion, and thereby balked in the winning run. That was in the first game of a double header and after dropping the second contest as well, Nashville's record stood at 7-11.

By the end of the month, however, the Vols were hot. They swept a double header against Birmingham on May 2nd, giving them nine wins in their past 12 games. Boots won the opener 5-4 while George Jeffcoat won the nightcap 3-1. Boots notched eight strikeouts and Raymond Johnson noted:

> Boots startled some 2,500 fans, the majority of whom were ladies who nearly froze in the marrow-chilling winds, when he struck out eight batters. Not since he graduated from Beaumont in the Texas League in 1938 [sic] has he baffled opposing hitters with the third strikes as he did last night. He fanned more in that nine-inning span than he had in all his previous trips to the rubber during this youthful campaign.[20]

Boots pitched decently throughout May, picking up an occasional win and a couple no-decisions despite his continued propensity to surrender a high number of hits. In back-to-back victories in mid June, however, he two-hit Knoxville and then one-hit Atlanta in a seven inning complete game. Against the Smokies on June 12th, Boots gave up only one unearned run when his pickoff throw to second sailed into center field. He struck out six and walked only one while hitting two batters in the 5-1 victory. Raymond Johnson wrote that "his performance was equal, if not superior to that he gave on Men's Night last summer when he shut out the Smokies on three hits."[21] In Boots' 6-1 victory in game two of the double header against Atlanta on the 15th, he also hit a double. The Vols had swept the twin bill and according to Raymond Johnson,

> *Larry Gilbert's Vols made the pace-setting Crackers look like the cellar club in a kindergarten league here today as they buried the Atlantans in a double defeat before 10,283 startled fans. The scores were 11 to 0 and 6 to 1, which, even as one-sided as these figures are, do not accurately show how pathetic was Paul Richards' club.*[22]

For his part, it appeared that Boots was enjoying himself more than ever as this undated, unsigned newspaper article portrays:

> *When he's cute and cunning as he has been in the last two starts, there's no one I had rather watch pitch than Boots Poffenberger.*
>
> *Main reason is that the Baron himself gets such a bang out of racking up the hitters and cannot conceal his own delight. Immodest, perhaps, but honest.*
>
> *Atlanta fans were booing him at every move Sunday, and did he love it! When he would goose a slow curve up to the plate, causing Mailho to pop up, Poffenberger would put his glove up to his face and snicker. When some Cracker bounced back to him, he would have a few little words to say before tossing him out at first.*
>
> *The Baron has spun two great games, a two-hitter and a one-hitter. And it isn't just a flash in the pan, either. He has come up with a real curve ball.*[23]

Boots had not been as happy, however, as appearances indicated, a fact which would soon become obvious.

The Baron picked up his seventh victory against two losses at Birmingham on the 20th with a complete game effort in the 3-2 win and he appeared to be on the kind of roll that might take him straight back to the majors. His next start on Tuesday the 24th at Sulphur Dell against New Orleans would be his last for Nashville, however, and not because he was purchased by a major league club. Incensed at home plate umpire Dutch Hoffman's strike zone, Boots had liberally cursed the umpire throughout the game. This was unusual for Boots, but according to all reports and Boots' own admission, he took the mound drunk. By the fifth inning, Hoffman decided to tolerate no more and ejected the inebriated Baron, who promptly nailed Hoffman with the baseball. Hoffman was uninjured as he warded off the ball with his balloon chest protector, but Boots' prospects of ever returning to the majors were permanently damaged. Southern Association President Trammell Scott suspended Boots for 90 days and Larry Gilbert released him.

"I'm through with him," Gilbert was quoted as saying in the Nashville papers the next day. "He won't pitch for Nashville anymore."[24]

Interestingly, Raymond Johnson had written a story the previous September about how Gilbert handled "problem guys" such as Boots.

> "I tell 'em what I want 'em to do, and they do it—or else," the Vol manager says. "When I get a player that is supposed to be hard to handle, I tell 'em that I'm not going to try to reform any of them. I don't care if they have a few beers after a game, but I am positively not going to have a player who gets full of whisky. They all know it and that makes it easier. I tell all my pitchers when they are going to work and I expect them to be ready at that time. If they are not, then it's me and them for it."[25]

This time however, Gilbert didn't have the luxury of telling Boots ahead of time that he was going to pitch the game on the 24th. The Nashville skipper was running short on pitchers and with a double-header on the 25th and George Jeffcoat nursing a blister, Gilbert had few options and apparently only notified Boots shortly before the game that he would pitch. Thinking that he had the day off, Boots had been drinking rather heavily, telling Fred Russell that he had had a few beers,[26] but telling Raymond Johnson that he'd "had a few Tom Collins."[27] Whatever the specific cause, the result was that Poffenberger took the mound drunk and began to complain to umpire Hoffman from the very first pitch of the game according to Johnson:

> He fussed and fumed on every pitch that Hoffman called a ball, regardless of where it was.
>
> Twice, while he was maneuvering around on the mound, Poffenberger nearly fell down. Once he started his windup and the ball flopped out of his hand toward second base. On several

*occasions he let the return throw from Catcher Hank Helf hit
his glove and drop to the ground.*[28]

With two out in the 5th, a ball four to New Orleans center fielder
and clean up hitter Tom Winsett prompted a profanity laced tirade from
Poffenberger who "wobbled" toward home plate to deliver it.[29] Catcher
Hank Helf tried to restrain Boots who eventually turned his back on
Hoffman, but it was too late as the umpire finally ejected him. Fred
Russell wondered the next day what took Hoffman so long to give Boots
the thumb.[30] Realizing that he had been tossed, Boots fired the baseball
at Hoffman who knocked it to the ground with his protector. Boots then
sailed his glove towards the screen and Larry Gilbert raced out to make
sure that Boots' unruly behavior went no further.

Gilbert, however, disputed the notion that Boots appeared to be
drunk, at least at the start of the game telling Fred Russell that,

> *Before the game Boots acted no different than he does all the
> time. He's always clowning around, as everybody knows.*
>
> *Not for a second am I trying to take up for him, but it is
> incorrect to say that he was wobbling and about to fall off the
> mound and couldn't control himself. The best proof of that
> is that Poffenberger was getting the ball over the plate, was
> getting the batters out.*
>
> *A drunk man can't do that. A drunk man can't throw strikes.*[31]

Gilbert acknowledged, however that by the 2nd inning it was clear
that Boot's behavior was amiss and that he would need to come out early,
but Gilbert, thin on pitching was trying to squeeze four or five innings
out of him.[32] The Baron might clown around and he definitely drank
too much, but he was never one to curse, especially before 3,500 fans on
Ladies Night, most of whom could hear every word thanks to the tiny
dimensions at The Dell.

Two days later, Boots repeated a familiar story of remorse, saying
he had no body to blame but himself. He apologized to Larry Gilbert,
his teammates, and the Nashville fans and talked again about going back
to Maryland and pitching in the semi-pros. He explained why he had

started drinking again, trotting out the familiar refrain about not having enough money. He told Raymond Johnson that he "was always owing the club and it didn't look like I'd ever get square. I couldn't on the money I was making."[33] Johnson parenthetically noted that Boots was one of the highest paid players on the team in 1940. Boots talked about an insurance policy he bought while with Detroit and never received, but "still they kept hounding me for the money."[34] He talked about the debt he incurred in 1939 when he was suspended. At the end of his recitation to Johnson regarding his money troubles, however, Boots described what might have been the real reason for his renewed heavy drinking:

> *I was so disgusted when I didn't get to go up after winning 29 games last year that I felt like quitting. Yes, I started to leave the club the day after we got back from training camp this spring. If it hadn't been for Jo, I'd have gone home then. I felt like quitting again a few weeks ago. I don't know why, except I got in those moods. I just can't seem to get ahead of even any more.*[35]

Indeed, Fred Russell was reporting that Larry Gilbert had told Senators' owner Clark Griffith during the off-season to simply name his price for Poffenberger, but that Griffith had declined.[36] Only the week before, according to Russell, the Baltimore Orioles, then of the International League were not interested in trading for the home state boy.[37] Disgusted at himself and depressed, Boots took a common and unhealthy approach by treating his symptoms with alcohol.

In a June 29th column, Dick Hudson back in Charleston wrote

> *Boots Poffenberger never was exactly a puritan, but the screwball former Senator pitcher has had more than his share of tough breaks . . . although mostly self inflicted.*
>
> *The Williamsport, Md., whiz threw himself out of the Southern association last week (and perhaps organized baseball) when he threw a ball at an umpire following a squabble. To Boots' credit . . . the pitch was true, but the ump deflected the ball with his chest protector.*
>
> *It's hard to defend a boy who has been in so much sizzling water as has Boots since he started playing baseball in the last*

*month of 1934 under the name of Zimmerman at Charleroi, Pa.
He's best described as a carefree, careless, modern version of
Huckleberry Finn. We've always thought that Boots didn't get
the right start in life. Living in a house divided, the carefree
Boots got much of his education in the streets. He apparently
didn't know discipline and doesn't yet.*

*As far as baseball is concerned . . . the saddest part of the
Poffenberger tragedy is that a boy with a more level head
blessed with better breaks wasn't born with the natural talent
Boots carried in his stout right arm.*[38]

Vincent X. Flaherty of the *Washington Herald* wrote on July 2nd,

*For all of his lunacies and notoriety, Poffenberger was never a
bad or belligerent sort.*

*For all of his deviltry and disobedience, Poffenberger was loved
by the Detroit sports writers, who protected him at every turn.
For they saw in him a big overgrown kid with a mischievous,
rather than malevolent, glint in his eyes. Poffenberger meant to
go through life playing hookey from school and making faces at
the teacher. And when fines depleted his funds, he went around
wearing a why-was-I-born look. It always won him a reprieve.*

*We'd like to see some good manager bring Poffenberger back
to the big leagues. He would be good enough to win his way
in any company if he observed training—even on a part-time
basis. And like all of the Grover Alexanders and Rube Waddells
of baseball, the impish Poffenberger has a way of endearing
himself to the fans.*[39]

Boots indeed returned to Maryland in search of a semi-pro team.
Factories and businesses all over the country sponsored semi-professional teams, so called because the players were paid to play, but usually
not enough to make it a full-time job. Most then worked in one capacity
or another for their sponsor. Baseball became the national "pastime" for
a reason; it was the most popular way to pass idle time before the days
of televisions. Even cities such as Washington, which had a major league
team had a semi-professional league and upon his return to Williamsport,

Boots was recruited by the Heurich Brewers. Heurich Brewery was the Capital's oldest, and the sponsor of the aptly named Brewers. That Boots might join a team sponsored by a beer company was not lost on one writer whose unattributed article appeared in the 1941 scrapbook:

Cletus Elwood Poffenberger, the former Detroit pitcher, who left the Southern League unexpectedly a few days ago when he whizzed a horsehide missle at the head of Umpire Dutch Hoffman, arrived here the other day, was received by Chris Heurich, and forthwith announced that he meant to get serious. He wasted an opportunity to make his mark in the brewery business.

Having studied the beer business from the outside ever since he caught on with the Tigers a couple of years ago, and able to distinguish Pilsner from the lesser brews any old time, Poffenberger was interested, or seemed to be, in going a little deeper into his favorite hobby. He said he would pitch for the Heurich baseball team, and wouldn't mind doing a little work along with his pitching. So Heurich took Poffy on a tour of his domain of malt and hops.

First, Heurich introduced him to "Fee" Colliere, one of the greatest all-around athletes in the history of anywhere, who is still playing ball for Heurich. "Fee," working feverishly in the bottling department, shook hands with Poffy hastily and hustled back to work. Next, Heurich escorted up to "Pepco" Barry, the outfielder, who quit a promising minor-league career to play ball in his own home town. "Pepco" was tossing cases of beer around like nothing at all. A worried look grew over Poffenberger's face. "But for the grace of a few gallons of gasoline," Poffenberger must have meditated, "this might be me."

Anyhow, Poffenberger promised to report for work the next morning, bright and disgustingly early, and this is where the story ends. Poffy didn't show.[40]

Major league, minor league, or semi-pro, the pattern never deviated with Boots. After promising he had reformed, he immediately went back to his old ways. Within 10 days, however, there was an Associated Press report from Atlanta that Boots had joined the Bona Allen Shoemakers of Buford, Georgia, one of the best semi-pro teams in the country.[41] Buford is located in Gwinnett County about 40 miles north of Atlanta and the Shoemakers had won the 1938 national semi-pro championship held in Witchita, Kansas as well as the *Denver Post* Tournament in 1940. Bona Allen, Inc. was the nation's largest tannery and in addition to manufacturing shoes, they supplied sporting goods giant Spaulding with all its leather for gloves and baseballs. The company sold no stock and never borrowed money, which meant that Bona Allen was one of the few manufacturers to not only survive, but thrive during the Depression.[42] Hence, the company had money to spend on ball players.

Lost to time is whether the Shoemakers reached out to Boots or vice-versa but it is reasonable to assume that Boots ended up in Buford, Georgia because the Shoemakers were willing to pay him to play baseball without asking him to work in the factory. In any case, the 1941 scrapbook contains an undated newspaper photo of a grinning Boots Poffenberger, "Bona Allen" across his chest looking at John Allen, "chief scion of the famous family" of shoemakers according to the caption. Allen, in white double-breasted suit and straw hat, doesn't seem to know what to make of Boots.[43]

The Shoemakers were heading west for several tournaments including ones in Denver and Wichita. They stopped in Birmingham, Alabama where Boots was knocked out by the "Goslin-Birmingham amateur team" in the first inning.[44] The *Birmingham News-Age Herald* reported that "Baron Boots Poffenberger was supposed to have been the whole show Saturday. He popped off plenty before the game, telling about how the night before he had hurled five hitless and runless innings against Dixie."[45] Indeed, Boots had thrown six innings on Friday night, which may have explained his early exit on Saturday.

Boots went on to say that he was quite satisfied to be playing for Bona Allen:

"It only costs me $12 a month for rent and meals cost only $3 a week. They pay us $2 a day for meals on the road and we stay at the best hotels. That's better than it was at Nashville."[46]

His one complaint, however was that "Beer costs more in Buford. And, boy, what a lonesome town. Why they don't even sell beer on Sundays."[47]

Boots sounded a familiar refrain about his new team in a July 25 interview with AP correspondent Romney Wheeler, which ran under the headline, "Baseball's Huck Finn With Semi-Pros." Saying that the Shoemakers were a "first-class team" and that Bona Allen treated him "right," he waxed enthusiastic about working in the factory during the off-season and stated that Jo liked Buford as well. Boots said that he didn't expect to return to the majors and claimed that he had no desire to "kick around the minor leagues until I'm worn out," adding that, "I'd just as soon stay right here in Buford."[48]

The Shoemakers stopped in Waco to play the Dons, which was the semi-pro team in that Texas town. The *Waco News-Herald* of July 22nd noted that while the Dons had won 11 straight and had not lost a game since acquiring several players including future major leaguer Grady Hatton, they would face a tough match in Buford who arrived with a 60-10 mark.[49] They also arrived with pitcher Sig "Jack" Jakucki on the roster. Jakucki had been a member of the Dons just the week before, but jumped the team and ended up signing with Buford. He was now back in Waco and, pitching the first game against the Dons, he defeated his former teammates 10-5. Jakucki had pitched 20.2 innings for the St. Louis Browns in 1936 going 0-3. He pitched in the minors for two years after that before disappearing into the vast baseball landscape that included towns such as Waco and Buford. Thanks to a shortage of players caused by World War II, however, he returned to the major league spotlight in 1944. Re-signed by the Browns, he went 13-9 and defeated the Yankees on the last day of the season to clinch the Browns' one and only pennant. He lost his only World Series start that year, returned in 1945, but was kicked off the team by manager Luke Sewell for poor behavior, including a fight with teammate and one-armed outfielder Pete Gray. Jakucki, who apparently derived great pleasure from riding Gray, kept one arm behind his back during the fray.[50]

The Shoemakers arrived in Denver at the end of July for one of the most famous tournaments in the country. Known as "the Little World Series," the *Denver Post* Tournament featured the best semi-pro teams from the Rockies to the Atlantic. Sixteen teams were scheduled to participate in 1941 including among others, Aurelia, the Iowa semi-pro champs, Centennial Coal of Louisville Colorado, Champlin Refiners of Enid, Oklahoma, the 1939 tournament champions, Duvall-Davison, a team made up of players employed by Coors Brewing Company; the Fort Leavenworth Soldiers, the top military team, the Greeley (Colorado) Jaycees, a collection of college all-stars; the Tractolubers of Lexington, Nebraska; and the Ethiopian Clowns, a talented, all-black, barnstorming team out of Miami.

Bona Allen and Greeley would open the tournament on Thursday, July 31st at 8:30, while the remaining first round games were played on Friday and Saturday. All the games were played at Merchants Park.

That day, the *Denver Post* ran a photo of Bona Allen player manager Mercer Harris holding tightly to a chain, the other end of which was attached to Boots' neck. The Baron does not look particularly thrilled at this photographic gag which was headlined, "Bona Allen Manager finds Way to Hold Poffenberger." The caption read in part,

> It will be Denver's first chance to see the man said to be the
> most colorful player in the game today. Poffenberger will be
> seen against the Greeley Jaycees, a fast-stepping group of col-
> lege players who know how to perform under the lights. The
> Greeley club has announced it has no fear of Poffenberger and
> his dizzy slants.[51]

Whether or not they feared Boots, the young Jaycees should have been scared to death of the Shoemakers' offense. They trailed 18-0 after four innings and Boots himself was two-for-three with a double and an RBI. Poffenberger was removed after those four innings by order of John Allen who, listening to the game description off the telegraph back in Buford, decided that it would be prudent to save his former major leaguer for tougher tournament opposition. Bona Allen won by a final score of 22-0.[52]

Bona Allen sailed through the double-elimination tournament and reached the finals through the losers' bracket with a 4-1 mark, losing only to the Ethiopian Clowns 6-1 in a game started by Boots and that was much closer than the final score indicated. The Clowns swept their five games and so would face the Shoemakers for the championship on August 12th. Boots would once again face "Macan," the stage name of Roosevelt Davis, one of the Negro Leagues' premier pitchers of that era. Davis, who had fanned 11 Shoemakers in the first contest, went by what he considered to be an African-sounding name and donned face paint when he pitched. The Clowns, as their name might suggest were baseball's equivalent of basketball's Harlem Globetrotters, only for the Clowns, the games were never pre-determined. Ultimately, Abe Saperstein, who had in fact formed the Globetrotters, would invest in the Clowns and the team would move to Cincinnati in 1943 and from there to Indianapolis in 1944.

Boots and Macan both pitched brilliantly. The Clowns picked up a run in the fourth but the damage could have been worse had not Boots made a spectacular fielding play. Left fielder "Selassie" who possessed blazing speed was on first when center fielder "Mofike" lined a smash through the box. Boots deflected the ball off his shin toward Shoemaker third baseman Mercer Harris, who ran in, fielded the ball, and heaved it toward first in a futile attempt to record the out. Seeing that third was uncovered, the speedy Selassie never broke stride coming around second base. Boots, who was in obvious discomfort from the ricochet off his shins, immediately broke for third and called for the ball. Catching it on the run, Boots dove toward Selassie, tagging him out much to the delight and amazement of the crowd. It was *the* defensive play in a game that saw several, but when Bona Allen came to bat in the bottom of the eighth, they still trailed 1-0. With a man on and two out, Boots strode to the plate. Macan quickly got two strikes on "The Baron." Then, as Frank Haraway reported in the *Post*,

> *You could have heard a pin drop as the crowd held its collective breath while Macan wound up for the pitch he hoped would retire the side.*
>
> *But crack! Poffenberger caught it square on the nose and sent a tremendous drive out to far-distant left-centerfield fence, more than 400 feet away. Mitchell easily scored from first with the tying run and Poffenberger steamed into third with a triple.*[53]

Boots, standing at third, and perhaps huffing and puffing after his three-bagger—columnist Jack Carberry reported that Boots was 30 pounds overweight[54]—began dancing off the bag and proved such a distraction that Macan balked him home. Consecutive doubles followed and when Boots retired the side in order in the top of the ninth, the Shoemakers had won 3-1 and forced a second game. Heading into the ninth inning of Game Two, it appeared that Bona Allen would retain their tournament title, but the Clowns rallied for six runs after Manager Harris removed Sig Jakucki in a 9-7 comeback victory.

Haraway, who was in just his fourth year with the *Post*, but who would cover Denver sports, particularly baseball long enough that the press box at Coors Field is named in his honor, was enthralled by the evening, writing about the first game:

> *Earlier in the night of gilt-edged baseball that sparkled with brilliance throughout, Bona Allen, or rather Cletus Elwood (Boots the Baron) Poffenberger, handed the Clowns their only loss of the tournament in a sensational 3-1 contest that will go down in annals as the greatest game in the history of THE DENVER POST tournament—and one of the greatest games ever played anywhere.*[55]

Jack Carberry, a *Denver Post* sports writer stated in his "The Second Guess" column that Boots "pitched his heart out. It may be that he pitched his arm out, too" noting that Boots couldn't straighten it after the game. Carberry also wrote that Boots was seen crying after the second game, not because the Shoemakers had lost, but because he felt that an error by shortstop Johnny Collins in the fateful ninth inning would be unfairly regarded as the play that lost the game for the Shoemakers. Carberry's column was apologetic for having portrayed Boots as "'Peck's Bad Boy of Baseball' and a lot of tripe like that." Indeed, Carberry stated that *Post* photographers had taken all kinds of photos of Boots "razzing the fans."[56] One AP photo in particular shows Boots on top of the dugout with his hat cocked over his left shoulder with his left arm outstretched, his right thumb in his ear, and wearing an expression of pure merriment.[57]

Bona Allen placed seven players on the post-tournament All-Star team, including Boots as one of three pitchers named. Macan was also named to the team.

Given his performance in the tournament, Boots could have no doubt secured a spot on the Shoemakers for some time to come. He may have even settled down in Buford as did his teammate Gerald McQuaig, the Shoemakers' hard hitting centerfielder who had played a handful of games for the 1934 Philadelphia Athletics before joining Bona Allen. McQuaig ultimately coached the high school baseball team and served as principal of a nearby elementary school.[58] Despite his statements about how much he and Jo liked Buford, however, and that he didn't expect to make it back to the majors, the Associated Press was quoting him during the tournament as saying:

> *Boy, oh boy, if some club would just give me one more chance. Sometimes I feel like giving up baseball for keeps, but you gotta make a living and baseball's the only thing I know. I've never made too good a living from it, either.*[59]

Far from settling in Buford, it appears that Boots never returned to Georgia once the tournament was concluded. The Shoemakers traveled from Denver to Wichita, Kansas for the 1941 National Semi-Pro Baseball Championship, which was being held from the 15th to the 28th. The 1941 scrapbook contains a tournament pass made out to Mrs. Boots Poffenberger "Buford, wife." It also contains a 12" x 20" broadside reading at the top:

> *EXTRA! Baseball Battle of the Year at Aurelia (Home of the 1940 Semi-Pro Champs—-Third Place Winners at Denver Post Tourney, 1941) Storm Lake Friday, August 29th Both Teams Unwilling to lay down the bats for the 1941 season until the issue is settled. This will be the last chance to see them battle this year.*

At bottom of the poster is printed:

> *Attraction Deluxe: Boots Poffenberger, major league hurler late of Detroit and Brooklyn has joined the history making Aurelians pitching staff and may be seen in action in both contests. The moniker, "Bad Boy of Baseball", means that he is bad news for opposing batters.*
>
> *Visit Aurelias Farmers Picnic and see this baseball treat of the year*
>
> *Games start at 2:30 O'clock   Admission 15c and 45c Inc. Tax*

Somehow, Boots was now pitching for Aurelia in the "Southwestern Iowa Baseball Tournament. Perhaps, the thought of returning to the "lonesome" town of Buford was more than The Baron could take and so, like Jack Jakucki, he simply joined another team. A player pass in the 1941 scrapbook reads, "Admit Player and Lady" for August 16, 17, 23, 24, 30, 31 Sept 1. The 31st is punched out and indeed the scrapbook contains a photo dated September 1st, of Boots in an Aurelia uniform, the caption telling of his 6-0 loss to the Omaha Storz, a team sponsored by the Storz Brewery.

From there, Boots ended up in Washington, D. C. no doubt with a stopover in Williamsport. Bob Addie, who would be named a J. G. Taylor Spink Award winner in 1981 by the National Baseball Hall of Fame noted in the *Washington Times-Herald* that

> Boots" Poffenberger, once regarded as one of the most promising pitchers in the big leagues when he was with the Detroit Tigers, now is a laborer for the Tompkins Construction Company here in town . . . Boots is living in a rooming house on Twenty-third Street Northwest . . . He's only 26 years old now . . .[60]

In actuality, Boots was living with his in-laws who had moved from Charleston and resided at 903 23rd St. NW. Jo and Boots had been living with her step-father, Herman Burte and her mother Bessie in Washington during at least part of the off-season since 1940 and perhaps earlier. Census data from that year shows that Burte had taken a job as a sewer inspector and that Jo's brother Carl along with six boarders were also living at the residence. This extended family no doubt reminded Boots of the household in which he was raised.

The next entry in the scrapbook is a clipping dated September 20th, stating that the Nashville Vols were headed to their third Dixie Series in a row. (The Vols would sweep the Dallas Rebels four games to none.)[61] The inclusion of this lone newspaper story of what might have been is the only suggestion of regret that Boots Poffenberger ever expressed. Perhaps it reflects more on Jo's regret than his.

Boots' baseball journey was not quite finished for the year, however. On December 6th, Fred Russell of the *Nashville Banner* reported that Boots' contract had been sold to the San Diego Padres of the Pacific Coast League for $2,500.[62] The Associated Press reported:

Today and with a kind word—Nashville Manager Larry Gilbert said he had sold Boots to the San Diego Padres of the Pacific Coast League in a straight cash transaction.

"Boots can win anywhere," said Gilbert, "if he behaves himself."

That "if" is about the biggest thing in Poffenberger's life—so far, he has never been able to get over it for any length of time.[63]

Boots' chaotic world would land in San Diego in 1942. The next day would land the entire country in chaos.

Notes

1   Frank Colley, "The Colley-See-Um Of Sports," *Morning Herald*, September 25, 1940.
2   *The Sporting News*, "They Set Hot Pace in Dixie," November 21, 1940, p 6.
3   Unattributed, "Nats' Chief 'Poofs' Poffenberger Deal," undated, possibly from the *Washington Post* in SB 37-40.
4   Unattributed, undated, possibly from the *Washington Post* in SB 41.
5   Fred Russell, "Sideline Sidelights," *Nashville Banner*, undated; filed during first two weeks of spring training 1941.
6   Raymond Johnson, "One Man's Opinion," *Nashville Tennessean*, undated, but appeared end of February/beginning of March.
7   *Ibid.*
8   Associated Press, March 13, 1941.
9   Leo Durocher with Ed Linn, *Nice Guys Finish Last*, (New York: Simon & Schuster Pocketbook Edition, 1976) pp 151-152.
10 Dewey Holden, "Noisy Nashville Hurler Determined to Crash Majors Again Before 1942 Campaign," *State-Times*, undated, but during spring training 1941.
11 Raymond Johnson, *Nashville Tennessean*, March 17, 1941.
12 Raymond Johnson, "One Man's Opinion," *Nashville Tennessean*, March 19, 1941.
13 Unattributed, March 31, 1941 in SB 41.
14 Unattributed caption of photo, April 3, 1941 in SB 41.
15 Unattributed, undated in SB 41.
16 John Steadman, "Boots was made for walking onto list of great characters," http://articles.baltimoresun.com/1996-06-30/sports/1996182039_1_beer-williamsport-tavern, June 30, 1996.
17 Buss Walker, "Burrows Opposes Nashville Today; Evans, Poffenberger to Hurl Sunday," probably in the *Chattanooga Times* around Easter weekend, 1941, when Nashville was playing the Lookouts in Chattanooga. SB 41.

18   *Ibid.*

19   Unattributed, undated in SB 41.

20   Raymond Johnson, "Vols Take Twinheader From Barons, 5-4, 3-1,"
     Nashville Tennessean, May 3, 1941.

21   Raymond Johnson, "Boots' Box Work Tumbles Smokies In Final Fracas,"
     Nashville Tennessean, undated, but undoubtedly from June 12, 1941.

22   Raymond Johnson, "Meers Gives Two Hits, Baron One," *Nashville
     Tennessean*, June 15, 1941.

23   Unattributed, undated in SB 41. Appears to be clipped from a Fred Russell,
     "Sideline Sidelights" column.

24   Fred Russell, "Vol Pitcher May Be Through With Baseball After Throwing at
     Ump," *Nashville Banner*, undated, but clearly June 25, 1941.

25   Raymond Johnson, "One Man's Opinion," *Nashville Tennessean*, September
     7, 1940.

26   Fred Russell, "Sideline Sidelights: Roll Out the Baron," *Nashville Banner*,
     undated, but clearly June 25, 1941.

27   Raymond Johnson, "One Man's Opinion: Suspended Boots Poffenberger
     Feels Badly Over Letting Gilbert, Teammates Down," *Nashville Tennessean*,
     undated, but clearly June 25, 1941.

28   Raymond Johnson, "Poffenberger, Put Out of Game For Cursing, Hits Ump
     With Ball," *Nashville Tennessean*, undated, but clearly June 25, 1941.

29   *Ibid.*

30   Fred Russell, "Sideline Sidelights: Roll Out the Baron," *Nashville Banner*,
     undated, but clearly June 25, 1941.

31   *Ibid.*

32   *Ibid.*

33   Raymond Johnson, "Poffenberger, Put Out of Game For Cursing, Hits Ump
     With Ball," *Nashville Tennessean*, undated, but clearly June 25, 1941.

34   *Ibid.*

35   *Ibid.*

36   Fred Russell, "Vol Pitcher May Be Through With Baseball After Throwing at
     Ump," *Nashville Banner*, undated, but clearly June 25, 1941.

37   *Ibid.*

38   Dick Hudson, "Warming Up," *Charleston Daily Mail*, June 29, 1941.

39   Vincent X. Flaherty, "Straight From the Shoulder," *Washington Herald*, July
     2, 1941.

40   Unattributed, undated in SB 41.

41   Associated Press, "Boots Will Play Semi-Pro Ball," July 11, 1941 in SB 41.

42   http://www.museumofbuford.com/shoemakers.html

43   Unattributed, undated photo in SB 41.

44   Jack House, "Goslin Beats Buford Team in 11 Frames," *Birmingham News-
     Age Herald*, July 20, 1941.

45   *Ibid.*

46   *Ibid.*

47   *Ibid.*

48 Romney Wheeler, "Baseball's Huck Finn With Semi-Pros," Associated Press, July 25, 1941.

49 Jinx Tucker, "Strong Georgia Team Also Plays Here Wednesday," *Waco News-Tribune*, July 22, 1941.

50 http://en.wikipedia.org/wiki/Sig_Jakucki

51 Unattributed, undated photo with heading of "Bona Allen Manager Finds Way to Hold Poffenberger," no doubt from the *Denver Post* in SB 41.

52 Frank Haraway, "Bona Allen Runs Over Greely In Night Game," *Denver Post*, undated, but most likely August 1, 1941.

53 Frank Haraway, "'Boots' Poffenberger Of Losing Team Hero Of Thrilling Battle," *Denver Post*, undated, but most likely August 14, 1941.

54 Jack Carberry, "The Second Guess," *Denver Post*, undated, but most likely August 14, 1941.

55 Frank Haraway, "'Boots' Poffenberger Of Losing Team Hero Of Thrilling Battle," *Denver Post*, undated, but most likely August 14, 1941.

56 Jack Carberry, "The Second Guess," *Denver Post*, undated, but most likely August 14, 1941.

57 Associated Press, undated photo in SB 41.

58 http://www.museumofbuford.com/shoemakers.html

59 Associated Press, "'Reformed' Poffenberger Eager For Another Major Chance; 'Just Broke Few Rules,'" August 8, 1941 in SB 41. The same scrapbook page contains the same article cut from a different paper and is attributed to Loudon Kelly, a reporter at the *Rocky Mountain News* who went to work for the AP. This one is entitled "Poffenberger Longs For Major Leagues."

60 Bob Addie, "Monday Wash," no doubt from the *Washington Post*, undated.

61 Norman Bradley, paper unknown, September 20, 1941.

62 Fred Russell, "Vols Sell Boots Poffenberger to San Diego Club," *Nashville Banner*, December 6, 1941.

63 Associated Press, "Poffenberger Getting Comeback Chance With San Diego," December 6, 1941.

CHAPTER 7

San Diego

At some point after arriving in San Diego, Boots or Jo or both apparently visited Professor F. W. Raymond a "minister-spiritual medium" and a member of the San Diego Spiritual Mediums' Guild. Located at 1554 Fifth Avenue, the professor also broadcast the *Psychic Hour* radio program which was "recognized as the best of its kind" according to his two-fold business card found in the 1942 scrapbook. Readings were $1.50 and satisfaction was guaranteed. No one knows what Professor Raymond said about Boots, but if he had been on his psychic game, he should have told The Baron to throw more strikes. Boots did not have a very good year in 1942.

Posting nine wins and 10 losses in 168 innings, Boots recorded an ERA of 3.86 which was slightly better than the league average. The problem, as it had been in the past, was that he walked 80 batters and struck out only 40. He was surrendering a runner and a half per inning and impressing no one. Perhaps, he had indeed injured his arm during the *Denver Post* tournament. By his own admission, he did not throw as hard as he once did, telling A. R. Hardman, a writer for the *Charleston Gazette*, whom Boots had stopped to see on his way to the West Coast, "I'm not as fast as I used to be, but I don't have to be. I'm pitching smarter and don't have to rely on speed so much."[1] His weight was affecting his pitching as well, having admitted to the Associated Press the previous August, "I'm a little too heavy. Weighed 168 when I went up to Detroit from the Texas League and now I'm 205. Got too much up here [indicating what the AP described as a "bass drum chest"]. Can't get over my fast one the way I used to."[2]

Regardless, Boots was still full of bravado, telling Hardman that "This Coast league should be easy for me" because the hitters weren't nearly as good as the ones in the Southern Association, where "three-hundred hitters are a dime a dozen."[3] Of course, it was the Pacific Coast League (PCL) that had within the past decade produced the DiMaggio brothers and Ted Williams among others. It was considered the best minor league in the country and in the next decade, there was talk of making it a major league. None of this made an impression on The Baron who went on to claim that winning in the big leagues was actually easier because of better travel conditions, better defenses, and "the finest of everything."

The Padres held their Spring Training in El Centro, California and Boots as usual, won praise from Padre manager Cedric Durst for his hustle and enthusiasm on the first day of camp, February 23rd.[4] He was also commended for his quick acclimation to his new teammates who responded to the fun-loving Baron by telling him that he was being farmed out to Twin Falls or Ponca City. A blurb in the 1942 scrapbook noted, "The eccentric one started to blow up but one of the ribbers started to laugh, giving the gag away . . . Incidentally, Cletus says he's not eccentric—he's colorful."[5]

No medium was needed to predict that Boots would once again claim that he had reformed, a claim that at this point in his career, was viewed with decided skepticism by PCL sports writers. Morton Moss of the *Los Angeles Examiner* wrote on February 26th:

> *San Diego, which upped and belted the experts on the chops by finishing third last year, apparently has decided to shift its attack to the funnybone this campaign. Otherwise how can you explain the presence of Cletus Elwood (Boots) Poffenberger, one of baseball's premier jesters, on Major Lott's payroll?*
>
> *We also know that Boots notified his new employer that he was fired by a reborn seriousness and will to succeed. However, we also know something of Poff's former shenanigans, which is why we are laying in a stock of splints for our sides when they begin to split.*
>
> *We predict that you'll get many a kick out of Boots.[6]*

An unattributed blurb from the 1942 scrapbook reads:

The grape and the grain have been the downfall of many a baseball player.

But you no longer can class Cletus Elwood Poffenberger the eccentric, pardon us, colorful, ex-big league pitcher now toiling for the Padres, in this category.

If we are to believe Cletus, from now on in he is a changed man. For two whole days now he has walked past the schnapps shops looking the other way.

"I'll show you Pacific coast guys I have the will power," says Poff, looking you straight in the eye.[7]

George Herrick, a writer for the *San Diego Tribune-Sun* wrote:

Cletus (Boots) Poffenberger, screwballish chucker San Diego got from Nashville, is a dead ringer for Lou Costello, the comedian—and just about as daffy . . . Poff hasn't done anything screwy yet, but he's only been in camp three days.[8]

The trouble for Boots in the spring of 1942, however, was that he simply was not performing very well. Earl Keller, a writer for the *San Diego Tribune-Sun* did not mention Boots as a likely member of the starting rotation in his column for the March 26th *Sporting News*, saying only, "Also in the battle for a spot on the starting staff is ol' Boots Poffenberger, bought from Nashville. Boots has been a little slow in rounding into form."[9] Nevertheless, Boots pitched eight innings for the Padre rookies who bested the Padre regulars in a 5-3 victory on the next to last day of camp and there was talk that he would be named the Opening Day starter. Certainly, he was hitting well enough, so much so that one fan suggested he become an outfielder.[10]

While his arm may not have been in mid-season form, his sense of humor was in tip-top shape as always. An item from the 1942 scrapbook notes that "Boots Poffenberger, who looks like and is just as daffy as Lou Costello, the comedian, was burned the other day when he read where a writer called him screwy three times in the same story . . . 'Twice would have been enough,' cracked Boots."[11]

Still out of shape, Boots started the first game of an Easter Sunday double header on April 5th, giving up two runs to Portland and receiving a no-decision in the Padres 6-3 victory. He also stroked a triple. Earl Keller wrote:

> *Although shakey at times, Poffenberger turned in a right nice performance in the opener to convince the Padre bosses he figures to be a big winner. "Poff" needs to take a couple more pounds off to get at his best pitching weight, then he should show us something.*

> *If Boots hadn't hit a triple in the sixth inning, he might have lasted the route, but the run around the sacks apparently was too much for him. Poffenberger hit a terrific drive to left center to score Mel Skelly with the third run for the Padres.*[12]

Ten days later, Boots came on in relief in the 3rd inning and finished the game allowing only one earned run and collecting two more hits, including another triple which traveled some 440 feet. Keller wrote, "Poffenberger looked to be in better shape last night, what with more weight off and he surely should be in line for his regular turn on the mound from now on."[13] Boots indeed received fairly regular work, functioning as San Diego's fifth starter, not an unimportant role given that the PCL played a 178 game schedule in those days. That was 24 games longer than the then major league schedule of 154. Boots was fifth on the team with 168 innings (Wally Hebert's 319 led the team), fifth in games started with 21 (out of 38 appearances which was sixth on the Padres.) His 10 complete games, which would lead any current major league team by a considerable margin, tied him for fourth on the Padres. The 34-year-old Hebert again led the Padres in this category with a remarkable 33 out of 39 games started. Boots also threw two shutouts and judging from the numbers and the newspaper accounts, he was either really good or really bad with most of his success coming in the first three months of the season.

When Boots was bad it was either because he lost his effectiveness in the middle innings or his wildness got the better of him. Boots started the second game of a July 4th double header against the Los Angeles Angels at Lane Field, the Padres home park, which stood at 906 West Harbor Drive, the site of which is now a parking lot. He shut out the Angels through the first five innings, but tired in the sixth, allowing three runs. The Padres eventually won the game 4-3. Later in the month, he walked six and hit a batter, giving up seven runs in four innings to Sacramento in a 7-5 loss. Through July 16th, however, Boots was the Padres leading hitter with a .378 average.

The Padres themselves had an up and down year, reaching as high as second place and sinking to fifth in the eight team league before ending the season 91-87 and squeaking past the San Francisco Seals for the fourth and final spot in the Shaughnessy playoffs. The Padres lost in the first round to Los Angeles in seven games. Boots relieved in Game Seven, walked one and struck out one in a non-descript performance. The Padres split $1,250 and Earl Keller penned this epitaph for the season: "Another San Diego Padre baseball season had been written in the books today, and the players were on their way to their homes throughout the country. Some will stay here to help America's war cause by working in the aircraft plants."[14]

Indeed, the War cast a long shadow over all of baseball in 1942, especially in places such as San Diego which was home to the Navy's largest air base, as well as the repair and operations base for many aircraft carriers. After World War II began, San Diego and its environs were home to many Army and Marine camps, and its aircraft plants, referenced by Keller, began 24-hour a day/seven days per week production.

According to a Keller article that appeared in the June 11th edition of the *Sporting News*, the Padres, on June 5th, experimented with "twilight ball."[16] The game was played in the late afternoon/early evening in an effort to avoid turning on the lights as there was no telling if and when the Navy would deem it imprudent to have the lights at Lane Field serve as a beacon to a Japanese air attack, still a real possibility at least as far as anyone knew on June 5th. Ironically, about the time the twilight game was being played, the American Pacific Fleet was busy tracking and destroying straggling enemy ships after decisively defeating a Japanese Naval Task Force at the Battle of Midway. While that battle was understood later to be the decisive action of the Pacific Campaign, the war effort was just beginning, and baseball was doing what it could to contribute to it.

One of the game's major contributions was simply continuing to play. The Padres published a booklet entitled, *San Diego "Padres" 1942: Published by San Diego Baseball Club For the Information of Our Local Fans* which contains an "extract" from President Roosevelt's famous "green light" letter to Commissioner Kenesaw Mountain Landis stating that baseball should continue to be played in order to maintain morale on the home front. The booklet also contains statements regarding the war from owner, Major Charles Lott and Manager Cedric Durst, as well as the "Padre Roll of Honor" at the center fold, which lists seven players already serving in the military.

The booklet also features player photos and profiles, and the one that Jo taped into the 1942 scrapbook includes the autographs of some of Boots' teammates. Hand written notes appear under some of the photos including one under Chuck Eisenmann, a right hander who got into three games with the Padres before he, as the note says, "joined Navy in April."

The Padres contributed directly to the war effort by playing three exhibition games in June against the Naval Training Station team. The final game, which the Navy lost 6-1 "much to the disgust of highly partisan sailors who comprised more than half the crowd," drew 700 fans.[17] The series was sponsored by the Elks Club and realized "a tidy sum to be split between the Naval Relief society and the Camp Lockett athletic fund."[18] Boots played left field in the final game and went two-for-three.

Boots was not at all certain that he wanted to return to San Diego for the 1943 season and because of restricted travel, there was no telling if he could even make it out to the West Coast. Frank Colley of Hagerstown's *Morning Herald* noted that,

> When the majors and Class AA teams go into training this spring transportation may figure in quite a few deals. For instance there is "Boots" Poffenberger of Williamsport, who at the present time is employed in his home town. Boots belongs to the San Diego club of the Pacific Coast League. That is a mighty long way to travel from coast to coast and there is a possible chance that some major league club will take Boots on if the San Diego club figures there is no way to get the right handed chucker out to the coast this spring. Poffenberger didn't have such an excellent season winning 9 and losing 10

games for the Padres, but his hitting kept him active, being
used many times as a pinch hitter, and he finished up with a
better than .300 average. San Diego took a chance on Boots
and he came through for them and perhaps the majors or the
eastern clubs of a Class AA league will endeavor to gain the
services of the reformed hurler.[19]

Whether Boots would accept San Diego's contract or if so, whether he could make it to California became a moot point when Boots received a post card from the local draft board that read simply, "Please report at the Antietam St. School, E. Antietam St., at 3:30 p.m. on Friday, Feb. 19, 1943 for Blood Test." In a letter dated March 31, 1943, Boots was told to report to Room 301 at Hagerstown's City Hall at 7:00 a.m. on April 9th at which point the local board would "furnish transportation to an induction station. You will there be examined, and, if accepted for training and service, you will then be inducted into the land or naval forces."

The Baltimore & Ohio train that took Boots to the induction station in Baltimore stopped in Brunswick to allow passengers to eat, and Boots became immediately immersed in a table tennis tournament.[20] Continuing to Baltimore and arriving at the Post Office Building, Boots was given his physical which revealed that he was 5'7" and 208 pounds as well as the fact that he had slightly high blood pressure with a reading of 146/90. On the lines for recording physical "defects" was typed "OVERWEIGHT."

Being overweight was hardly a disqualification for military service in 1943, especially since a recruit was likely to be cured of that particular malady during boot camp. Boots passed his physical and chose to enter the Marine Corps. His induction was widely covered in regional newspapers and when asked for a comment, he replied, "I might have joined the Navy if I thought I could have passed the physical the Navy gives you," completely unaware apparently, that the physical was the same for all branches of the service.[21] Baltimore's *Sun* carried a photo of Boots holding a Marine Corps dress hat, his white collar over his sport coat, standing next to Sgt. John J. Iaricci.[22]

Boots, and the eight others inducted in Baltimore that day, were offered a two week furlough before they would report back to the Post Office Building for shipment to Parris Island, South Carolina and boot camp.

Naturally, there was plenty of speculation as to how well Boots would do in the Marines, considering the difficulty he had in following the orders of his managers. An Associated Press story that ran in the April 24th edition of the *Morning Herald* explored this very subject:

"When they bugle me out at five o'clock in the morning, I'll be a different man right then." So vowed Boots "baseball's bad boy" Poffenberger as he left Baltimore Friday for the Marine Corps "boot camp" at Parris Island, S. C.

Boots admitted his many previous promises to be good hadn't meant much, but this time he was serious.

The madcap pitcher said all his much publicized "messing around" never did anybody any good but from now on he hopes to help the U. S. Marine Corps quite a lot.

"You know, I never gave baseball my best. But the Marines are going to get my best."

He credited all his notorious exploits as a problem child to too much money too suddenly when he made the big leagues and to the fact he hates to be bossed.

"But taking orders as a Marine will be different. The way I feel about getting back at those Japs who executed our flyers [a reference to the Doolittle raiders who were shot down over Tokyo and then executed] is something I can't put into words. It's just different from anything I ever did before. This is the only thing I've ever been able to take to heart."

Six or eight weeks will trim Boots down from his 208 pounds to about 185, he said, and then he'll be in "real good shape and ready to go after 'em."

"I've missed plenty of games I should have pitched," he confessed, "but this is one affair I'm not missing."[23]

Boots did miss it, although this time it was not because of his own poor behavior. In fact, he proved to be a model Marine, but like many professional ballplayers who were in the service, he spent the war in home whites and traveling grays rather than in khakis or camouflage.

Notes

1   A. L. Hardman, "Sports Notes," *Charleston Gazette*, undated.
2   Associated Press, August 8, 1941.
3   A. L. Hardman, "Sports Notes," *Charleston Gazette*, undated.
4   Unattributed, "Poffenberger, Dasso Sparkle," February 23, 1942 in SB 42.
5   Unattributed, "Boots Is Ribbed," undated in SB 42.
6   Morton Moss, "The Moss Code," *Los Angeles Examiner*, February 26, 1942.
7   Unattributed, "Shuns Grape and Grain," undated in SB 42.
8   George Herrick, "Calling the Shots," *San Diego Tribune-Sun*, February 27, 1942.
9   Earl Keller, "Padres Big Four Mound Staff Threatens To Become Big Six," *The Sporting News*, March 26, 1942, p 2.
10   Unattributed, "Poff Outfielder?" undated in SB 42.
11   Unattributed, undated in SB 42.
12   Earl Keller, *San Diego Tribune-Sun*, undated, but undoubtedly from April 6, 1942.
13   Earl Keller, "It's Padres Pay Day—Now Will They Win?" *San Diego Tribune-Sun*, April 15, 1942.
14   Earl Keller, "Padres Head For Homes After Losing," *San Diego Tribune-Sun*, undated.
15   *Ibid.*
16   Earl Keller, "Hebert Sets Pace For Padres' Crack Staff With Nine Wins," *The Sporting News*, June 11, 1942, p 16.
17   Unattributed, "Errors Bring Easy Victory," undated in SB 42.
18   *Ibid.*
19   Frank Colley, "The Colley-See-Um of Sports," *Morning Herald*, December 11, 1942.
20   Frank Colley, "The Colley-See-Um of Sports," *Morning Herald,* April 10, 1943.
21   *Washington Post*, undated but probably April 10, 1943.
22   *The Sun*, undated photo, but again probably April 10, 1943.
23   Associated Press, "Boots Is Headed For The Marines," April 24, 1943.

CHAPTER 8

Boots Poffenberger, U.S.M.C

Boots' official Marine Corps service record gives no indication of the fact that he spent his three year hitch playing for the Parris Island baseball team and the Fleet Marine Force team in Hawaii. In fact, only occasionally, and then only in an obscure line or two does it tell us about Boots' time in the service at all. Boots' Professional and Conduct Record shows that from the time of his enlistment in April of 1943 through his mustering out in April of 1946, he received nothing but the highest score of five in the categories of "Obedience" and "Sobriety."

John McNamara, a fellow Marine who played with Boots at Parris Island in 1944 has a ready explanation for that. "I'll tell you how that happened. He was a big leaguer and whatever officer was in charge of the ratings immediately gave him a high rating. That's how he got that. If you were famous or semi-famous you always got high marks."

McNamara (not the John McNamara who managed the Boston Red Sox in 1986) was a pitcher himself who was being scouted by the Red Sox. "Boots always used to say, 'If I had your curveball Mac, I would have gone a little higher!' I said, 'You did damn well!'" McNamara states that he would sit next to Boots in the dugout whenever possible to "pick his brain" and learn all he could about the art of pitching.

Boots' record does contain one citation for "willfully and wrongfully wearing chevron of a platoon sergeant's field jacket" on April 9, 1944, which happened to be the one year anniversary of his enlistment. One can only imagine that it was a cold day on the baseball diamond and someone handed him a jacket or he borrowed a jacket or he simply picked up the first jacket that was handy.

"He'd wear anything," laughed Jerry Knode when informed of the charge against Boots. "He'd go down the street and I'd say to Mom, there goes my coat!"

The charge was "proved by plea" the next day and Boots was docked $10.00 pay in each of the succeeding two months.

Boots was playing for the Parris Island Marines within a month of his arrival on base and long before his official promotion from recruit to private first class which occurred on July 17th. His official Marine Corps occupation is listed as a "recreation instructor." He remained in that position at Parris Island until mid-December, 1944 when his post is listed as "44th Replacement Draft" at Camp Lejeune in North Carolina. McNamara, who served as a drill instructor states that Boots was a military policeman, a claim that is supported by the only war story of Boots' that has turned up in print. Speaking to John Steadman in his 1967 *Sporting News* interview, Boots said,

> "Yeah, I was in the South Pacific for 15 months and never saw a _ _ _ _ Jap. Once they told me to take care of a prisoner, a kid in the Navy who had jumped ship. They told me to take him to Pearl Harbor, but to try not to embarrass the boy or make it look like I was guarding him.
>
> "The kid was a son of a lieutenant colonel in the Marines and they didn't want to show up his old man. But how could I wear a .45 on my side and not look like I was guarding him? I haven't figured that out yet."[1]

On the home front, Jo moved back with her family on 23rd Street in Washington D. C. shortly after Boots left for Parris Island, and began working at Red Cross Headquarters.[2] Connie Cole recalls that Jo wasn't eager to stick around Williamsport. "She didn't like this little town as far as I can remember," states Cole.

Whether or not Jo cared for Williamsport, she certainly seemed to still care for Boots and vice-versa, for if the Official Records tell us little about Boots' life in the Marines, the scrapbook that Jo kept from this era certainly does. It is full of post cards from Boots to her and of mementoes from the time they had together when she would visit him or he would come home on leave. A "Greetings from North Carolina" postcard dated May 26, 1943 is a typical example of both his affection for Jo and his new routine. It reads:

Dear Wife,
We arrived here on the plane and you sure had one sick husband. Honest I believe that's about as sick as I've ever gotten. And we have to ride it the way back. Gee [?] we leave for New river tomorrow and two games. Will write you from there. Love, Boots.

Boots' service was national news, as were most of the inductions of high profile ballplayers, and the Associated Press snapped a photo of Boots running over a log while wearing his cloth cap with an ammo belt around his waist and a rifle in his hands.[3] One unaccredited blurb from May 1st referred to him as "Boot Poffenberger" referencing his status in the Marines.[4]

Boots' induction was very big news in Williamsport where the townsfolk published The *Dug Out: A Morale Builder For The Armed Forces,* an 8.5" x 11" newsletter filled with news about the local boys in the service, and with news for them about their home town. Boots' best man Abner Kaplan served as an assistant editor. The April 29th edition had this to say about the town's favorite son:

He's been inducted in the Marines and action goes with these guys like icing goes with a cake, if you can get the sugar. Never one to be too concerned by money or the lack of it, Boots will probably do all right for himself as long as he gets his three meals. He'll have to do without his hunting and fishing, probably his only regrets in leaving the old home town, but if he can catch a few Japs or hunt down a couple hundred Nazis he won't be too much put out. Anyway we hope to see him in there pitching. The competition is big and strong and they're playing for keeps.[5]

Boots apparently wrote to the editors about his time in the Marines thus far, and he received this reply from George "Hooper" Wolf, the newsletter's general manager who signed his columns "Unk" as in "Uncle." Wolf was still a bit skeptical about whether Boots would always remain at his assigned post:

> *Hello Boots:*
>
> *I received your card and was pleased to know you like being a Marine. Getting up at 4 A. M. and being drilled for a few hours before breakfast may be new to you but finally you will observe the good you derive from regularity and will be glad you are in a branch of the armed forces.*
>
> *The boys on the corner (and in the taverns) miss you as do the fish in the streams, but we will see that there are some left for you when Adolph and his likes are liquidated.*
>
> *You should be tops in your marksmanship tests as I never knew you to miss a sitting bunny. I am convinced that you will again gain promotion easily, and I will be looking for your stripes and medals when you get home on furlough. Of course, you can't go A.W.O.L. and still get stripes.*
>
> *When drilling be careful not to use your rifle for a bat, for I know baseball will be on your mind. The Dug Out which you requested was sent.*
>
> *Yours for luck,*
> *Unk.*[6]

Far from "liquidating Adolph," Boots was mowing down Coast Guardsmen, soldiers, sailors, and factory workers on diamonds from Florida through the Carolinas. Boots shut out the Jacksonville (FL) Coast Guard team, walking none and striking out 10. An undated blurb noted that,

> *Burly Boots Poffenberger, still a hefty individual even with the loss of 15 pounds in boot camp, turned in a masterful three-hit pitching performance yesterday afternoon at the ball park as the Parris Island, S. C. Marines shut out the Jacksonville Coast Guard nine for the fourth time this season.*[7]

Jo received a post card from Camp Wheeler, an Army training facility near Macon, Georgia dated June 21st on which Boots noted that he had "been waiting three hours on phone to reach you. Have to head for ball park now—I'm pitching today's game."

One week later Boots mailed another postcard, this one from Augusta, Georgia showing the "beautiful sunken gardens" near the town.

Won our game last night but looks like rain out today. However, I'll pitch upon our having to play. Will write you Mon when we reach the Island. Send the present you have for birthday. Love, "Boots"

Jo received a telegram from Boots one week after that asking her to wire some money so that he would have enough to travel home on leave. This furlough was not recorded in his Marine Corps record, but it clearly took place because according to the July 20th edition of the *Dug Out*, Boots pitched for the "Old Wildcats" against the current "Wildcats." The game resulted in a 1-1 tie after seven innings, Boots allowing a home run to "current Wildcat" Glen Anderson. He pitched a second time for the "Old Export Wildcats" before returning to Parris Island, where Boots resumed hurling for what was fast becoming the best Marine Corps baseball team in the country.

Every base and camp had baseball teams during the war and the intra-service rivalry was fierce. The best players in a given branch were funneled to the best teams. Most of Boots' teammates were former professionals like himself with players from the International League, the Eastern League, the Southern Association, the Georgia-Florida League, the Western International League, and the Coastal Plains League filling the Parris Island roster.[8] Second baseman Cal Ermer, who had begun his professional career in 1942, gained three at-bats as a big leaguer in 1947, but would enjoy an extensive career as a manager culminating with the Minnesota Twins in 1967-1968. In fact, when the Parris Island team ventured to Greenville, South Carolina and a two game weekend set with the 334th Bomb Group Jay Birds, the local press was fearful that star shortstop Billy Hitchcock would not make it back in time for the Saturday game. He had been flown to New York to play on an Army All-Star team that would face a collection of players from the Yankees, Giants, and Dodgers.[9] Hitchcock, who had debuted with the Tigers the year before, enjoyed a nine year playing career and then turned to managing. In 1962, Hitchcock would manage the Baltimore Orioles, where Cal Ermer served as one of his coaches.

The games against the Jay Birds were played at Meadowbrook Park, which was only six years old and home to the erstwhile Greenville Spinners of the South Atlantic League. The Marines won by respective 9-3 and 12-5 scores. Boots pitched six innings of the Sunday game, finishing the contest in the outfield and enjoyed a four-for-four day at the plate. Jo came down to see Boots and recorded on the back of a post card,

> Came to see Boots for weekend. Stayed at Greenville Hotel. Met all the fellows and they're really a grand bunch. Hope I see them all again.

Labor Day saw the team in Georgetown, South Carolina, a seaport on the Winyah Bay some 60 miles north of Charleston and home of the largest kraft paper mill in the world in 1943. The squad was there to take on the Charleston Port of Embarkation team as part of the culmination of a month-long effort to sell war bonds.

> With army bombers and speedy pursuit ships droning over-head Georgetown celebrated its biggest Labor day as a climax to a month of intensive bond selling as marine, navy, army, and state guard units marched in a colorful parade here today.
>
> This afternoon Governor Olin D. Johnston and Lieutenant Governor Ransome Williams and hundreds of others saw the Parris Island marine baseball team defeat the Charleston Port of Embarkation nine, 5-1. Managers decided the field was too wet to play and the teams departed by bus for their respective bases only to be called back by highway patrolmen and city police cruisers after officials had the field dragged and the sun came out.
>
> A militaristic parade this morning inaugurated the festivities. Led by the crack Parris Island marine band, military units marched two miles through Georgetown streets. Other outfits

*included a platoon of sailors form the Charleston navy yard,
the Charleston Port of embarkation band, units of the South
Carolina defense force, army tank corps, Boy Scouts, floats and
marching labor union members.*

*Despite the slow, wet playing field, the nine innings were run off
in an hour and a half. Admission to the game was by purchase
of $1 or more in war savings stamps.[10]*

Boots pitched and won, allowing only one unearned run.

When the season ended later in the month, the Parris Island
Marines could boast a 51-11 record. Boots was 15-4 and batted .377. Bob
Revels who had played with Norfolk in the Piedmont League led the
team with a 21-3 mark, while Johnnie Barrett, formerly with Hartford of
the Eastern League, led the Marines with a .417 average. The team's photo
appeared in the October 7th edition of *The Sporting News* which now
featured a page entitled, "In the Service" and covered former pros now in
the military as well as the exploits of military teams.[11]

Boots continued to fascinate fans and sports writers alike. Carter
Latimer, sports editor of the *Greenville News*, who actually signed his cor-
respondence "'Scoop' Latimer," wrote to Jo, apparently in response to her
request for a clipping about Boots. It is possible that they met when Jo
came to Greenville at the end of August. Noting that "fans in Greenville
greatly enjoyed the opportunity of seeing your famous husband in action,
and they got their money's worth from his performance in the box and at
bat," he then requested a letter, asking Jo to explain "how you managed
Boots at home when he was playing ball, what were his favorite dishes,
how you felt watching a game he was pitching, just anything you can
think of." Latimer stated that he would turn this into a column, which he
did for the October 31st edition of the *Greenville News*.

In his "Scoopin' 'Em Up" column, Latimer reminds his readers that
they probably saw Boots pitch and "enjoyed his clowning antics," which
certainly indicates, that Marine or not, Boots had not changed the way
he conducted himself on the baseball diamond. Latimer then introduces
"the lovely, petite Mrs. Poffenberger" to the readers and quotes from her
letter at length. Jo admits that their marriage did not begin smoothly
and that "it took us about a year to get my Irish and his German temper

to cooperate. Every club we were on always demanded things of Boots, which of course he wouldn't do."[12] Implying that those demands were unreasonable, Jo apparently never specified what those demands were. Perhaps after Boots explained situations in his charismatic way, showing up on time did seem unreasonable to Jo or perhaps she was simply defending her husband as a duty to her marital bond and not because he actually deserved defending. She may well have been biased towards Boots because she added that,

> *At home, I ask that he do something and he usually did. . . . he has always been wonderful to me. I can't remember ever wanting something I didn't get. He's given me all of his salary checks to place in the bank in my name. He's always taken me on all the trips possible, and . . . well . . . he's what I can call a good husband no matter what the papers have said.*[13]

Jo went on to explain that she became "terribly tense" watching Boots pitch and had to keep her arms folded so that no one, especially Boots could see her emotions. She also addressed Latimer's request to relate Boots' favorite foods which she said were "sea food and raw vegetables." Jo also related that Boots weighed only 164 pounds in July of 1937 when he was called up to Detroit, but by September had gained 36 pounds and had never been under 200 pounds since, not even after basic training. "We used to watch his diet because he was so heavy but found it was natural, so he now eats all he wants."[14]

Latimer sent Jo a copy of his column along with a type-written note thanking her for her "swell letter. It's a pip, as we say 'way down South in the old apple orchard,'" and inviting her to return to Greenville.

Boots returned to Williamsport for another 15 days of leave in September and apparently wasted no time in heading out on the town. Pasted into the Marine Corps scrapbook is a pristine napkin from the Vogue Room, with a date of September 24, 1943 written under it. Located at 57 South Potomac Street, The Vogue Room was a nightclub in Hagerstown, which like many towns was booming thanks to the war effort. Fairchild Aircraft was headquartered in Hagerstown and churned out PT 19, PT 23, PT 26, and C 82 cargo planes. The napkin was emblazoned with a red dancer and *Swing it!* printed in blue, the exclamation point being especially large. A red swizzle stick in a blue martini glass on top of a blue piano appears in the lower right corner. A red border of musical notes snakes its way along the bottom and up the right hand side. Like the proverbial sea shell, it seems that one can hold the napkin to the ear and hear the sounds of laughter and a hot Lindy Hop tune. It is the sole witness to how many martinis were consumed, how many rugs were cut, and whether Boots perhaps really did hop onto the stage this night and lead the band until the small hours of the morning. Whatever the night held, it certainly meant something to Jo as evidenced by its placement in the scrapbook.

Boots returned to Parris Island and with the baseball season complete, he spent the winter refereeing basketball games.[15] Jo returned to Washington and in November began working or volunteering at Walter Reed Hospital.

Jo traveled to Parris Island in January to spend a week with Boots and while she was there, she gave another interview, this one to reporter George Theeringer of *BOOT, The Parris Island Weekly*, which misspelled Boots' surname in the headline reading, "Inside Story On Poffenberg."

Theeringer wrote that Boots' differences with Mickey Cochrane resulted in "unfavorable" publicity, apparently never having read the very favorable rationalization of Boots' behavior that sports writers in three different cities had by now put forth. In any case, Theeringer wrote that he had believed all the bad things until he heard "the petite young wife . . . refute the many stories written about her husband."[16] Jo then repeated to Theeringer what she had told Scoop Latimer, that her husband took her on road trips whenever possible and always sent home his pay check, adding that while "Boots loves baseball, [he] refuses to become a slave to the game."[17] Jo would have made an excellent publicist and indeed, Boots, or at least his arm, was still highly regarded in major league circles. Philadelphia A's owner and manager Connie Mack told a *Dug Out* reporter that "Most of the managers around the loop agreed that Boots had as much natural ability as any young pitcher in the majors."[18]

Boots was one of four returning players in 1944 along with pitchers Joe Catapano and Bob Revels, and first baseman Bob Feiderlein on what was again a strong Parris Island team. On June 24th, for example, the

Marines won their 24th consecutive game, 7-2 over an army all-star team from Fort Jackson in Columbia, South Carolina. Boots pitched into the seventh and collected the win. Newly arrived catcher Gene Desautels had already spent 11 seasons in the big leagues when he joined the team in 1944. Desautels was the very first batter that Boots had faced in his major league debut. It was he who grounded into a double play allowing Boots and the Tigers to escape further trouble in the third inning in Boston back in 1937.

Desautels, whom McNamara described as "one helluva guy" was one of Boots' drinking buddies while in the service. "After the games, when we were on the road, both Boots and Gene asked me to make sure that they made their way back to the bus because the bus left on time and they would have been in big trouble [had they missed it.] This was the service!" remembers McNamara.

Boots' former exploits continued to be written about. The "Breakfast of Champions" story appeared in the July issue of *Coronet* which was picked up by *BOOT, The Parris Island Weekly*. The Marine newspaper added an interesting twist:

> *Sidney Carroll, writing in the current issue of Coronet, reports that Parris Island pitching ace Boots Poffenberger (whom he described as one of "baseball's bona fide eccentrics") once called a hotel clerk and ordered—"Send me—the breakfast of champions—six bottles of beer and a scrambled egg."*
>
> *When several of Boots' Parris Island teammates suggested that he sue Carroll for libel, the fun-loving Poffenberger squirmed his face in an over-all smile and said: "He may be telling the truth."[19]*

The *Dug Out* also noted the Coronet story, commenting wryly, "We question the accuracy of this story. What in the heck would Boots want with an egg?"[20]

The July 22nd edition of *BOOT* contained a photo of Boots juxtaposed with Lou Costello who had visited the base. Boots, his eyes up and to his left, his mouth agape in mock surprise bore an especially remarkable resemblance to the famous comedian who was holding the same pose. The caption noted that Boots was often mistaken for Lou while playing for San Diego.[21] This photo was picked up by *The Sporting News* in their September 14th edition with a caption that read in part: "Lou Costello, film and radio comedian, ran into a facsimile of himself in Boots Poffenberger, who was somewhat of a fun-maker, too, in his diamond days."[22]

Lou Costello was not the only Hollywood celebrity who Boots encountered as this passage from the August 21st *Dug Out* notes:

> *Incidentally, Boots recently wrote and stated that when his club played in North Carolina recently they were grounded because of bad weather. The following morning when they took to the air their plane was piloted by Tyrone Power of movie-land fame. Boots says that Tyrone is quite handsome, but also looks to be in fine condition and from his appearance could well take care of himself in time of trouble.[23]*

Power, who starred in a variety of film genres, and who already had some training as an aviator, enlisted in the Marines, becoming a transport pilot. But then all branches of the service were filled with famous people. One of Boots' Marine Corps friends was Pat Harder, whose black and white photo appears in the Marine Corps scrapbook. Harder had been an All-American fullback at the University of Wisconsin in 1942 before enlisting in the Marines. He would go on to an 8-year NFL career and win championships with the Chicago Cardinals and Detroit Lions, before becoming an official.

Indeed, there were more major league players in the armed forces than there were in the major leagues, at least if judged by actual major league talent. Thirty-six eventual Hall of Famers served in the military during World War II in addition to almost 500 other bona fide major leaguers.[24] The Army all-star team that Billy Hitchcock played for on August 26, 1943 featured future Hall of Famers Hank Greenberg and Enos Slaughter. Played at the Polo Grounds, the game raised $800 million in war bond pledges and saw the "War Bond All-Stars" defeat the team comprised of the three New York professional teams 5-2.[25]

The talent pool was so shallow that 15 year old Joe Nuxhall pitched two-thirds of an inning for Cincinnati on June 10th, 1944 giving up five runs and not returning to the majors until 1952. (The next year would see Pete Gray, a one-armed outfielder for the St. Louis Browns amass 253 at-bats while hitting .218. That he hit anything says something about the quality of the pitching, which included his tormentor teammate Jack Jakucki, resurrected from the semi-pro leagues.)

The *Armored News*, the newspaper of the Army Armor Divisions, even proposed a Service World Series and nominated the Parris Island Marines, the Great Lakes Naval Station (headed by Lt. Commander Mickey Cochrane), and the 20th Armored Division from Camp Campbell, Kentucky to be the representative teams.[26] Proceeds from the series would go towards the war bond effort. Nothing came of that proposal, but an Army-Navy Series was held in Hawaii in October of 1944 with the sailors pounding the soldiers, nine games to two. The Navy team included future Hall of Famers Johnny Mize, Pee Wee Reese, and Phil Rizzuto. Virgil Trucks and Johnny Vander Meer starred on the mound for the Navy squad that was managed by future Hall of Famer, Lt. Bill Dickey.

For Boots, the end of the season in which he went 18-3, meant another two week furlough beginning on October 5th. He had hoped to return to Williamsport on furlough in September at which time he was going to bring three teammates with him to play in a game to benefit the *Dug Out*. His teammates had read so much about his home town in the *Dug Out* that they wanted to see the place,[27] but those plans were canceled when Boots' furlough was postponed. When Boots' leave was finally granted, however, he returned to town and the game was held on Sunday the 8th. Heavy rains had left the diamond "very muddy," but Johnny Mallot furnished "time, truck, and labor" and hauled several loads of sand that was donated by Victor Cushwa & Sons, the local brickyard. The contest was held, $50.00 was raised to keep the *Dug Out* presses running, and Boots hit two home runs in a four-for-four effort at the plate, while striking out 10 in eight innings on the mound.[28]

Boots remained at Parris Island upon his return until mid-December, when he was transferred to Camp Lejeune. An undated blurb headlined, "Athletes Ship to Lejeune," noted that

> *numerous Parris Island athletes including Boots Poffenberger,*
> *popular and winning pitcher, and boxing coach Eddie Griffin,*
> *shipped out of [to?] Camp Lejeune this week.*
>
> *The sports contingent included baseball and basketball players, swimming and boxing instructors, and cage and diamond officials.*
>
> *Poffenberger squirming up his cherubic countenance in his best Costello-smile, expressed the sentiments of the crew when he remarked: "Well, I'm not going to say I'm glad I'm leaving good old P. I. but after all we got in the Marines to fight, so it's goodbye and we'll see you in Tokyo."*[29]

This "shipment of athletes" was probably a result of an order from Army Chief of Staff George Marshall who discovered in the spring of 1944 that of the 280 or so major league ball players in the military, most had never left their domestic bases and some had never even finished basic training. This seems to be the case with Boots for whom 11 different entries appear on his "Basic Training Record" each one of which is marked "no instruction completed." When Marshall discovered that such incomplete training for professional ballplayers was widespread, he eventually ordered most of the players to be sent overseas. This seems to have meant, whether it was Marshall's intent or not, that instead of playing baseball in the United States, the former ball players were now playing in the European Theater of Operations or, if they were truly lucky, in Hawaii, which, as it was not yet a state was considered an "overseas" assignment. Boots' service record shows a gap between the end of March 1945 and May 15 when he is clearly listed as having received his pay in Hawaii.

Boots obviously had received orders that he was headed overseas by the new year at the latest. The January 12, 1945 issue of the *Dug Out* contained a letter from Boots in which he stated that his vacation was over and that he was shipping out in 10 days, adding that he had "received my shots, zeroed my rifle and overseas equipment has been issued me." More than likely, Boots was referring to baseball equipment. He did not leave immediately, however.[30]

Family history says that Boots was pulled off a transport ship bound for Iwo Jima, but if he was ever destined for that Pacific Island, it was after the famous battle had been fought, because Boots' service record shows him still at Camp Lejeune at the end of March, 1945. The records also show nothing of Boots' time on Guam, but he was there during most of April, 1945. This is in keeping with McNamara's recollection that the entire baseball team was shipped to Guam to entertain the troops. The *Marine Corps Chevron* of April 28, 1945 noted that Boots had "recently reported to a Marine Raider nine following service on Guam," a statement that was repeated *ver batim* in an April 28th issue of the *Dug Out*.[31]

Upon his return to Hawaii, he was assigned to pitch for the Fleet Marine Force (FMC) where his teammates included George Staller and Willard Marshall. Staller played one season in the majors in 1943 for the A's, but enjoyed a long career in the game including a stint as Earl Weaver's first base coach in Baltimore. Marshall enjoyed a productive 11 year big-league career. Besides Staller and Marshall, Boots' teammates also included his old pitching pal from Parris Island, Bob Revels and "Private C. R. Medley, the only left hander on the squad and one-time member of the Homestead Grays of the National Colored league," according to an article by T/Sgt. Bill Goodrich, that is hand-dated July, 1945.[32] A photo of the FMF pitching staff appeared in the August 23rd edition of *The Sporting News* showing Boots, Medley, Revels, Ray Yokim, Oren Baker, Bob Green, and catcher Dee Moore. All but Green, who was a standout at Dartmouth College were professionals.[33]

The competition that Boots now faced was superior to the factory teams and local army base teams against whom he had pitched in South Carolina and Georgia. When FMF faced the Aeia Naval Hospital team, for example, they faced the likes of Billy Herman, Bob Lemon, Fred Hutchinson, and Hugh Casey. It was now estimated that 400 ex-major leaguers were in uniform and the *Dug Out* reported on a letter Boots had sent home saying that "all 400 must be down in the league" in which he played.[34]

The Fleet Marine Force played in what was known as the 14th Naval District Baseball League, which divided the season into two halves.

The league contained ten teams which included the FMF, Aeia Hospital, Aeia Barracks, Base 8 Hospital, Marine Flyers, NAS Barber's Point, NAS Honolulu, NAS Kaneohe, Ship Repair Unit, and Submarine Base. Furlong Field was the featured diamond and one game was held there on each day a game was scheduled, each team playing three times per week. Boots finished the first half with a 4-2 record. The FMF team faded down the stretch after considerable time in first place ultimately finishing fourth, three games back. A few days before the second half of the season started, Boots received a 3 day/ 2 night pass to the Royal Hawaiian Hotel. Opened in 1927, the Royal Hawaiian was one of the first hotels to be built in Waikiki. The Navy leased the entire hotel beginning in 1942 and used it as a rest and recreation retreat for Pacific Fleet personnel. One can only imagine the degree to which Boots Poffenberger enjoyed himself at the Royal Hawaiian or Hawaii in general for that matter. One undated personal photo in the USMC scrapbook shows a photo of Boots with a pineapple. The photo is inscribed, "Pineapples plentiful. Also Beer."

Another photo from the scrapbook shows Boots, his FMF manager, Harry Hughes, and Bill Goodrich, from *Pacific Leatherneck*, a magazine for Marines that would feature a story on Boots in its August 1st edition. Hughes, on the far left, was a career minor leaguer and had served as the player/manager of the Atlanta Crackers in 1943. Hughes has written, "To Boots, Hoping we meet in civilian life, Harry Hughes, Mgr." Boots has written beneath this "Mgr. Atlanta Southern League, 1943." Goodrich, in his Marine uniform (Boots and Hughes are in their baseball uniforms) has written "To 'Bootsie' a good pitcher." Boots' notation by Goodrich reads, "Photographer who wrote story for Leatherneck July issue." Across himself, Boots has written "'The 'Baron' Ha ha."

Despite not having pitched in the big leagues for six years at this point, Boots still drew the attention of sports writers, a pattern that would continue for the next 20 years. On May 5th, there appeared in the *Washington Daily News*, a story headlined, "Cletus Learns Sobriety or— Don't Believe All You Read" by Oscar Fraley.[35] Fraley was a UPI sports reporter from 1940-1965. (In 1956 he would meet Eliot Ness and write *The Untouchables*, the book upon which the TV series and movie were based.) Essentially, the story says that Boots learned training and discipline in the Marines and "plans to settle down in the glowing future and be a major league star."[36] Fraley recounts a couple familiar stories about Boots, particularly how he reported overweight to spring training in 1938. Fraley's tone is cynical and he expresses definite doubt that Boots will stay this disciplined, writing in conclusion, "Through it all he was a merry little man with a ball or at a brawl."[37]

Four days later, Frank Colley of Hagerstown's *Morning Herald* came to Boots' defense:

> *I wonder if Oscar Fraley, well known sports writer ever took into consideration what a wonderful lot of copy that the "Baron of Williamsport" has furnished for the writers in the majors, as well as the minors.*
>
> *I wonder if he delved deep enough into the history of "Boots" to know that while at Parris Island "Boots" worked himself up to a drill sergeant and then passed up the stripes to go back to PFC just because he couldn't hand out the dish that was expected of the drill sergeants in the Leathernecks?*
>
> *I wonder if Mr. Fraley ever took a look at the letter written "Boots" by the Brooklyn club where he was guaranteed so much salary and underlined in red pencil. I wonder if they ever stopped to consider that "Boots" fresh up from the bushes was a prey for the news hawks who later on had to lambast him in their columns. Asked for a story, "Boots" would give it without batting eye, but it was "Boots' not "Dizzy" Dean, the man who checked into every hotel and Y.M.C.A. in Omaha, Neb., just to let them know "Dizzy" Dean had arrived.[38]*

Colley continued in a similar vein, seemingly becoming more irritated at Fraley with every passing paragraph until he finally concluded with "right now he is pitching better ball than a lot of us and let's hope that his fast ball continues to mow the JAPS down and after all it'll be a great day when V-J Day arrives, so why don't you go out and BUY A BOND . . . Good morning."[39]

In between the appearance of those two articles, President Harry Truman declared May 8th Victory in Europe Day.

The *Pacific Leatherneck* story by Bill Goodrich was edited by Sgt. Ernie Harwell, the former Atlanta Cracker announcer who would enjoy a Hall of Fame broadcasting career, primarily with the Detroit Tigers. Harwell, as editor, was credited in the by-line. This edition of *Pacific Leatherneck* contained two and a half pages of casualty lists for May 15-June 15, a full page photo of actress/dancer Ann Miller, and a variety of articles including the one on Boots which was accompanied by a pen and ink illustration of him in his wind up. "If only I had this sort of training and disciplining years ago, there's no telling how far I could have gone in the big league," he told the *Leatherneck*.[40]

By early August, Boots was also pitching for and managing a Marine team from the Transient Center, although some evidence suggests that this was now his sole team. This squad did not face the same quality of competition but it did feature a young shortstop named Alvin Dark who starred in baseball, basketball, and football at Louisiana State University. Dark joined the Marines in 1943, entering the V-12 program which was administered by the Navy in an effort to ensure college educated officers. The Marines transferred Dark from LSU to Southwestern Louisiana Institute where in addition to the three sports mentioned, he also ran track and played on the golf team. He was drafted by the Philadelphia Eagles in 1945, but after the war, came home to play baseball, making his major league debut in 1946 and earning Rookie of the Year honors in 1948 with the Boston Braves. The three time All-Star played for six teams over 14 seasons, then managed five different teams, concluding his major league career in 1977.

***

Alvin Dark, Boots, and the rest of the Transient Center team took the field on a Saturday afternoon earning a 10-1 victory over the Hickam Bombers. Meanwhile, on that same day, August 6th, a B-29 bomber nicknamed the *Enola Gay* took off from its base on Tinian to drop the atomic bomb on Hiroshima.

***

Boots received a letter dated September 18th from Bill Starr, the owner of the San Diego Padres stating in part, "Please advise us of your status in the service and whether you will be available for baseball next spring." For whatever reason, and Boots never needed one when it came to doing something he didn't want to do, Boots did not answer, but instead seems to have simply forwarded it to Jo at the beginning of November. At the bottom of Starr's letter Boots has written, "P. S. Write him that my letter was forwarded to you from Williamsport. We'll try and get in touch with the club when I get out of service. Yes, I will be ready for spring training. Type the letter honey I never wrote the club yet." Apparently, Boots believed that Starr would believe that it would take six weeks for a letter to travel the 70 miles from Williamsport to Washington.

Jo, once again acting as a de facto agent for Boots, immediately responded to Starr on November 9th, apologizing for the delay, adding "the letter was forwarded on to me and I contacted Mr. Poffenberger so that I could write to you in order to cause no more delay." Like all good agents, she made sure that Owner Starr knew what a fine player he was getting: "He has been on a diet and in training for some time, and has his weight down to 190 pounds, and hopes to be lower still before coming home. Therefore, he is in excellent condition." Jo concluded with "We are looking forward to being in San Diego next season."

Jo and Starr got down to business right after Christmas, 1945. Jo sent a letter to Boots on December 28th for him to either sign and mail to Starr or to simply approve, which he did on January 11th. The letter contained several requests:

> Before leaving Hawaii, I am requesting that I be discharged on the West Coast, thereby signing away government privilege of paying my transportation to my home in Maryland. Since I will be discharged in California, I would like to request that the travel expenses due me from the baseball club from my home to San Diego be transferred to my wife, who is residing in Washington, D. C.

> I would also like to know the terms of my contract for the 1946 season. Although I have been in the service for three years, I well know living conditions have gone sky high, and therefore feel my contract should call for $700.00 per month.

> During my service in the Marine Corps, I have pitched ball each season and hold a good record. I am in excellent condition, in fact better than I can ever remember, with my weight down to around 180 pounds.

Perhaps I may be out of order in asking for all this informa-
tion, but I feel that I must have something definite before mak-
ing personal request for my release from the Marine Corps on
the West Coast, and in making plans for Mrs. Poffenberger to
meet me there.

Starr had to know that this attention to detail did not come from
Boots, but he kept up the pretense of directing his replies to his pitcher.
The reply that Boots received to his requests, however, was not only
direct, but immediate, and much more formal in tone. Whereas Starr's
initial inquiry in September was signed "Bill Starr," this one was signed
"William Starr" and read in part:

Dear Mr. Poffenberger:

We have your letter of January 11th.

Your request that we pay the transportation expenses of your
wife from Washington, D. C. to San Diego in lieu of such
expenses being paid directly to you, by reason of your coming to
the West Coast, is very irregular. However, I will not make any
issue with you over this and will assure you that your wife will
be reimbursed for her expenses from Washington to San Diego
upon her arrival. This only applies to this instance and will not
establish a precedent as far as we are concerned.

Regarding your salary, I find that you were paid $400 per month
in your last year in San Diego. Your record for that year was 9
wins and 10 losses. I can't see anything in this record to jus-
tify the type of increase that you ask. It was my intention to
send you a contract, upon your discharge, for $500 per month.
However, I will increase that to $550 per month which is all that
we can pay you this year. Naturally, if you produce for us you
are in a much better position to command a better salary next
season. As you know this is the customary procedure.

Perhaps sensing that they had no more room to negotiate, the
Poffenbergers accepted Starr's offer:

I received your letter of January 11 stating the terms of my con-
tract for this coming season. I feel that the terms are quite

*satisfactory, and I also wish to thank you for your agreement
to pay the transportation expenses for my wife to San Diego.*

With Jo handling all his negotiations, Boots did what he always
did, which was play ball and generally have as good a time as possible. In
November, on Veterans Day to be precise, he attended a football game at
Furlong Field between the Hawaiian Flyers Army team and the FMF Pac
Marines. Boots took many photos that day and despite the best efforts of
his baseball teammate, halfback Alvin Dark, Army won 19-13. Boots also
played for and managed the Transient Center during its winter season.

In February, Boots was once again in the nation's sports pages when
famed sports writer Grantland Rice wrote a story entitled, "Rice Names
All-Time Baseball Team With Greatest Appeal to Writers." A couple of
Babes appeared in the outfield in the persons of Herman and Ruth, while
Boots was part of a pitching staff that included some familiar names in
Rube Waddell, Dizzy Dean, and Bobo Newsom.[41]

Boots was also in the pages of the *Dug Out* which reported that
he had sent the Williamsport Wildcats two dozen baseballs (stamped
"USMC" no doubt.)[42]

At a March 8th banquet for the naval baseball teams Boots was
presented a "team manager trophy" by Col. Herbert. A. Vernet, Jr. the
Commanding Officer of the Transient Center. Boots, in turn presented a
signed ball to Col. Vernet.

The San Francisco Seals ventured to Hawaii as part of their 1946
spring training regimen to play against the Hawaii All-Stars, a Marine
team comprised of professional ball players including Boots, Mel Queen,
Willard Marshall, Dee Moore, Nippy Jones, and Bill Shea. Boots defeated
the Seals on Sunday the 10th. The following Saturday, he boarded a transport ship for home or more accurately, for San Diego, to await his discharge. Seasick for the entire six day voyage, Boots arrived back in the
United States after a 15 month absence on March 21st, the first day of
spring. Ken Bojens, sports editor of the *San Diego Union* wrote on the 22nd:

*Cletus (Call Me Boots) Poffenberger, the dark-haired right
hander whose throwing arm is expected to slip into the uniform
of the San Diego Padres again this season, came home yesterday aboard the transport U. S. S. Grimes to await discharge*

orders which will enable him to return to baseball. Poffenberger, once one of the sports "bad boys," has spent nearly three years as a Marine, the last 15 months of which were overseas, and his return was preceded by reports that service life has converted him into a serious and conscientious sort of fellow.

Bronzed by tropical sunshine, but admittedly a bit shaky after six straight days of seasickness, the 185 pound hurler said he hoped to get a liberty and have a pow-wow with Bill Starr, Padre president. So far he hasn't signed a contract for the 1946 campaign.

Barring changes in his plans, Poffenberger probably will go on furlough shortly, and by the time that is over he will be eligible for discharge.

"I don't recall that I've ever been in better condition," he commented. "You know, my last season here I weighed around 210 pounds and that's too much. I pitched against the San Francisco Seals a week ago Sunday and let them down with eight hits. We won 7 to 4."[43]

The story was accompanied by a photo of Boots on the dock talking to Jo, and Bojens devoted his entire "Off The Main Line" column to Boots and his arrival home. It reads in part:

There were hundreds of whistling, shouting, laughing Marines crowded on the forecastle deck of the docking transport.

From the pier we looked up at the mass of faces and yelled, "Any of you fellows know a pitcher named Poffenberger who is supposed to be on board?"

The name didn't register, but there was an immediate reply.

"Don't know anybody by that name, but there's a ball player here called 'Boots.'"

"Boots" Poffenberger is possessed of the kind of personality that make friends and he had acquired a lot of them during the rough passage from the Central Pacific where he had spent the last 15 months with the Marines.

But nobody knew him as Cletus Poffenberger. He was just plain "Boots" which is as he would want it.

In fact, if you ask him his first name, that's the one he will give you.

Stories about him are numerous, and a majority of them are of a nature which tend to classify him as one of baseball's madcaps.

"Boots" denies the veracity of many of those tales, but admits they all meant good publicity for him from the public standpoint. In the same breath, he regrets that some of the more fantastic ones were carried to extremes and hurt his career in the sport.

"Such a thing as that can be overdone," he explained. "Then, the first thing you know, every manager or owner and a lot of the ball players get the idea that the fellow they've been hearing about never has a serious moment."

At 185 pounds, Poffenberger is in the best condition of his career, and insists it wasn't six days of seasickness during the voyage home that took off the excess weight.

Credit for that goes to the grand old military custom of griping.

"Everybody in the service does a lot of griping, and I've done my share of it," he explained. "I guess I just griped myself into shape."

Although he hadn't discussed contract matters with President Bill Starr yet, he is anxious to get started as soon as Uncle Sam releases him.

The good-looking athlete insists his period in the service has helped him forget his so-called escapades and to live down most of the stories about him. At the age of 29 he believes his best pitching years are ahead of him, and there isn't much doubt that Pepper Martin [San Diego's new manager] could use another good thrower.

The comely Josephine Poffenberger, to whom "Boots" has been married for nine years, was at the pier for his arrival.

She showed up with two envelopes for him, and then, because his outfit was whisked away in buses bound for the separation center, she didn't have a chance to deliver them.

*One of the envelopes contained some money; the other carried
a piece of paper on which was written Poffenberger's home telephone number.*

*"Boots never thinks to carry any money with him, and he always
forgets the phone number," she said, "so I thought I'd be able to
take care of both items for him today."*

*Mrs. Poffenberger didn't know then that "Boots" is a changed
man.*[44]

On the contrary: Mrs. Poffenberger by now knew better.

Notes

1   John Steadman, "Meet One and Only Boots Poffenberger," *The Sporting
    News*, August 19, 1967 p 5, 6.

2   Carter "Scoop" Latimer, "Scoopin' 'Em Up: Mrs. Poffenberger Bares Inside
    Story of Famous Hubby, Boots," *Greenville News*, October 31, 1943.

3   Official U. S. Marine Corps photo from Associated Press. There are actually
    two clippings of this photo in SB USMC. One is from the Knoxville Journal
    while the other is from *"Sunday News,"* May 23, 1943.

4   Unattributed, "Poffenberger Now Marine 'Boot' at Parris Island," May 1,
    1943 in SB USMC.

5   *The Dug Out: A Morale Builder For The Armed Forces*, April 29, 1943, p 5.

6   *The Dug Out: A Morale Builder For The Armed Forces*, May 22, 1943, p 4.

7   Unattributed, "Poffenberger Blanks Coast Guard By 2-0," undated, but prob-
    ably late May to early June, 1943 in SB USMC.

8   *The Sporting News*, caption to an unattributed photo headlined, "Marines
    Keep Situation Well In Hand On Diamond," October 7, 1943, p 9.

9   Unattributed, "Jay Birds Lose, Play Again Today," undated, but probably
    August 28 or 29, 1943 in SB USMC.

10 Unattributed, "Parade Climaxes Georgetown War Bond Sales Drive,"
    September 8, 1943 in SB USMC.

11 *The Sporting News*, caption to an unattributed photo headlined, "Marines
    Keep Situation Well In Hand On Diamond," October 7, 1943, p 9.

12 Carter "Scoop" Latimer, "Scoopin' 'Em Up: Mrs. Poffenberger Bares Inside
    Story of Famous Hubby, Boots," *Greenville News*, October 31, 1943.

13 *Ibid.*

14 *Ibid.*

15 Hy Goldberg, "Sports in the News," *Newark Evening News*, undated.

16   George Theeringer, "Inside Story on Poffenberg [sic], BOOT, The Parris Island Weekly, undated, but article states that the interview was conducted "a few weeks" after Jo's January visit.

17   Ibid.

18   The Dug Out: A Morale Builder For The Armed Forces, May 8, 1944, p 6.

19   SB USMC contains the July, 1944 Coronet story in Sydney Carroll's "Carroll's Corner" column, as well as the original clipping from Boot. The July 20, 1944 edition of The Sporting News cites the Boot piece in a page 13 blurb authored by "Pvt. Red O'Donnell."

20   The Dug Out: A Morale Bulder For The Armed Forces, July 31, 1944, p 2.

21   Boot, The Parris Island Weekly, unattributed photo, July 22, 1944.

22   The Sporting News, "Two Holler Guys Look Alike," unattributed photo, September 14, 1944, p 13.

23   The Dug Out: A Morale Builder For The Armed Forces, August 21, 1944, p 10.

24   Gary Bedingfield's excellent website, www.baseballinwartime.com provides a complete list.

25   William B. Mead, Baseball Goes To War. (Washington DC: Broadcast Interview Source, Inc., 1998) p 5.

26   Armored News, undated in SB USMC.

27   The Dug Out: A Morale Builder For The Armed Forces, September 11, 1944, p 8.

28   The Dug Out: A Morale Builder For The Armed Forces, October 26, 1944 p 1.

29   "Athletes Ship to Lejeune," attributed to Boot, The Parris Island Weekly, from Dec. 1945 according to a handwritten note SB USMC. A certain mistake, however, as Jo meant to write "1944"; Boots had been in Hawaii for seven months by December of 1945.

30   The Dug Out: A Morale Builder For The Armed Forces, January 12, 1945.

31   T/Sgt. Bill Goodrich, "Poffenberger, Casey Play Pacific Ball," Marine Corps Chevron, April 28, 1945 and p 10 of the May 15, 1945 edition of The Dug Out.

32   T/Sgt. Bill Goodrich, "Fleet Marines Tabbed As Team To Watch." Goodrich contributed to both the Marine Corps Chevron and Pacific Leatherneck. The item has "July, 1945" handwritten next to it in SB USMC.

33   The Sporting News, unattributed photo, August 23, 1945, p 11.

34   The Dug Out: A Morale Builder For The Armed Forces, July 11, 1945, p 12.

35   Oscar Fraley, "Cletus Learns Sobriety or—Don't Believe All You Read," Washington Daily News, hand-dated May 5, 1945.

36   Ibid.

37   Ibid.

38   Frank Colley, "The Colley-See-Um of Sports," Morning Herald, May 9, 1945.

39   Ibid.

40   Sgt. Ernie Harwell, "Poffenberger Shows Corps," Pacific Leatherneck, August 1, 1945, p 39. T/Sgt. Bill Richardson is not credited in the article.

41 Grantland Rice, "Rice Names All-Time Baseball Team With Greatest Appeal To Writers," *Honolulu Star-Bulletin*, February 18, 1946.

42 *The Dug Out: A Morale Builder For The Armed Forces*, undated in SB USMC. Despite our best efforts to locate the exact issue in which this information appeared by reviewing the bound copy of the entire run of issues housed at the Williamsport Museum, neither Jerry Knode nor I could find it. Which doesn't mean it isn't there! Jerry's recollection is that Boots would send catcher's equipment and anything else that he could get ahold of.

43 Ken Bojens, "Poffenberger Returns in Glowing Condition," *San Diego Union*, March 22, 1946.

44 Ken Bojens, "Off the Main Line," *San Diego Union*, undated, but most likely March 22 or 23, 1946.

CHAPTER 9

Same Old Boots

Boots was given a 30 day furlough beginning March 29th, pending his official discharge from the Marines. Both the Padres and Boots believed that he would be allowed to pitch while on leave, but W. G. Bramham, president of the National Minor Baseball league, ruled that neither Boots, nor any enlisted man was eligible until his official discharge took place. Boots was given his exit physical on April 17th, promoted to corporal along with 11 other men in his separation company on the 19th, and discharged the same day. A civilian once more, Boots resumed his career with the San Diego Padres.

After appearing once in relief, Boots made his first start on May 4th against Sacramento, giving up six hits and three earned runs in seven innings. The Padres lost 4-0, in a game that took all of one hour and 44 minutes to play, but Earl Keller of the *San Diego Tribune-Sun* reported that, "Boots was lightning fast and pitched well enough to win."[1]

On the 6th, Boots lost to Sacramento again while pitching in relief, gave up three runs to the Hollywood Stars in the 8th inning of an 8-0 defeat in his next appearance, then took the loss against the Stars in the first game of a May 12th double header. Finally, on May 23rd, he defeated San Francisco 5-2, despite yielding four walks and 12 hits. The June 5th edition of *The Sporting News* mentioned Boots' victory, but the highlight of the game was outfielder Johnny Jensen scoring in the ninth inning on a triple steal.[2]

Boots was held back a day from his next start against the Los Angeles Angels after complaining about a sore arm, but defeated the Angels when he next took the mound, giving up only two runs.³ He then defeated the Portland Beavers at Lane Field, pitched well again, then poorly in a relief outing against the Seals at home, when the Padres dropped a double header to San Francisco. Earl Keller mixed his historical metaphors when reporting on the double header loss to the Seals:

> The atomic bomb must have backfired yesterday and sank the San Diego Padres instead of the battleship Nevada! At any rate, an atomic bomb, summer fever or something struck 'em and the best they could do in a twin bill with San Francisco at Lane field was get three tallies while losing 2 to 1 and 9 to 2. . . . They got to him [Tom Seats] for four hits and three runs in the first inning and for four runs and four hits in the fifth. Boots Poffenberger succeeded him in the fifth and the Seals hit him like they owned him, too.⁴

Boots was dramatically inconsistent as were the Padres who had won five straight coming into the seven-game series with San Francisco only to lose the next six to the Seals. Boots faced only four batters in a start against Portland and gave up a run before coming out of the game with a sore arm, then defeated Hollywood 5-3 in the second game of a July 4ᵗʰ double header. On the 13ᵗʰ, he gave up five runs in a 7-2 loss to San Francisco.

In the *Pacific Leatherneck* article that had appeared the previous August, Boots claimed that he "never owned a fast ball" but that he was smarter than ever and that "I don't think I need one."⁵ This is contrary to what Boots said about himself early in his career as well as contrary to what the hitters said. Perhaps Boots was simply trying to put a good face on a bad situation, in essence saying to prospective major league clubs, "I haven't lost anything, because I didn't have it in the first place." He also stated that "It was during my first season at Parris Island that I discovered how much better I could pitch with my weight down and spirits up."⁶ It would only be natural if Boots had lost something off his fastball as he had not pitched professionally for three years and was approaching his 31ˢᵗ birthday, one which would prove to be eventful.

Clearly, he was not the same old Boots on the mound, but he definitely reverted to form off it. Hit hard in a 7-2 loss in San Francisco, Boots

was relieved in the fourth inning, and in his usual pattern told reporters that he was quitting. After he refused to suit up for a Sunday double
header on July 15th, his 31st birthday, Boots was suspended by Padre manager, Pepper Martin. Watching the double header from the stands, Boots
stated that he was going to "talk things over" with Padre officials, but
Martin vowed that either the suspension would be made permanent or
that Boots would be sold.[7]

Ironically, John Leonard "Pepper" Martin had been an integral
part of the St. Louis Cardinals Gashouse Gang of the early 1930s, a
fun-loving, wild and wooly bunch that included Dizzy Dean. Star of the
1931 World Series in which he batted .500 and led the Cards to victory
over the Philadelphia Athletics with not only his hitting, but also his
aggressive base running, Martin was a determined competitor. Playing
with Dizzy Dean was one thing, but managing anyone who marched to
any drummer other than Martin's own fierce percussionist was something else entirely. The year before, he reportedly punched pitcher
Vallie Eaves, telling the Associated Press that Eaves, "had it coming to
him. He let me down during the game . . . besides upsetting the discipline of the club and setting a bad example for the rest of the players."[8]
(Eaves, who was a stalwart of the '45 staff, going 21-15, pitched in four
games for the Padres in 1946.) In 1949, Martin was fined and suspended
by the Florida International League for choking an umpire. Two years
later he was arrested when he went into the stands in Lakeland, Florida
to punch a spectator.[9]

In further keeping with Boots' well-established pattern, he was
remorseful the next day saying, "I have nothing against Martin. I'm just
home sick and I'm going so lousy I figure a change would be good for
me."[10] Ken Borjens reported on the 16th that Boots declared, "I just lost
my head."[11]

Pepper Martin and the Padres, however had more problems than
Boots Poffenberger. They were in the midst of an incredibly bad run, losing 14 of 18 including 13 straight to the Seals, having dropped the entire
seven game series in San Francisco. Furthermore, reports now surfaced
that more than a few players had complaints about Martin who was in
his second year of managing San Diego. Reporter Mitch Angus of the
San Diego Union noted that, "Padre players last week were quoted freely

by San Francisco-area scribes in their complaints of Martin's tactics. The two principal charges blamed him for constant lineup changes and his failure to maintain a high team spirit." Angus also noted that some of the Padres were "openly hostile to their manager."[12]

Padres owner Bill Starr who had been traveling with the club met with the players and let it be known that he was backing his manager, but he was immediately threatened with a $100,000 lawsuit by Carl Parlapiano, owner of Carl's Baseball Inn, which stood at the corner of 16th and Island Streets in San Diego.[13] Carl's Baseball Inn was a favorite hang-out of Padre players and Parlapiano was a huge Padre fan who claimed that he had missed only five ballgames at Lane Field in the past 10 years. In fact, he had driven to San Francisco to see the Padres play over the weekend.[14] Apparently, Parlapiano had his own theories about how the Padres should be managed, with which the players who frequented his establishment strongly concurred. Martin, getting wind of the mutinous talk brewing at Carl's Baseball Inn banned his players from visiting the place and threatened any more patronage with a $100 fine. In fact, any player even seen with Parlapiano would be fined.[15] Hence, Parlapiano threatened a lawsuit.

It takes no imagination to envision Boots Poffenberger as a frequent patron of Carl's Baseball Inn, and one not hesitant to tell the barkeep how the Padres should be run. By Tuesday the 16th, everyone's temper had cooled. Starr, who had threatened to sell or trade away the troublemakers had changed his mind and even the fiery Martin was quoted as saying, "Again I say let's bear down and get some runs and forget everything."[16] Neither Starr nor Martin, however were willing to forget the fact that Boots had quit the team on Saturday night. Ultimately, Parlapiano dropped his lawsuit, Pepper Martin was fired in early September, and Boots Poffenberger with his 5-6 record was sent home to Williamsport. Rumor had it that Boots would be sold back to Nashville or to Louisville in the American Association or even to a team in the Mexican League.[17] Those were merely rumors, however, but the August 14th *Sporting News* reported the fact that Boots "who recently went on the retired list of the San Diego Pacific Coast League club, is now playing semi-pro ball in his home town Williamsport, Md. In his first start, however, he dropped a 9 to 3 decision to the Frederick, Md., Hustlers."[18]

* * *

The 1947 season followed the exact same pattern as the 1946 season, which was the same pattern more or less as every season except 1940 when Boots was with Nashville. In 1947, Boots was now with his home town team, the Hagerstown Owls, which ironically enough was an affiliate of the Detroit Tigers. The Owls were a Class B outfit in the Interstate League—Boots was as far away from major league competition as he had been at any time since he played for Charleston in 1936, only now he would be 32 at mid-season.

It had been Boots' intention to quit baseball altogether. In a fascinating interview with Al Cartwright who was in his first year as sports editor of Wilmington's *Journal-Every Evening* and would go on to become a revered figure in the Delaware sports scene, Boots revealed that he had "had enough of ball-playin' all over the country."[19] Cartwright had called on Boots at his hotel when the Owls were in Wilmington for a series with the Blue Rocks, and he noted that Boots was dressed in "beautiful blue pajama bottoms and contrasting skivvy shirt." Cartwright added to the scene by further noting that during the interview, Boots did his best to prevent his roommates, Gene Crumling and Jack Lance from falling back to sleep. The "garrulous" Boots began his explanation of his attempt to quit baseball by saying almost ominously, "Things are happening in the family, you know." He then went on to explain at length his attempt to leave baseball for another line of work:

> *"My wife and I thought it was about time for me to get a year-around job. I went to work for the Bureau of Standards in Washington during the winter but they started throwin' all that atomic stuff at me and bein' a guy who didn't have much of an education, I pulled out.*
>
> *"This Hagerstown deal is good. I'm close to home, which cuts down the expenses, among other things. I took inventory the other day and found out that I was in the same shape financially*

as I was the year I started playin' ball in 1935. You can't save any money bouncin' around the country."[20]

More likely Jo did the inventorying. According to Laco Anderson, she was making "good money" working at Fairchild Aircraft in Hagerstown, now that they had returned to the area.

Cartwright gave "homesickness" as the reason Boots left San Diego and made no mention of his suspension for jumping the team, apparently taking Boots' explanation of events at face value. Clearly, for Boots, playing ball even at the Class B level in places such as Allentown, York, Harrisburg, and Trenton was better than working an actual job and he persuaded San Diego to "unretire" him and then release him so that he could sign a contract with Hagerstown. According to the April 2nd edition of *The Sporting News*, Boots had contacted Larry Gilbert about returning to Nashville, but "received a polite 'no' for an answer."[21]

At some point, probably during this winter of 1946-1947 Boots was featured on a Marine Corps recruiting poster. Measuring 2' x 3', the poster illustrates what a wonderful time a young man could have as a Marine as it featured six black and white photos of sailboats and rodeo and someone throwing a javelin. There was a photo of Johnny Weissmuller (who never served in the military) in a pool, his arm around the shoulder of someone, who also possessed Tarzan-like muscles. The featured photo, almost as large as the poster itself, was a cutout of Boots in mid-windup wearing his Parris Island team uniform.

The Owls held their training camp right at their home ballpark, Municipal Stadium, in Hagerstown as Class B teams couldn't afford to travel very far. Frank Colley of Hagerstown's *Morning Herald* reported a familiar refrain: "'Boots' is turning out to be one of the hardest workers on the team. He is hustling from the time he hits the park until a halt is called." Manager John "Bunny" Griffiths allowed Boots to "get himself into "condition in his own manner. 'Boots' is really in earnest about it all and when the grind is all over he will have shed a lot of that extra weight he has been carrying around."[22]

Boots was given the assignment to start the home opener on May 1st which he did against Allentown, defeating the Cardinals 9-3 in a complete game, nine-hit victory. Boots walked four, struck out one and was one-for-three at the plate. Frank Colley wrote:

Before a crowd of 2500 chilled fans "Boots" Poffenberger displayed the same wizardry that made him one of the most feared hurlers while he was toiling in the livery of the Detroit Tigers in the American League.

Outside of a pair of solid wallops by Frank Hecklinger which cleared the right field fence, "Boots" was master of the situation, scattering Allentown's blows over the route, besides turning in an excellent job in fielding his position.[23]

As May moved along, Boots was enjoying as much success at the plate as on the mound. He homered in a pinch hitting appearance against Lancaster on May 4th, then hit a grand slam on the 16th in a 10-4 win in which he pitched. He also had a two-run single in the fifth and the 1,000 or so locals in attendance were so impressed by his performance that they passed the hat and collected $90.92 to give to their Williamsport neighbor. Frank Colley reported that the fans also donated "several other prizes."[24] Laco Anderson remembers that home run. And what followed.

He hit that sucker clean across Cannon Avenue. Oh man, what a shot! Well, some screwball, he goes through the stands and they come up with all this money. "Collection for Boots! Collection for Boots!" Well, they didn't see him for four days. He never come back! For four days! He got this money and I guess he went to who knows? Stadium Tavern or somewhere.

By May 20th, Boots was six-for-seventeen with seven RBI and one binge.

Jo was hospitalized at the end of May, with what appears to have been a non life-threatening condition. Dick Kelly of Hagerstown's *Daily Mail* wrote, "Did you know that Boots Poffenberger hurled that fine game against York last night with very little warm-up practice. He was with his wife, who is confined at the Washington County Hospital, until nearly time."[25] Jo's release was listed in an undated blurb that appeared among the 1947 clippings.[26] Perhaps Boots was in a hurry to return to the hospital as he struck out five and walked none in what, at 1:40 was the fastest game of the season to date.

On June 12th, Boots scattered six hits and struck out eight in a complete game, 14-2 victory at Allentown, then lost to Lancaster on the 17th, walking the bases loaded in the first and eventually giving up four runs in only 2.1 innings. On June 20th, Manager Griffiths suspended Boots for disappearing for three days. Dick Kelly reported:

> *Just before the Owls took the field to oppose the Sunbury Yankees, Manager "Bunny" Griffiths released the news that Poffenberger had been suspended for 10 days for failing to report to the local club for three days running. It was with deep regret that the Owl's pilot made this decision as pitching is one of his biggest headaches at the present time. The suspension, without pay, will be continued indefinitely if "Boots" fails to report at the end of the 10 days.*
>
> *Poffenberger could not be contacted for a statement today, but it has been reported by a very reliable source that the big right-hander has decided to quit the Hagerstown club.*[27]

Perhaps, this is the four day absence that Laco Anderson believed occurred earlier in the season. Just as likely, if not more so, this was a second (or third) absence from the club.

When the 10 days was almost up, Boots in his customary fashion announced, "that he is ready to take up where he left off when his suspension expires today. Nothing official has been released by the Owls' front office concerning Poffenberger's standing with the club but it is rumored that he will be given his release."[28]

Boots was indeed given his release and as sure as day follows night, the rumors as to where he would play next appeared in the newspaper. One rumor had him playing for the Lancaster Red Roses and there was substance to this report.[29] Among the clippings is a telegram from Lancaster directing Boots to call. On the right side of the telegram, someone, probably Boots, has scribbled, "Bonus for signing," "What salary you'll pay," "Sign for remainder of season—or for this season and 48." Boots' record stood at 5-3 and he was hitting .267 with a robust .600 slugging percentage, but it is highly unlikely that even had his record been 10-0 with a 1.000 slugging percentage, that a team was going to sign him since he had just quit the team that he was on. Such considerations never mattered to Boots who indeed, did not go to Lancaster or probably more accurately stated, Lancaster refused to sign Boots. Boots did sign a contract, however—with the Cumberland Amvets Red Sox in the Bi-State League, a semi-pro league operating in Allegheny County, Maryland about 50 miles west of Williamsport.

Cumberland is only some 16 miles from Lonaconing, the town in which Lefty Grove was raised and to which he returned following his retirement in 1941. J. Suter Kegg of the *Cumberland Sunday Times* in his "Tapping on the Sports Keg" column of July 20th wrote about Grove's reaction to Boots pitching for the Amvets.

> *When Lonaconing's "Lefty" Grove heard the other day that Cletus "Boots" Poffenberger would pitch for the Cumberland Amvets this afternoon at Taylor Field, he recalled that "Boots," in his major league debut, decisioned him by a 4-2 [sic] score.*
>
> *Grove, of course, was pitching for the Boston Red Sox at the time while Poffenberger was with the Detroit Tigers. "Lefty" asserts that Poffenberger looked "mighty good" during his stay in the majors.*
>
> *Although he may have slipped, "Boots" is far from being washed up and could undoubtedly win a lot of games in a high-class league if he decided he wanted to be "tied down" during the summer months.*
>
> *Bobby Williams, who is recuperating at his home here from an injury received in a Pony League game last month, saw Poffenberger pitch while both were in the Marines and states that although not exceptionally fast, "Boots" has plenty of stuff on the ball.[30]*

Boots made his debut that Sunday, defeating the Queen City Brewers 6-4 before 1,500 fans. It was his first start in five weeks and he fanned seven to keep the Amvets, who at 20-5, were only one half game behind Westvaco who were 20-4. Grove was not in Cumberland to see Boots pitch, however, for on the 21st, he and Boots' first big league manager, Mickey Cochrane (along with Frankie Frisch and Carl Hubbell) were inducted into baseball's Hall of Fame.

Boots pitched well for the Amvets, if not spectacularly and he drew big crowds whenever he took the mound. When he wasn't pitching, he often played first base. Semi-pro baseball is but an echo of the game that is played in the major leagues and plays occur that aren't seen at higher levels. For example, Boots' debut victory was taken down when Queen City's protest of an illegal steal of home was upheld by league President Alex "Pop" Nicol. It seems that the Brewers believed that time had been called by ump Ray Middleton who was dusting off the plate, when the ball was thrown back to pitcher and got away. That allowed the runner on third, player-manager Norm Gerdeman to steal home. In another game, the Amvets stole 17 bases. This was not Detroit or Nashville or even Hagerstown, but Boots didn't seem to mind playing against the Lonaconing Republican Club or the Hyndman Firemen or the Frostburg VFW.

On Labor Day, September 1st, Boots won both games of a seven-inning double header over Barton American Legion. The Amvets took the first game 16-0 and the second 8-3 and the entire day of baseball took only two hours and five minutes to play.

The Bi-State League playoffs began six days later with Boots defeating Lonaconing 8-3, giving up only six hits (four of the scratch variety) and no walks in a complete game effort. In addition to his stellar work on the mound, Boots was three-for-four with two doubles and two RBI. A standing room only crowd estimated at 2,500 turned out to witness the contest. Boots' mound opponent that day was Robert Moses Grove, Jr., Lefty's son. Junior was right-handed and on this day was roughed up for 11 hits.

Before the second game of the best of three playoff series continued, the Amvets traveled to Hagerstown for a highly anticipated exhibition game. The *Morning Herald* excitedly proclaimed:

> *The Boonsboro Yellow Jackets announced last night that Dave Cole, 17 year pitching sensation of the Morris Frock Post Junior American Legion team would be their starting pitcher in tonight's battle with the Cumberland AMVETS at Municipal Stadium in a contest to decide the mythical amateur championship of Western Maryland.*

And opposing young Cole on the firing line for the Mountaineers will be one Cletus "Boots" Poffenberger, his loquacious fellow townsman from Williamsport and mainstay of Cumberland hill corps since receiving the pink slip from the Owls some weeks back.

The outcome should be interesting—will youth be served, or will the veteran Poffenberger have the edge on the highly regarded Cole?[31]

The Amvets won 10-4 "to the dismal disappointment of a surprisingly large turnout of 1250 fans at Municipal Stadium."[32] Boots pitched only 3 innings and left with the game tied 1-1. For his part, Cole who was already being scouted by the Boston Braves, went the distance, striking out 10 and giving up only 2 extra base hits (including a double by Boots) but was hurt by 8 errors including 3 of his own.

We may reflect on the irony of defeating the immortal Lefty Grove for his first victory, only to be reduced 10 years later to pitching against his far less talented son or a high school prospect, but clearly that never occurred to Boots. It was a ballgame and he enjoyed himself thoroughly as J. Suter Kegg described in the September 14th edition of the *Sunday Times*:

When the Cumberland Amvets turned back the Boonsboro Yellow Jackets Friday night at Hagerstown's Municipal Stadium, Cletus "Boots" Poffenberger, the former major leaguer, walked away from the park with a satisfied look on his face.

The scheduling of the exhibition engagement was Poffenberger's idea. He had boasted to Washington County friends that the Amvets had a better ball club than the best in the Hagerstown district and had the locals lost, he would have had a tough time living down his "undue assumption of superiority."

Because he had deserted Hagerstown's professional Owls in mid-season after words with Owner Oren E. Sterling, a lot of Hub City fans turned out just to give Poffenberger the Bronx cheer. But "Boots," noted for his flair for showmanship, acknowledged the boos in a spirit of fun and let the spectators in the vicinity of the Red Sox dugout know that the Amvets would win with ease.

He also told members of the Amvet team that young Dave Cole, the promising Williamsport chucker whom he is tutoring, might be tough to hit, "but you can bet your boots, "Boots" won't have any trouble with him."

Every member of the club seems to take on a feeling of superiority when he's on the mound. That Poffenberger knew what he was talking about was proven his first and only time at bat. After his protégé had sneaked two strikes over on him, "Boots" parked Cole's next pitch against the right-center wall for a double.

Poffenberger is a big favorite among district fans because of his eager-beaver attitude. There's no other player on the Amvet team who hustles any more than he does.[33]

That same Sunday, Boots again defeated Lonaconing 10-0 while facing only 29 batters. The Amvets would take on the Hyndman Fireman for the Bi-State League championship; Cumberland lost the first of the three game series in a big way, 22-7, but Boots defeated the Firemen 3-1 in Game 2. The *Cumberland News* reported:

"Boots" Poffenberger for the Amvets, and Paul Clapper, of Hyndman, hooked up in a peach of a hurling duel but "lady luck" deserted Clapper, for the day at least, and two unearned runs enabled the Amvets to get even with Clapper for the licking he gave them a week ago. Clapper gave up only five hits, two of those of the scratch variety and Poffenberger yielded only seven.

Hundreds of Cumberlanders went to Hyndman for the game and the crowd was so large that it was necessary to put up ropes to keep the spectators off the field. Hundreds lined the field down the first and third base foul lines and countless others watched the contests from windows in houses and barns.[34]

Boots started the deciding contest, tiring quickly and leaving after only five innings. It didn't matter much as the Amvets held a 14-6 lead when he departed and they coasted to a 16-11 triumph and the Bi-State League crown. Boots had won seven games during the regular season and four more in the playoffs. It was a great half a season, even if it was semi-pro baseball in the hills of Western Maryland.

And despite being relegated to those hills, Boots showed up in the September 9th edition of the *Saturday Evening Post* in Stanley Frank's article entitled, "Baseball Needs Some New Fools." Several photos accompanied the story including the one of Boots thumbing his ear in his Bona Allen Shoemakers uniform and another, ironically enough of Pepper Martin riding on a fire truck with a caption that read "Fire Chief Pepper Martin used to race midget autos and liked to pour water on his manager." Frank argues that the game has become too business-like and could use some more colorful characters such as Boots, in a story that could have as easily been written in 2007 as 1947 if the names were changed:

> *A gifted clown like Rabbit Maranville, who convulsed fans a generation ago, probably would be barred now for conduct detrimental to the dignity of the national game. Immunity from that offense is enjoyed only by executives.*

> *The old-time, dyed-in-the-wool fan was a raconteur who could kill a pleasant evening recounting the zany antics of his favorite screwball without mentioning a batting average, a score or a court decision. Quick now. When did you last hear a funny story about a grim, frozen-faced ballplayer in the major leagues today?*

> *Feller, Greeenberg, Musial, Newhouser, DiMaggio and Reiser would have been outstanding in any era, but they go through the motions with the detached efficiency of a bank clerk checking his accounts.*

> *"Nobody gets fun out of baseball anymore," [Maranville] says, "because big salaries have made it a serious career. Don't get me wrong. I'm all in favor of players getting all they can from the owners. It's great that a man can set himself up for life by sticking in the big leagues for eight or ten years. Guys in my time played for the love of the game."[35]*

Boots' name appeared prominently in print again in the spring of 1948 when Leo Durocher's controversial book *The Dodgers and Me* was released. Durocher pulled no punches in describing the daffiness of his Dodgers. Many critics panned the book including Red Smith, a Hall of

Fame baseball writer who penned a scathing criticism that appeared in the May 26th edition of *The Sporting News*. Smith, however, conceded that the stories concerning Boots "are not malicious. They are meant to be humorous."[36] He questioned Durocher's accusation, however, that Boots had kept the $150.00 supposedly given to Boots for a return train ticket to the Dodgers after he (Durocher) had been convinced by Larry MacPhail to forgive Boots. (Durocher is not likely to have "forgiven" Boots and may have been confusing Boots' adventures in trying to reach Montreal.)

There is no evidence that Boots had any reaction to the book whatsoever; he probably never read it although he had the time since he did things a little differently in 1948. Instead of being the hardest worker in the spring and then jumping the team in July or so, he didn't join the Owls until mid-August. By then, the Owls were desperate for a pitcher. The August 13th edition of the *Morning Herald* noted that "Owner [Oren] Sterling has been in contact with "Red" Rolfe of the Detroit Tigers in an effort to land a hurler to aid the overworked Owl corps and there is a possibility that a pitcher will be sent in here to finish out the season."[37] The Owls also contacted the Senators, but ultimately, perhaps as a way to also boost the gate for a team fighting to escape the basement of the Interstate League, the team signed Boots.

Indeed, there had been speculation throughout the summer that Boots would once again sign with the Owls, and Dick Kelly reported that he had been offered "a very lucrative contract when Gene Crumling was managing."[38] Crumling, a catcher on the squad, had 12 at-bats in the big leagues in 1945, but was otherwise a career minor-leaguer. One of three managers the Owls employed in 1948, he and Boots were fast friends. Also on the team was Boots' former Marine teammate Cal Ermer as well as Hal Keller, who would spend three years as a catcher with the Washington Senators before serving in the front office, primarily as a farm director for the Senators/Rangers and the Seattle Mariners.

Signing with the Owls, however, was hardly the most significant event in Boots' life that August. Jo had finally had enough and filed for divorce in Washington, D. C. There were signs that the marriage was disintegrating. The 1947 clippings themselves give an indication of trouble: None of the clippings are actually pasted in any scrapbook.

Boots' comments to Al Cartwright that "things were happening in the family," and that "*My wife* [my emphasis] and I thought it was about time for me to get a year-around job," indicate that there was friction over the fact that Boots rarely worked. In fact, Boots never worked steadily until 1960. Laco Anderson believes that that fact, along with Boots' drinking, ultimately destroyed the marriage. Indeed, he was a witness to the moment that the marriage ended:

> *Here was Jo getting up and going to work every day. Most likely she would be coming home at 5:00 or in that area—no Boots! Where is he? Who knows? I can tell you that the one day she was supposed to have gone to work and he left, that the moving van popped up within an hour. She was out of there and took everything. She might have left him a table and one chair, a plate and a knife and fork. [The move] had to've been lined up and it had to be lined up way in advance.*

Boots and Jo had been living downstairs in a house in which Boots' mom Sophia lived upstairs. Sophia was now divorced from Herb Connelly who remained in Williamsport. Anderson saw firsthand the sparsity of Boots' downstairs apartment after Jo left:

> *I'm going down by Murray's tavern right across from City Hall in Williamsport and here comes Gene Crumling . . . Gene Crumling and Boots hooked up many times. Here are them two comin' out of Murray's. They had a case of beer and said, "Lac, how about carrying this case of beer down home for us?" Well, I can understand why they would want help carryin' that out of there. We got down into where [Boots] and his wife lived and it was all vacant except what I just told you was there.*

> *You have to have someone who's going to keep you motivated to do the best you can do. Jo had to be or she wouldn't have kept all those scrapbooks. She had to be something to keep him in line. But then again, be honest: It ain't hard to get out of line. That's probably what the hell led her to just get that van in there and say "We're gonna load up and I'm out of here!"*

Boots never expressed any bitterness that Jo left, and left him with precious little. Nor did he try to persuade her to change her mind. According to Anderson:

> He made no effort to go get her. He never said, "Well this is all she left me."... I never, never heard that man ever say anything negative. But me, knowing her as I knew her and then my wife [Jeanne] knew her well at Fairchild. She had a good job; she made good money, but the bottom line was she got sick and damn tired of the life they were livin'!

Boots, no doubt, felt that Jo had done what was best for her and he simply went on living, which for Boots meant having fun whenever and where ever he could find it—even if it was settling faux arguments with Gene Crumling in his nearly empty apartment. Boots would tell the catcher that he could never tag him out and Crumling, quite naturally, disputed the claim. To settle the argument, Boots would retreat into his near empty kitchen, get a running start and then slide into a pillow that had been placed on the empty living room floor as a base. "That's just the way he was," says Anderson.

Anderson himself spent three weeks in Boston in June of 1948 when the Braves invited him and his Williamsport High School teammate Dave Cole to work out at Braves Field. Boston had already signed Cole who would make his major league debut just two years later, 11 days after his 20th birthday. The summer of 1948 was an exciting time to be in Boston with the Braves who would capture the National League pennant that year, thanks in large part to the outstanding play of rookie shortstop Alvin Dark and pitcher Johnny Sain. Dark batted .322 and was the NL's Rookie of the Year. Johnny Sain, the young part-time pitcher, part-time outfielder with Nashville in 1940 won 24 games for Boston and combined with Warren Spahn, fresh out of the Marines for the best 1-2 punch in baseball. Their work gave rise to the cry in Boston, "Spahn and Sain and pray for rain!"

While Cole and Dark and Sain were on their way up, it was clear that Boots was, at 33, just about finished in professional baseball. He struck out the only batter he faced in his first appearance with the Owls on August 15th in an 8-5 loss to Allentown. The next day, another of baseball's colorful characters and its greatest player died. Babe Ruth had succumbed to cancer in New York. As if to salute a fellow good-time loving Marylander, Boots performed a little Ruthian magic of his own in a 7-2 victory at Trenton the following evening:

> *In the seventh . . . Poffenberger batted for pitcher Don Belton with the bases full. The ex-major leaguer promptly clouted one of Paul Lapalme's pitches over the fence in left-center for a grand slam home run. . . . At 8:01 p. m. the crowd of 2,187 stood for a minute of silence in tribute to the memory of Babe Ruth.*[39]

The next night, Boots was given the start and like Ruth, both pitched and hit the Owls to victory. The *Daily Mail* had this to say and though there is no byline, it was no doubt written by Dick Kelly who after all these years, still could not get the correct order of Boots' name:

> *Elwood Cletus [sic] "Boots" Poffenberger, the loquacious pitcher from Williamsport, assumed the starring role for the Hagerstown Owls again last night. The former major leaguer turned in a five hitter and clouted a home run with two mates aboard in the Owls 8 to 2 victory in the opener.*

> *Poffenberger, ex-major leaguer, made his first mound start of this season for Hagerstown in the opener. He helped his own cause by clouting a homer in the second inning with two mates aboard. His tricky delivery and mound mannerisms had the crowd of 1,261 in a constant uproar. He proved a puzzle to Trenton batters, however, allowing only four singles and a pinch double by Dilorenzo over the seven inning route.*[40]

Boots won again on the 23rd, a 5-3, seven-inning complete game over Lancaster. It was the final win of his professional career. In his final pitching appearance of the season on September 3rd, he took a loss against Sunbury 9-7, giving up 12 hits and nine runs in 6.1 innings. He also walked six while striking out only three.

Perhaps because he felt invigorated by his experience and perhaps because the Owls recognized a drawing card when they saw one, Boots returned to the club for the 1949 season. The Owls trained just 20 miles south of Hagerstown in Martinsburg, West Virginia that year, and Boots, along with Gene Crumling, were among the first to report when camp opened on April 3rd.[41] Boots seemed to realize that this was his last chance in professional baseball:

> *"This is the year, if I am going to turn the trick, this is the year that I will have to do," said "Boots" Poffenberger as he jogged around Municipal Park in Martinsburg yesterday afternoon bundled up in a rubber sweat jacket and a heavy woolen jacket over that.*
>
> *"Owner Sterling gave me a good contract and anyone who can't play ball for [manager] Woody Wheaton shouldn't be in the game," stated "Boots." "My legs and wind are in excellent shape and with some warm weather the old flipper should be just as good as it ever was, perhaps that high hard one won't be as hard but I'll have plenty of what it takes to win games."*
>
> *Poffenberger is working just as hard as any of the youngsters in camp and Manager Wheaton likes his attitude. "Boots" has been out long enough to know how to condition himself and I am letting him solve his own problem. I feel that he will be fit and ready when I call on him to work and that is all that counts," said Wheaton.*
>
> *Fans who have seen Poffenberger pitch know that he has the stuff and with a good club behind him this year there is every reason to believe that he will come through with close to fifteen or more wins.*[42]

Boots was having trouble even getting into an exhibition game, however, for he had come down with a sore arm. On the 19th Colley reported that

> *Despite the gloomy weather there was some brightness as "Boots" Poffenberger worked several rounds of batting practice and although he has a hitch in his arm, he was getting the ball over and calling his shots. Some good warm weather and "Boots" will be ready to take a turn on the hillock against any and all opposition.*[43]

Boots' arm was still sore a week later as was that of manager/ outfielder/pitcher Woody Wheaton who played 37 games for the Philadelphia A's in 1943-44 and spent a total of 17 seasons in the minors. Sore arm or not, Boots was still a local favorite and his photo, as well as Gene Crumling's, appeared on either side of the Interstate League schedule on page 24 of the April 29th edition of the *Morning Herald*. The page, as well as its opposite was filled with sponsors' ads many of which promised prizes to the Owl who accomplished certain feats. For example, Jacobson's at 16 W. Franklin St. offered a "beautiful $10 bedspread to the 'Owl' who has the highest batting average for the season," noting that, in case of a tie, "duplicate awards will be given."

One week into the season, Boots had amassed only one at-bat, apparently as a pinch-hitter for he had yet to pitch. Finally, on May 12th, Boots got his first start at Municipal Stadium against the league leading Wilmington Blue Rocks. Dick Kelly of the *Daily Mail* was anxious to see how Boots would fare:

> *Anything can and usually does, happen when Boots Poffenberger toes the rubber. The unpredictable Lou Costello of the Hagerstown Owls will make his first start of the season tonight—and this itself should be well worth the price of admission.*
>
> *Regardless of whether you like the Baron or not, you must admit he supplies plenty of thrills, laughs and excitement when he's on the firing line. The unpredictable Boots has a way of coming up with some of the darndest things at the darndest times . . . just like the time in 1947 when he hit a home run with the bases loaded at the Stadium to win his own game.*
>
> *Boots might get his ears knocked off tonight, or he might turn in a shutout. But you can rest assured, he'll be out there trying.*[44]

In his game story for the evening contest, Kelly reported that others in town were anxious to see how Boots would fare as well.

> *Indications point to a large turnout of fans for tonight's finale with the league leaders. The loquacious Poffenberger's appearance alone is enough to make the turnstiles sing a merry tune.*

Unpredictable and colorful, Boots has always been a good drawing card.

The one-time major league hurler wouldn't make any predictions on the outcome of tonight's tilt, other than to say "I'll be out there charging 'em." And he'll do just that.

Although noted for his antics off the diamond, Poffenberger has always given his best when the time came for him to take his turn on the mound. At 33, Boots has lost some of the zip on his fast ball, but he usually comes up with something new when the occasion calls for it.

The one-time Peck's Bad Boy of The Detroit Tigers appears to be in excellent physical condition. During the spring training grind, Boots was one of the hardest workers on the local squad, giving all he had to round into shape for the 1949 campaign.

A sore arm, as a result of his over-anxious work in training, has kept the big hurler on the shelf but he appears to be ready for his initial start.[45]

Giving up only five hits over eight innings, Boots nevertheless gave up four runs (not all of which were earned). He surrendered six walks while striking out only three and took the loss 4-0. Frank Colley thought that he pitched well, however.[46] Kelly agreed, writing, "Not bad at all, when you consider that he hadn't thrown in 10 days—not to mention the fact that he pitched the eight innings with a sore arm."[47]

It was Boots' final professional appearance. Six days after this start, the *Daily Mail* reported that Boots would go on the voluntary retirement list with a sore arm:

Elwood Cletus "Boots" Poffenberger has broken into the headlines once again.

The veteran righthander from Williamsport announced last night that he will ask to be placed on the voluntary retired list by the Hagerstown Baseball Club. Bothered by a sore arm since spring training, the one-time major league hurler said he has decided to call it quits "until my arm feels a lot better."

Poffenberger did not make the trip to Trenton with the Owls yesterday, deciding instead to remain in Williamsport. He was originally scheduled to take his turn on the mound against the Giants last night.

"If my arm rounds into shape," commented the unpredictable righthander, "I may rejoin the club in a month or so. The way it is now, I'm not doing the club or myself any good."[48]

A sore arm had eliminated Boots' last chance at professional baseball, but there was no bitterness or regret. Boots just kept on being Boots.

Notes

1 Earl Keller, "Southpaw Jinx Stymies Padres," *San Diego Tribune-Sun*, May 4, 1946.

2 *The Sporting News*, June 5, 1946, p 24.

3 Unattributed, "Poffenberger Subdues Los Angeles, 6-2," May 29, 1946, in SB 46.

4 Earl Keller, "O'Doulmen Drop A-Bomb on Padres," *San Diego Tribune-Sun*, undated in SB 46.

5 Sgt. Ernie Harwell, "Poffenberger Shows Corps," *Pacific Leatherneck*, August 1, 1945, p 39. T/Sgt. Bill Richardson is not credited in the article.

6 *Ibid.*

7 Mitch Angus, "Padre Pilot 'On Spot;' Poffenberger Suspended," *San Diego Union*, July 15, 1946.

8 Associated Press, July 23, 1945, as quoted in http://boblemke.blogspot.com/2011/06/latest-custom-card-for-vallie-eaves.html

9 http://en.wikipedia.org/wiki/Pepper_Martin

10 Unattributed, "Confidence Vote Given To Pepper," July 15, 1946 in SB 46.

11 Ken Borjens, "Poffenberger's Ban To Stick," *San Diego Union*, undated but most likely July 16, 1946.

12 Mitch Angus, "Padre Pilot 'On Spot;' Poffenberger Suspended," *San Diego Union*, July 15, 1946.

13 Earl Keller, "Starr, Martin Face Lawsuit," *San Diego Tribune-Sun*, July 15, 1946.

14 Ken Bojens, "Off The Main Line," *San Diego Union*, undated, but most likely July 16, 1946 in SB 46.

15 Earl Keller, "Starr, Martin Face Lawsuit," *San Diego Tribune-Sun*, July 15, 1946.

16   Earl Keller, "'Start Anew' Padres' Slogan," *San Diego Tribune-Sun,*
     July 16, 1946.

17   Unattributed, "Poffenberger May Join Louisville," undated in SD En.

18   *The Sporting News,* August 14, 1946, p 34.

19   Al Cartwright, "New Job as Hagerstown Ace Is Peachy With Poffenberger,"
     Journal Every-Evening, undated, but most likely May 24-25, 1947 in Owls En.

20   *Ibid.*

21   *The Sporting News,* "Gilbert Turns Down Boots," April 2, 1947.

22   Frank Colley, "Owls' Skipper Anxious To Get Men On Infield," *Morning
     Herald,* April 9, 1947.

23   Frank Colley, "Poffenberger Hurls Owls To Win Over Allentown Cards,"
     Morning Herald, May 2, 1947.

24   Frank Colley, "Poffenberger's Grand Slam Homer Gives Owls 10-4 Win,"
     Morning Herald, May 17, 1947.

25   Dick Kelly, "Spotlight on Sports," *Daily Mail,* May 29, 1947.

26   Unattributed, undated, but some time before May 27, 1947 in Owls En.

27   Dick Kelly, "The Spotlight on Sports," *Daily Mail,* June 21, 1947.

28   *Daily Mail,* "Double Exposure," caption to an unattributed photograph,
     June 30, 1947.

29   *Daily Mail,* "Poffenberger Is Still Unsigned," July 8, 1947.

30   J. Suter Kegg, "Tapping on the Sports Keg," *Sunday-Times,* July 20, 1947.

31   "Cole To Pitch For Boonsboro,"*Morning Herald,* September 12, 1947.

32   "Amvets Defeat Jackets 10 To 4,"*Morning Herald,* September 13, 1947.

33   J. Suter Kegg, "Tapping on The Sports Keg," *Sunday Times,*
     September 14, 1947.

34   *The Cumberland News,* "Amvets Down Hyndman 3 To 1 To Even Series,"
     September 29, 1947.

35   Stanley Frank, "Baseball Needs Some New Fools," *The Saturday Evening
     Post,* September 9, 1947, p 25, 70-77.

36   Red Smith, "View of Sports," *The Sporting News,* May 26, 1948, p 13.

37   "Owls Meeting Allentown In Twin Bill At Stadium Tonight," *Morning Herald,*
     August 13, 1948.

38   Dick Kelly, "The Spotlight on Sports," *Daily Mail,* August 21, 1948.

39   *Daily Mail,* August 18, 1948.

40   *Daily Mail,* "'Boots' Stars For Owls Once Again," August 19, 1948.

41   Frank Colley, "Hagerstown Owls Start Training Grind Today," *Morning
     Herald,* April 3, 1949.

42   Frank Colley, "Colley-See-Um of Sports," *Morning Herald,* April 7, 1949.

43   Frank Colley, "Cinders Being Removed From Stadium Infield," *Morning
     Herald,* April 19, 1949.

44   Dick Kelly, "The Spotlight on Sports," *Daily Mail,* May 12, 1949.

45   Dick Kelly, "Boots Poffenberger Ready To Charge 'Em At Stadium Tonight," *Daily Mail*, May 12, 1949.

46   Frank Colley, "Wilmington Shuts Out Hagerstown, 4-0," *Morning Herald*, May 13, 1949.

47   Dick Kelly, "The Spotlight on Sports," *Daily Mail*, May 15, 1949.

48   *Daily Mail*, "Boots Poffenberger Will Ask To Go On Voluntary Retired List," May 18, 1949. No author is listed, but the tell-tale mix up of Boots' name indicates that it was Dick Kelly.

CHAPTER 10

The Legacy of Boots Poffenberger

Although his professional career was over, Boots continued to play baseball. As late as 1957, at age 42, Boots was playing for the Williamsport Wildcats in the South Mountain League[1] and he would draw good crowds wherever the Wildcats played. Laco Anderson recalls playing in Charles Town, West Virginia, some 30 miles south of Williamsport.

"Charles Town would draw top flight teams in because they would pay for you to come play there. They would invite us down on Saturdays and they would have a helluva crowd because they knew Boots was going to be there."

While it might not have been major league baseball, the competition was no less intense. Jerry Knode worked the concession stand and served as a ball boy for Williamsport and recalls when the Wildcats used an unusual variation of the hidden ball trick.

"Some of the things you seen, you never forgot. They played to win! And I don't care how they won, they played to win. Some of the things they done was unbelievable. One time Glen Anderson was catching. It was the last inning and Williamsport was ahead by one run and Hancock had the bases loaded with two out. Anderson threw the ball over the head of the third baseman, *way* over his head, out into left field. Here come the runner just trotting in and Glen tagged him out! He had the ball in his glove! They went out into left field to see what he threw and here it was an old potato! And that started a big fight."

Boots never learned to accept failure even on these smallest of diamond stages. John Frye the curator of the Washington County Room at the Washington County Free Library remembers seeing Boots pitch in the early '50s when Frye served as the batboy for a team in Gapland, Maryland.

> They hit him hard down in Gapland one afternoon and I can see him now going into the dugout, pulling off his cleats and changing into his shoes; he went up and sat on a railroad trestle overlooking the park and watched the rest of the game from there. He might've even pulled himself out of the game because it was one hit after the other. I know why I remember that, because it was Boots Poffenberger! He was still a big deal around here back then.

Connie Cole remembers a similar incident in Sharpsburg when Boots left a game.

> They put on the loud speaker that song 'Bye, Bye Blackbird.' He was walking off there so mad! I don't know what the reason was [why he was taken out]. I just remember them playing that song and him leaving the ballpark. That's when he and dad played together.

Connie's dad, of course, was Jack Krebs who had signed with the Tigers along with Boots in 1934. Twenty years and a World War later, they were still playing together.

Boots managed the Wildcats on occasion, but just as he often did when he was playing, he never stuck around for a full season.

"He was a good man to play for because he was always that guy that tried to get the best out of you," says Anderson. "He just had a way to encourage guys to play. The sad part about that—and I knew him and I loved him—is that he didn't give more of [himself to the game]. He'd go 3-4-5 weeks maybe and then you wouldn't see him. He never went a full season."

Boots' cousin, Jack Rupp, notes, however, that some guys didn't like to play for The Baron. "He'd point out their faults and they didn't want to hear that," says Rupp with a laugh. "He told it like it was."

Boots also continued to pursue fun wherever he could find it. Laco recalls that Boots could often be found in the Vogue Room or the Rainbow

Room or Beck's in Hagerstown. Boots never learned to drive, "And never had no problem getting' anywhere!" according to Anderson who along with his girlfriend Jeanne (whom Anderson would marry and to whom he would stay married for 57 years before her death) would often meet Boots at a nightclub despite the fact that Anderson was under-age at the time.

> We were going places that I shouldn't have been in and there were dances and things . . . They would be packed and that was no problem; we'd wait for Boots to get up on the floor and we'd follow him. He had those big broad shoulders and it wasn't no problem knowing where he was going to be on Saturday night and sometimes Friday night. There's where we would go because we knew we wouldn't have any problems. Just get up on the dance floor when he's there and follow him.

A natty dresser who always wore a suit and a bow tie on a Saturday night, Boots kept his eye on the ladies. On the dance floor as on the diamond, however, he didn't win them all.

"He'd be dancing and I would hear some women just give him a blast you wouldn't believe," relates Anderson, laughing at the memory. "But I never heard him ever curse a woman, in fact I never heard him curse. I never heard him disrespect a woman no matter what she said to him."

What "she said to him" is lost to the ages, echoing around Hagerstown's long-defunct night clubs, but it does leave the imagination flush with wonder.

Boots spent 10 years working for Fairchild, according to an interview that he gave in January of 1963 to Raymond Johnson of the *Nashville Tennessean* who was writing a "where are they now" piece on Boots.[2] According to the Knodes, Boots would get laid off periodically and spent such occasions hunting and fishing. Johnson also wrote that Boots no longer drank beer, a claim that was decidedly not true and which could be verified by most of Williamsport's citizens.

Boots changed jobs in 1960 when he began working construction for Deron & Armstrong, the company that was building a Mack Truck plant in Hagerstown. In keeping with Boots' charmed life, it just so happened that Deron & Armstrong was headquartered in Detroit. Company officials knew him from his playing days there and essentially looked out for him, for he was as likely to be in the office telling stories as he was to be working the business end of his shovel. Once the plant was completed in July of 1961, Boots went to work on the inside as a heat treater which involved softening metal parts to make them more pliable and, therefore, less likely to cause damage to the tools.

Boots endured some damage to himself however, when he lost the index finger of his right hand while working in the plant. Jack Rupp, who worked with Boots on the second shift remembers.

> He come runnin' out of this heat treater, which was like a sepa-
> rate part of the world. And I was workin' right outside there and
> I seen him comin' out that door and he had his hand up in the
> air like this. Big glove on because they had to wear them heat
> treat gloves.
>
> "What's a matter, Poff?"
>
> "I gotta go!" he said, and I didn't even know what had happened.

"He called Mom and said he was at the hospital," relates Jerry Knode. "Mack Truck put him in a taxi and took him to the hospital. He come home and he said, 'Cut my finger off.' Of course, we ended up down at Ern's [Tavern]. He didn't say nothin' more about it."

"It was a tough job," adds Jerry. "Hot, but that's the job he wanted. He knew the President and he'd walk into the President's office at any time. He took my boy over there to get a job and said 'Let's go see the President' and the secretary said, 'You can't see him for that,' but in went Boots and talked to the President for a couple of hours and my boy is still working over there!"

Jerry relates that Boots secured a job for Dave Cole at Mack as well, although not before he almost kept Cole from a chance to extend his baseball career. Connie Cole recalls that Dave had grown tired of minor league life, and with small children at home had returned to Williamsport. Nevertheless, the Washington Senators offered him a try out (likely in 1957 or 1958) and Dave decided to go.

"Dave was going to go down to Washington the next day and Boots was going to go with him," recalls Connie. "The night before, Dave and Boots got into that Peck Carter's tavern and I called for him to come home; and he didn't come home and he didn't come home. He was with Boots! I went down there and I went in Peck's tavern and I said, 'I'm comin, here to get you and I'm going out that door and you better be right behind me! And he was," laughs Connie. Cole was offered a minor league contract by the Senators, but turned it down and ultimately, as noted, went to work at Mack Truck with Boots.

Joan Knode states that Boots "was not an employee who would show up all the time," a fact which would not surprise Walter Briggs, Mickey Cochrane, or Leo Durocher.

"He's the only guy I would haul to work regular," said Jack Rupp, "because if I didn't show up, he didn't care. Him and a guy named Freddie Herbert. 'Cause that's the way he was! He'd say, if you don't show up buddy, that don't bother me none!

Boots' job change may have been motivated by a monumental change in his life: He married for a second time. He and Hanna Knode, who was a year younger than Boots, had known each other since childhood and they became husband and wife in 1959. Neither Jerry, Hanna's son, nor Joan, Jerry's wife, knows the exact date. Jerry went to the Washington County Courthouse at one point to find out only to discover that his mother and Boots did not marry in Washington County, nor has he ever found out where the couple did indeed take their vows.

"I didn't ask him and he didn't tell me," chuckles Jerry. "Boots never told you anything about anything. The only way you find out about Boots was to read it in the newspapers or somebody told you something about him.

"I guess they just fell in love. Of course, they argued and fought just like everybody else."

"They looked good together, Hanna and Boots," states Joan. "He was always dressed to the hilt and she looked beautiful."

Indeed Hanna often appeared in Fairchild Aircraft promotional photos, where she worked from 1941 until her retirement in 1977. Two days after the attack on Pearl Harbor, Hanna secured a job at Fairchild making a robust $.50 an hour. Hanna managed Boots' money just as Jo had done.

"When he worked at Mack, he'd come home and give Mom the check. She took care of the money; she'd give him $5.00 or $10.00 and he'd get drunk," says Jerry.

"He won the lottery one time," states Jerry, "He got a $30.00 ticket. Mom gave him the ticket and told him to go cash it. Well, we didn't see him for three days! Mom said, 'It's a good thing that wasn't a $50,000 ticket!'"

Boots and Hanna kept a cabin along the Potomac where she raised flowers and he raised vegetables and they partied and fished.

"When you went fishin' with him, you fished! You didn't sit there and bullshit. If you caught more on that side of the boat, he'd change seats with you! That's the way it was. He was a good hunter and a good fisherman. And he was lucky!" says Jerry who often accompanied Boots on his hunts. "He'd go deer huntin' and them deer knew he was there and they'd come down outta the woods! They'd come down and he'd shoot 'em!" Boots particularly enjoyed rabbit hunting, but no matter the game, he was known for his marksmanship. "He was one helluva hunter," states Anderson. "He was always able to get whatever he was after."

Boots was still quick and athletic enough that he could catch a setting rabbit with his bare hands. Jack Rupp recalls that, "He'd always say, Nat—that's what he called his mom—wants one with no shot in it, so he'd catch one settin'. I've seen him do it more than once. All the rabbit huntin' I ever done and I only ever seen one guy do that and that's him."

According to Jerry Knode, Boots' hunting and fishing buddies included more than just relatives and friends, however.

> He had this general from the Air Force would come up to the cabin. He was flying over one time and he wanted to land in Hagerstown and they wouldn't let him land because he had too big of a plane. So he went down to DC and landed and this sergeant brought him up. Boots went and got these hellgrammites [the larval stage of the Dobson fly and a popular bait] and put 'em in a bucket. Of course, with Boots drinkin', he tipped over the bucket and these hellgrammites were crawlin' up the curtain. Well, this general come up the next morning and Boots was getting the hellgrammites and pulling down the curtains and putting them in the bucket. And this general was looking at him and said, 'Well I never seen anybody keep bait like that in the house!' And Boots never told him any different!

> The sergeant stayed there all day while they was up there fishin'. He sat there at the car and wouldn't come in the cabin. He sat

*there and I took him drinks; he wouldn't drink any beer, but I'd
take him Cokes and sandwiches and stuff. And then he'd leave.
But Boots and this general would sit down and talk; now what
they'd talk about I have no idea. They'd sit down and talk and
laugh and carry on and then he'd get up and leave. Six months
later I'd see him up at the house again. I have no idea who he
was. He was just one of Boots' friends who would just show up.*

Everyone in Williamsport speaks of Boots' many friends.

"He'd walk in a tavern not knowin' anybody in there and when he
left, everybody knew him. With $2.00 or $3.00 he'd go down the street [to
a tavern] and stay all day. If I went down with $2.00 or $3.00 I'd be back
in 15 minutes!" says Jerry.

"And he didn't have money to buy anybody drinks, so it had to be
something else," adds Joan. It certainly wasn't his "celebrity status" around
Williamsport and Washington County because if you didn't know he was
a former major leaguer, he didn't mention it. Bud Britner, whose father
used to hunt with Boots, rubbed elbows and raised glasses with Boots in
Ern's Tavern for some time before discovering that this particular "Boots"
was *the* Boots.

"It didn't matter where you went, he'd run into someone he knew. I
don't care where he went," recalls Knode who illustrates with a story about
a visit to Baltimore's Memorial Stadium when a group of Williamsporters
traveled east to see the Orioles play the Tigers.

"We was raising cain, drinkin' and carryin' on and this fella in the
next section there said, 'Hey, I wish you all would settle down. I'm here
with my wife; I just want to enjoy the night.' I told him, 'I'm sorry but
we're here with a fellow that used to play for Detroit; they won't own him,
but he used to play for Detroit.'" In disbelief, the man asked Jerry who it
was. Jerry pointed to the press box where Boots was being interviewed
and told him that it was Boots Poffenberger.

"'Christ sake! My daddy used to take me to ballgames to see him
play in Detroit.' And then, of course, he left his wife and came over with
us and he was talking to Boots. When we left he said, 'I'm a lawyer; here's
my card. Just call me anytime. If you all get in trouble, just go on home!'"

During the 1970s, Boots was involved in the Williamsport Bass
Club a third of whose members were serious fishermen who sought to

land the biggest bass out of the Potomac. The winners, which included Boots a couple of years, "got a real nice prize" often a couple of hundred dollars worth of fishing gear from Wolf's on the Square, a store in Williamsport that sold beer, bait, and general merchandise. All entries had to be weighed at Wolf's and more than one argument ensued about "who caught what and where" according to Anderson who added that Boots "was never the president or the vice-president, but he was always in charge!" Using his local fame and winsome personality to garner sponsors, the annual bass club feed would often draw 500-600 people or about one-third of Williamsport's population.

Boots retired from Mack Truck "as soon as he could" according to Knode, at age 62 in 1977.

"Money never seemed to be his thing. He might have wanted more, but he wouldn't have done no different if he had more," says Anderson.

"If he had money he spent it!" comments Jerry Knode. "That never worried him. If he had a pocketbook with a $5.00 bill in it he thought he was rich!"

"I don't recall him ever having any money," adds Anderson. "I don't recall him havin' any whenever we went somewhere. He traveled at one time with another Anderson, Jim Anderson. They'd travel around on Saturday night to different places. Now how the hell they got there I don't know because neither one of 'em had a car! I don't ever remember Boots reaching down and paying for it. He never had to."

Boots continued to follow the game at the major league level, although he didn't have a particular team. "He'd holler at the TV," says Knode. "He just liked to watch 'em play and he'd tell 'em when they did wrong." Boots continued to be revered by those still in the game who remembered him. A 1979 Baltimore Orioles game program contains the following inscription:

Dear Boots—

I'm sorry I missed seeing one of my real heroes. Next time please try to make it.

Best wishes,
Ernie Harwell

Harwell, now well on his way to a Hall of Fame career with the Detroit Tigers had broadcast Atlanta Cracker games during Boots' great 1940 season some forty years before. The page was also signed by Oriole public address announcer and former Dodger hurler Rex Barney, as well as the Orioles' future Hall of Fame broadcaster, Chuck Thompson.

Boots also continued to find adventures large and small that would have made Huck Finn proud. Knode relates the story about a "mean parakeet."

> We had this parakeet and everybody would get him out and put him on their shoulder, but this son of a bitch was mean! He was a mean parakeet. Boots and me were drinkin' this one day and we come up there and this parakeet was chip! chip! chip! And I said, 'We're gonna train this son of a bitch. So I put my finger in there for him to jump on and he pecked it and he stayed right on there. Well, I hit him and he fell over. Christ, he was out for a minute or two and I thought he was dead! I'm there blowin' in his face and everything so finally, we got him up and got him runnin' again and Boots threw him back in the cage. 'Give him here,' Boots said, 'I'm tired of this shit. And he got him out and took him out back and threwed him up in the air and said, 'Go south you son of a bitch; go south!' Mom come home and the cage was empty, but she never said a word! That's the way he was! He thought everything should be just right and if it isn't, he'd fix it!

Throughout his retirement from baseball, Boots' name continued to appear in newspapers and magazines. John Lardner, Ring Lardner's son, wrote a piece entitled, "They Walk By Night" in the February, 1950 issue of *Sport* magazine.

> Back in the days before arc-light games made major-league players work late at night, the bad boys of the diamond wrote history after sundown. The last outstanding night-walkers in baseball were Rollicking Rollie Hemsley, until he joined Alcoholics Anonymous, and Baron Boots Poffenberger, until he joined the Marines.[3]

Boots was referenced by Irving Zimmerman (no known relation) from Brooklyn in a letter to *The Sporting News* published on August 22nd, 1951. Zimmerman wrote to chastise Bill Veeck who had stated that there were "too few screwballs" in the game. Noting that many players were now college educated and aware of "the histories of such colorful screwballs as Boots Poffenberger and Art Shires," Zimmerman added that "only recently Chuck Connors admitted that being a comic set him back several years."[4] (Connors was in the second of his two major league seasons, splitting time between the Cubs and the Los Angeles Angels of the Pacific Coast League. He would play in another 113 games for L. A. in 1952, but put his "comic" talents to good use by pursuing a career in acting, a move made easier by playing in Los Angeles. That year he appeared in *Pat and Mike*, a Spencer Tracy/Katherine Hepburn comedy. Connors, of course would go on to star in film and television, most notably as Lucas McCain in *The Rifleman*.)

H. G. Salsinger was still covering the Tigers in 1956, and reported from Lakeland that Gene "Twinkle" Host might be the next Boots Poffenberger.[5] (Host, a highly regarded left-hander, would pitch in one game for the Tigers in 1956 and 11 games for Kansas City in 1957, compiling a lifetime 0-2 record with a 7.31 ERA.) Similarly, in 1963, *The Sporting News* asked if Bill Faul was Boots Poffenberger with a college degree.[6] (Faul, from the University of Cincinnati, finished a six-year big league career with a 12-16 record, the mirror image of Boots' 16-12. He also recorded a similar 4.72 ERA. His biographical page at baseball-reference.com notes that "although he had a non-descript career Bill Faul is remembered for eating a live frog in the clubhouse and using a hypnotist to control his pitches."[7])

Boots again appeared in a July 1962 *Sporting News*[8] article on great characters in the game and in a July, 1962 piece on great Tiger eaters.[9] In the latter, author Joe Falls repeated the "Breakfast of Champions" story in which Boots, who was supposed to answer "Wheaties" when asked what he had for breakfast, instead told a radio man that he had had a steak and a beer. That story, of course, mutated over the years, the usual variation, repeated in Falls' story, is that Boots calls room service and orders the "Breakfast of Champions" which he identifies as "two fried eggs and a bottle of beer." Indeed, the cartoon illustrating Falls' story features this version.

Both Joe Falls of the *Detroit Free Press* and Raymond Johnson, still writing for the *Nashville Tennessean* ran retrospectives on Boots in January of 1963.[10]

Baltimore sports writer John Steadman's interview with Boots appeared in a full two-page spread in the August 19th, 1967 issue of *The Sporting News*. Steadman sat down with Boots in Ern's Tavern, which was located across the street from a confectionery story run by Dave Cole in Williamsport, where Boots talked at length about his life and career.

Steadman, was another in a long-list of reporters who was obviously fascinated with Boots.

> *Off his performance and reputation, one of baseball's most unforgettable characters is Cletus Elwood (Boots) Poffenberger. There couldn't be another like Boots.*
>
> *Boots still has much of the naïve country boy about him. He's honest, even when the story he's telling doesn't make him look like an angel with a halo, and he can't understand why anyone would ever want to be any other way.*
>
> *Poffenberger is refreshing, like a cool breeze off the Potomac River.[11]*

Boots denied the Breakfast of Champions story but owned up to several others leading one to believe that the Breakfast story was indeed a bit of fiction. Jerry Knode believes it to be true. Steadman asked about his drinking and team-jumping. At the age of 52, and 19 years removed from his last professional game, Boots offered as full and reflective an answer as he would ever give. Of course, that doesn't mean that his answer was accurate.

> *"Yes, those things are true," he admitted. "But let me tell you why I often drank more beer than I could handle. When I was a kid in Williamsport, I never had a beer or smoked a cigarette.*
>
> *"If you don't believe me, then ask the people in this town. They have known me all my life. Want to know why I drank when I got away in Organized Ball? I was the backward sort. I'd go out*

with the other players after the game and they'd be talking or dancing with the girls and I was so shy I couldn't have any fun.

"I found a couple of beers gave me nerve and changed me from being a wall-flower."[12]

Steadman then describes Boots in greater detail:

He is still on the chunky side, physically, and is in surprisingly good condition.

His hair is still dark, the arms short but powerful and his step is fast. Hardly a man who is going to lose years off his life by what might have happened in a misspent youth.

Poffenberger has a colorful, frank way of talking. He says whatever pops into his mind. It comes out free and easy. Boots doesn't bother to be cautious about what he says or to guard the subject matter.

He seems a man without inhibitions—doesn't know what the word means—and it's this characteristic which made him No. 1 on every sports writer's list of all-time characters.

"I never fell out with a sports writer," said Boots. "The things I did might have been zany to them. But they weren't zany to me. It was my style."[13]

Asked about his many fines, Boots told Steadman, "I never paid a fine in my life. Those things were only bluff fines."[14]

The year after the Steadman interview, 1968, became known as the "Year of the Pitcher" and the October 5th edition of *The Sporting News* featured an article on Denny McLain's 30-win season. McLain told his pitching coach, Johnny Sain, that he was sure Sain had never seen anyone win that many before, but Sain told the eventual Cy Young Award winner that he had: Boots Poffenberger in 1940.[15]

Joe Falls wrote a two-part column in the early '70s detailing his attempts to connect with Boots when the Baron was in Detroit for a Mack Truck Convention. Falls would arrange a time to meet with Boots, but Boots would never show, until finally the two connected. Falls was bemused by Boots staying true to form and noted that there were an incredible 52 clips in the *Free* Press file for a player who played in only parts of two seasons in Detroit.[16]

The next year the September 7th issue of *The Sporting News* featured an article on baseball's biggest boozers and Boots, of course, was mentioned.[17] In 1975, Leo Durocher again discussed Boots in *Nice Guys Finish Last* which was essentially an update of *The Dodgers and Me* and which received similarly bad reviews.

While the baseball world kept periodic tabs on Boots, Boots never kept in touch with Jo, who remarried in Kanawha, West Virginia in 1953. She died in March of 1981. Neither Jerry Knode nor Laco Anderson can ever recall Boots even mentioning Jo after she left him.

Boots was honored locally in 1987 with his induction into the Washington County Hall of Fame, which had been established the year before. One of ten inductees, his plaque reads:

Poffenberger is still well-remembered outside of Washington County for his brief but colorful major league pitching career with the Detroit Tigers and Brooklyn Dodgers. With 41 wins in 2 ½ minor league seasons, Poffenberger earned a promotion to Detroit in mid-1937 and won 10 games for the Tigers. Among his victories was a win over a young Bob Feller, who was already pitching his way toward immortality. Traded to Brooklyn in 1939, Poffenberger returned to the minors and won 26 games for Nashville in the Southern League. He later pitched for San Diego in the Pacific Coast League and ended his career with the Hagerstown Owls in the late 1940s.

Boots celebrated the occasion in typical fashion according to Knode. "He went, enjoyed it that night, and got drunk, probably." (Laco Anderson joined his friend in Washington County's Hall of Fame in 2011.)

By all accounts, Boots remained in great shape until the very end, thanks to the fact that he walked everywhere. When Jack and his son Kelly took Boots to purchase his Pennsylvania hunting license, the clerk could not believe, upon seeing his identification, that he was 80 years old, remarking that he looked so good. "You should have seen me last week; I just got off an eight-day drunk," replied The Baron.

Boots lived to the age of 84, which may be the most remarkable statistic of his remarkable life given his drinking. By the summer of 1999, he had developed prostate cancer, a disease that would take his life on September 1st.

"A horrible death," states Jerry Knode. "We got him in the home out here and it took the whole day to get him in there and he only lasted overnight. We went out to see him the next morning . . . we were going to bring him home to let him die at home . . ."

"That was a blow," says Jack Rupp who relates how Boots confided in him concerning his condition one morning while cleaning up their hunting camp with Jerry Knode and a few others. Boots was burning trash in a barrel,

> And I was carrying stuff out and he said, "I want to talk to you"; and he told me about it. He said, "I've always lived what I wanted to live and I told the guy you're not going to butcher me. That's the way it is and that's what I'm gonna do." I said, "Poffy, you're your own man."
>
> "Yep," he said. But I want to tell you, he was in such good shape, if he'd have let 'em do the operation, he might have lived to be 100.

Fourteen years later, Jack has to work hard to control his emotions when relating this story.

Joan says he could have had an operation earlier "but chose not to. He didn't worry about anything; not even his cancer."

"Two weeks before he died, they give him drug and alcohol rehabilitation in the hospital," recalls Jerry. "I said, 'You gotta be shittin' me!' And this guy was chargin' $150 a shot for drug and alcohol rehabilitation. I said, 'You're a little late on that! He needed you 50 years ago!'"

Laco Anderson recalls his last conversation with Boots.

> I visited him in the hospital. I didn't know he had prostate trouble . . . and we talked. When I was leaving, I said good-bye, not knowing his condition. He hollered out, "Lac!" I turned around and looked back: "So long,' he said. Looking back, I realize that he knew what was going to happen.

He never ever said good-bye any other place we were ever at. He never said anything like that, but at the hospital he said good-bye. That was the last time I seen him alive. That tells me that he knew.

John Steadman sat right in front of me at the funeral and John said he was one of a kind.

Ten years later, Hanna died.

***

Boots' copy of Steadman's book, *The Best (and Worst) of Steadman: A Collection of Stories by the Sports Editor of The* Baltimore News American, contained the following inscription to Boots:

You will never know the respect and admiration I have in my heart for you. You are a man all the way and the world should have a million like you. Please tell Hanna she always has my best. You are both something special. As ever, John.

That Steadman would note that the ultimate boy is "a man all the way," is not necessarily a contradiction. The Baltimore sports writer recognized that Boots was man enough to remain a boy, to shun cynicism. Boots Poffenberger never became world-weary or bitter; he remained true to himself and true to his friends, the number of whom increased throughout his lifetime.

Jack Rupp had a similar assessment.

Boots was his own guy. It don't matter how much he liked to do something. If you do it with him 10 days in a row and the 11th day you said, 'Let's do that again, Boots,' he'd say, 'I don't wanna do 'er no more. He wouldn't do it. He was a man's man. He was a good guy. I miss him.

You know I asked him one time, "Do you ever regret what you did?" and he said "Nope, I have no regrets. You gotta figure where I was at. Born and raised in Williamsport; I didn't have nothing. I didn't have a nickel! This guy got me, put me on a

train, got me a suit of clothes, met me up there, bought me
more clothes, and gave me $600.00. I was the King of Detroit
for a while! No, no regrets."

Perhaps, the secret to his charm was that Boots was so true to himself that you felt more comfortable being yourself around him.

Boots was never self-impressed and never falsely modest. He was the least neurotic person whom I have ever met (and I feel as if I have) and if some long ago trauma from childhood led him to the bottle, then he never directed that destructive streak toward anyone else. Certainly, Jo and his managers, coaches, and teammates were affected by it, in Jo's case, rather dramatically. It was as if in the middle of a good time, Boots would spill a big mug of irresponsibility all over her and others. Ultimately, it's not enough to not mean to; responsible adults mean not to, but perhaps his clumsiness and sincere but unsuccessful efforts to clean up the mess made him all the more lovable.

In response to an email that I sent to Joan Knode, to which she provided the information requested, she concluded simply, but poignantly, "We miss Boots."

"Didn't matter if the sun didn't come up tomorrow, if he was doing it today and having fun that was it. And he never hurt nobody," says Jack Rupp.

"He was happy go lucky and he didn't care about the next day," states Connie Cole. "He didn't care. I don't think he realized he was in the big leagues. He probably would have been just as happy playing baseball in Williamsport. Everybody liked him. He was friends with everybody."

"I admired him all the time," says former Marine teammate John McNamara. "He was that kind of a guy. He had a helluva sense of humor. He could tell the greatest stories about baseball. He'd keep you laughing all the time."

"He was just a helluva nice guy," says Anderson, who laughed, then added wistfully, "They don't make too many like that anymore. We just talked about a guy that'll never leave."

Indeed, Boots Poffenberger is still a presence in Williamsport where anyone who knew him is happy to tell a story about him, just as John Steadman predicted in Boots' obituary that he penned for *The Sun*. It just may be, however, that the final story belongs to the man himself. When I first picked up the Steadman book, it opened easily to the chapter on Boots because it had long been marked with a playing card. Naturally, that card was the joker.

Notes

1 *The Sporting News*, May 1, 1957, p 40.
2 Raymond Johnson, "One Man's Opinion: After 22 Years, Boots Admits He Did Wrong," *Nashville Tennessean*, January 22, 1963.
3 John Lardner, "The Walk By Night," *Sport Magazine*, February 1950, p 28-30, 91.
4 Irving Zimmerman, "Kids Too Smart For Screwball," letter to the editor, *The Sporting News*, August 22, 1951, p 12.
5 H. G. Salsinger, *The Sporting News*, March 7, 1956, p 16.
6 *The Sporting News*, June 1, 1963, p 23.
7 http://www.baseball-reference.com/bullpen/Bill_Faul
8 Frederick G. Lieb, "Old-Timer Hijinks Drove Pilots Daffy," *The Sporting News*, July 21, 1962, p 1, 42. Boots is mentioned in the final paragraph.
9 Joe Falls, "Ball-Player Feats On Field Pale Before Knife and Fork Exploits," *The Sporting News*, July 31, 1965, p 19.
10 Falls' did a series of retrospectives on various Tigers. His one on Boots appeared January 18, 1963, entitled, "Tigers Famed Boots Just a Family Man." Johnson's, cited above, appeared on January 22, 1963.
11 John Steadman, "Meet One and Only Boots Poffenberger," *The Sporting News*, August 19, 1967, p 5, 6.
12 *Ibid.*
13 *Ibid.*
14 *Ibid.*
15 Watson Spoelstra, "McLain Man For All Seasons," *The Sporting News*, October 5, 1968, p 3.
16 Joe Falls, "Legend of Boots Not Exaggerated" and "'Joe, Joe, It's Me—Boots Poffenberger!'" *Detroit Free Press* undated, but from 1972 or 1973 during the Mack Truck Convention in Detroit, attended by Boots.
17 Pete Broeg, "Best at Booze, Bar-ring None," *The Sporting News*, September 7, 1974, p 22.

References

Books

Durocher, Leo. *The Dodgers and Me: The Inside Story.* Ziff-Davis Publishing Company, 1948.

Durocher, Leo (with Ed Linn). *Nice Guys Finish Last.* Pocket Book Edition, 1976.

Gershman, Michael. *The Evolution of the Ballpark From Elysian Fields to Camden Yards.* Houghton Mifflin, 1993.

Mead, William B. *Baseball Goes To War.* Broadcast Interview Source, Inc. 1998.

Nash, Bruce and Zullo, Allan. *The Baseball Hall of Shame 3.* Pocket Books, 1987.

Steadman, John. *The Best (and Worst) of Steadman: A Collection of Stories by the Sports Editor of The* Baltimore News American. Press Box Publishing, 1974.

Periodicals

Armored News
Atlanta Constitution
Birmingham News
BOOT: The Parris Island Weekly
Charleston Daily Mail
Charleston Gazette
Chattanooga Times
Colliers August 6, 1938 Kyle Crichton
Coronet

Cumberland News
Cumberland Sunday Times
Daily Mail (Hagerstown)
Denver Post
Detroit Free Press
Detroit News
Detroit Times
The *Dug-Out: A Morale Builder For The Armed Forces*
     (Williamsport, MD)
Greenville News (South Carolina)
Hartford Courant
Herald-Mail (Hagerstown)
Honolulu Star-Bulletin
Journal Every Evening (Wilmington, DE)
Knoxville News-Sentinel
Lakeland Ledger
Los Angeles Examiner
Marine Corps Chevron
Morning Herald (Hagerstown)
Nashville Banner
Nashville Tennessean
Newark Evening News
New York News
New York Post
Pacific Leatherneck
Pittsburgh Post-Gazette
San Diego Tribune-Sun
San Diego Union
Saturday Evening Post September 9, 1947 Stanley Frank
Sport Magazine February, 1950 "They Walk By Night," Ring Lardner
State-Times (Baton Rouge)
The Sporting News
The Sun (Baltimore)
Toledo Blade
Toledo News-Bee
Waco News-Herald

Washington Daily News
Washington Herald
Washington Post
Washington Times-Herald

Personal Interviews

Anderson, Donald "Laco." September 12, 2012 and August 10, 2013.
Cole, Connie. October 10, 2012.
Frye, John. August 3, 2013.
Knode, Jeremy and Joan. October 31, 2012 and August 11, 2013.
MacNamara, John. By phone, February 22, 2013 and March 3, 2013.
Rupp, Jack. August 21, 2013.

Websites

baltimoresun.com
baseball-reference.com
baseballinwartime.com
cinematreasures.org
gainesvilletimes.com
milb.com The Official Website of Minor League Baseball
museumofbuford.com
pitchblackbaseball.com
polaris.net
thediamondangle.com
sabr.org
sportsillustrated.cnn.com
sulphurdell.com
wikipedia.com (very helpful in finding information on various
    reporters and columnists)

Cletus Elwood "Boots" Poffenberger
Professional Baseball Pitching Statistics

MAJOR LEAGUE TOTALS

Year	Age	Tm	Lg	W	L	W-L%	ERA	G	GS	CG	SV	IP	H	R	ER	BB	SO	WHIP
1937	21	DET	AL	10	5	0.667	4.65	29	16	5	3	137.1	147	83	71	79	35	1.646
1938	22	DET	AL	6	7	0.462	4.82	25	15	8	1	125.0	147	74	67	66	28	1.704
1939	23	BRO	NL	0	0		5.40	3	1	0	0	5.0	7	3	3	4	2	2.200
TOTALS	3 Years			16	12	0.571	4.75	57	32	13	4	267.1	301	160	141	149	65	1.683

MINOR LEAGUE TOTALS

Year	Age	Tm	Lg	Lvl	Aff	W	L	W-L%	ERA	G	GS	CG	SV	IP	H	R	ER	BB	SO	WHIP
1935	19	Fieldale	BIST	D		16	15	0.516		40				241.0	225	141		74		1.241
1936	20	Charleston	MATL	C	DET	16	12	0.571	2.75	34				255.0	234	107	78	77	28	1.220
1937	21	Beaumont	TL	A1	DET	9	1	0.900	2.50	14	13			108.0	100	44	30	28	30	1.185
1938	22	Toledo	AA	A	DET	8	3	0.727	3.92	14	11			78.0	87	40	34	26	17	1.449
1940	24	Nashville	SOUA	A1	BRO	26	9	0.743	4.58	38	33			238.0	296	146	121	98	26	1.655
1941	25	Nashville	SOUA	A1		7	3	0.700	4.42	16	14			106.0	113	63	52	51	17	1.547
1942	26	San Diego	PCL	AA		9	10	0.474	3.86	38	21	10		168.0	173	86	72	80	40	1.506
1946	30	San Diego	PCL	AAA		5	6	0.455	3.86	16	10	5		70.0	80	39	30	32	19	1.600
1947	31	Hagerstown	ISLG	B	DET	5	3	0.625	3.86	9	9			63.0	64	36	27	19		1.317
1948	32	Hagerstown	ISLG	B	DET	2	3	0.004	4.01	7	4	2		33.2	31	17	15	17	17	1.426
1949	33	Hagerstown	ISLG	B	WAS	0	1	0.000	4.50	1	1	0		8.0	5	4	4	6	3	1.375
TOTALS*	9 Seasons					101	62	0.620	3.01	219	102	15		1327.0	1372	702	444	485	59	1.399

*Totals do not include 1948 and 1949 which were compiled by the author

Source: www.baseball-reference.com

Index

P

R

S

Printed in the USA
CPSIA information can be obtained
at www.ICGtesting.com
LVHW021304041223
765638LV00011B/453